Short Stories on Film

Short Stories on Film

Carol A. Emmens

1978

Libraries Unlimited, Inc.
Littleton, Colo.

LIBRARIES UNLIMITED, INC.
P.O. Box 263
Littleton, Colorado 80160

Library of Congress Cataloging in Publication Data

Emmens, Carol A
    Short stories on film.

    Includes indexes.
    1. Film adaptations--Bibliography. 2. Short
stories--Bibliography. I. Title.
Z5784.M9E46 [PN1997.85]   791.43'7   78-13488
ISBN 0-87287-146-0

TABLE OF CONTENTS

ACKNOWLEDGMENTS

My thanks to Nick Fiorentino, a movie buff, who read the manuscript, to Brian Camp and Maryann Chach of the Educational Film Library Association, to the Museum of Modern Art study department for film, to the many librarians who assisted in verifying whether or not a title was a short story, and to the distributors who sent catalogs.

STORY TO SCREEN

Since its inception and continuing to the present, the motion picture industry has relied heavily upon literary works for the story material that is adapted to the screen. Today, best-selling novels are frequently the original source of a movie, but a survey of film history reveals that short stories have most often served as the original source for movies, especially between 1910-1940, when films were shorter than they are today.

As the reference librarian for the Educational Film Library Association (EFLA), I was once asked what films were based on the short stories of Ring Lardner. I found no work that could readily answer the question, and the idea for a bibliography listing films based on short stories was born.

Short Stories on Film is intended to aid the reader in locating the original short story source of a movie. To date, there is no other work that lists all the important films—including non-theatrical films—produced between 1920-1976 and based on stories by American authors or outstanding international authors that were well-known in America. The only existing books on film adaptations of short stories are detailed analyses of selected short stories or films. *Short Story/Short Film* by Fred H. Marcus (Prentice-Hall) is an example of this kind of study. In its approach, *Short Stories on Film* is roughly equivalent to *Filmed Books and Plays* by A. G. S. Enser (Academic Press); both books direct the user to the original source(s) of a movie. *Short Stories on Film* also provides a complete Directory of Distributors for both feature and non-theatrical films listed.

To find films based on short stories, many reference tools and catalogs were searched, including the *Library of Congress Catalog—Motion Pictures and Filmstrips*; *Who Wrote the Movie?*, compiled and published by the Writers' Guild of America (Los Angeles, 1970); the *Title Guide to the Talkies*, by Richard B. Dimmitt (2 vols., Metuchen, NJ: Scarecrow, 1965; 1964-1974 supplement by Andrew A. Aros, published 1977); the reviews of the *New York Times* and other trade publications; and the *American Film Institute Catalogs of Motion Pictures*, 1921-1930 and 1961-1970 (New York: Bowker, 1971 and 1976, respectively).

Compiling *Short Stories on Film* was a monumental task because all too often the references merely said "based on a story by Ben Hecht." What I learned is that "story" is an all-encompassing word, and is used to refer to books, novels, short stories, original screenplays, and even plays. To add to this problem, authors such as Hecht wrote in several of these genres. During the 1920s and 1930s, many prolific writers such as James Curwood were lured to Hollywood, as well as acclaimed writers like F. Scott Fitzgerald, and often they wrote directly for the screen. To further complicate research, the definition of a short story varies widely. *Short Story Index* covers brief narratives as well as 150-page stories; other tools define a short story as a work of less than 60 pages. Because of this ambiguity, a few works that are generally considered novelettes are included in this bibliography.

To insure accuracy, all the titles were checked in at least two reference sources—movie records are notoriously poor. Often the information supplied to the Library of Congress did not identify the original story title or the original format, i.e., novel, play, etc. Sometimes the records read "based on the story by John Smith"; other times the reference gave "Story: John Smith." As a result, there are listings in this bibliography under "Unidentified story (stories)." If no title was found in any of the many reference sources I consulted, I made no further attempt to identify the story: reading the author's stories, in hope of finding the source of a film story, would require months if not years of work.

Publication of the stories was also difficult to ascertain because during the 1920s and 1930s pulp magazines abounded. Literary magazines were also numerous; *Ainslee's*, for example, published all the best authors of the day. Stories published in a magazine were generally not copyrighted individually. In one case the story was apparently published after the movie was released. The movie, "The Patent Leather Kid," based on the story by Rupert Hughes, was nominated for an Academy Award as an original story, yet it appears in *The Patent Leather Kid and Other Stories.*

Whenever possible, I have included the original place of publication or an anthology in which the story was published, though no attempt was made to provide publication information for all the stories. Titles by authors such as Edgar Allan Poe appear in many anthologies, and these can be obtained from the *Short Story Index.*

The guide is arranged alphabetically by author and subdivided by an alphabetical list of the story titles; therefore, all the films based on a story are listed in one place. The short story and film title indexes that follow the Directory of Distributors facilitate alternate access by title. The second part of this introduction identifies the particular information given in each bibliographical entry, and provides a brief list of abbreviations used.

The distributors cited in the entries are not the original theatrical distributors, but the current distributors of 16mm or 8mm prints of the films. A complete directory of the distributors is appended to the main bibliographical listing. Feature films are usually rented, but the distributors of non-theatrical films sell and rent. The non-theatrical films are generally less than 60 minutes and are readily identifiable by producer and/or distributor. For a more comprehensive listing of distributors, *Feature Films on 8mm and 16mm*, compiled by James Limbacher (Bowker), should be consulted.

Because the primary objective of this bibliography is to identify the films based on short stories, the descriptive annotations are brief, and occasionally no description is provided. The early LC catalogs do not always give descriptions, and often no review or other notice could be found for "poverty row" films. A surprising number of films were not listed in the LC catalogs at all, including those produced by such companies as Maurice Conn Productions.

Though based on the same story, in a few instances the annotations of the films are not alike. There are two reasons for this: first, different elements of the plot and sub-plot may have been given prominence in the different films; and second, Hollywood often used little more from a story than the title. When more than one short story or other source served as the basis for a film, the additional sources are identified in the source material notes, following the film title. Sometimes a film was based primarily on a play in turn based on a story. This information is also given in the source material notes. The notes may also provide information about characters, such as Sherlock Holmes, who originally appeared in short stories, and were subsequently used in original screenplays.

Frequently a reference source like the LC catalogs lists the number of reels rather than the running time. I followed suit. A reel runs approximately 12 minutes. A film's length is also indicated in feet (').

This bibliography is as complete as possible. There are over 1,300 entries of films based on well-known and lesser-known short stories. Film researchers now will be able to trace the literary sources for a substantial corpus of films produced between 1920-1976. Teachers will find it useful for literature and film courses. Librarians will find *Short Stories on Film* invaluable when asked that perennial question, "What was the movie based on?" Lecturers and community program coordinators will find it easier to identify and locate films, using the Directory of Distributors, to supplement their talks and programs.

I welcome suggestions, additions, or corrections for future editions, which will expand the information already provided.

> Carol A. Emmens
> 213 Highfield Lane
> Nutley, NJ 07110

* * *

Short Stories on Film is arranged alphabetically by short story author, and subdivided by an alphabetical list of story titles. If more than one film has been made from a single short story, these films are listed alphabetically under the appropriate short story title.

The following sample entry identifies the content of each bibliographic item: author's name, short story title, film title, source material note, technical information, production credits, cast credits, and annotation, with a note. The joint author's name, if there is one, usually follows the short story title, and a cross reference from the joint author's name to the bibliographical entry is provided. Occasionally, several stories (named in the source material note) have served as the sources for a particular film; cross references from the names of these stories to the appropriate bibliographic entry are also supplied. Where an author has used a pseudonym, cross references refer to the most commonly used form of the author's name, and this is where the entries are listed. Where possible, the genre of a film, such as western, melodrama, etc., is indicated at the beginning of the annotation.

Access to the entry by short story or film title is assured by the title indexes, which follow the Directory of Distributors.

Following the sample entry is a list of abbreviations used in this bibliography.

SAMPLE ENTRY

┌────────────────Author's name
MATSON, NORMAN

Larger Than Life──────── Short story title
He Couldn't Say No*──── Film title   — Note
──s.m. Larger Than Life, a play by Joseph Shrank in turn based on
    the story
7 reels   b&w   1937────Technical information
Dir: Lewis Seiler. Prod: Warner Bros. Dist: United Artists. ──Credits
Cast: Jane Wyman, Frank McHugh.──── Cast credits
──An office clerk is harrassed by his girlfriend's mother. *Note: Prior movie title was Larger Than Life.

└─Annotation, with note

Source material note

ABBREVIATIONS USED IN THE TEXT

Adap	adaptation
AFI	American Film Institute
AKA	also known as
b&w	black and white
Dir	director
Dist	distributor
'	feet
jt.	joint
min.	minutes
mm	millimeter
mus.	music
Prod	producer
rel.	released
sd.	sound
sil.	silent
s.m.	source material note
Sp	screenplay

Names of countries are also abbreviated, as necessary, in the text.

ALPHABETICAL LIST

OF

SHORT STORY AUTHORS

ADAMS, CLIFTON

The Desparado
    Cole Younger, Gunfighter
    78 min.   color   1957
    Dir: R. G. Springsteen. Prod: Allied Artists. Dist: Hurlock Cine World.
    Cast: Frank Lovejoy, James Best.
    Western. A couple of men cross the path of the notorious gunslinger Cole
Younger.

ADAMS, EUSTACE L.

Loot Below
    Desperate Cargo
    69 min.   b&w   1941
    Dir: William Beaudine. Prod: Producers Releasing Corp.
    Cast: Ralph Byrd, Carol Hughes, Jack Mulhall.
    Spies commandeer a giant clipper ship on which two girls are returning to
America.

Sixteen Fathoms Under in *American Magazine*
    Sixteen Fathoms Deep
    82 min.   color   1948
    Prod: Monogram. Dist: Ivy.
    Cast: Lloyd Bridges, Lon Chaney.
    Sponge divers discover a saboteur aboard a boat off the coast of Florida.

ADAMS, FRANK R.

The American Sex in *Munsey's Magazine* (June 1925)
    Meet the Prince
    6 reels   sil   b&w   1926
    Dir: Joseph Henabery. Adap: Jane Murfin, Harold Shumate. Prod: Metropolitan
        Pictures.
    Cast: Joseph Schildkraut, Marguerite De La Motte.

ADAMS, FRANK R. (cont'd)
Meet the Prince (cont'd)
Comedy-melodrama. Prince Nicholas Alexnov, now living in a tenement in New York, dreams of his elegant palace in Russia. He falls in love with Annabelle Ford and eventually wins her.

Circus Girl in *Cosmopolitan Magazine*
Circus Girl
54 min.   b&w   1937
Dir: John H. Aver. Sp: Adele Buffington, Bradford Ropes. Prod: Republic Picture Corp. Dist: Ivy.
Cast: June Travis, Robert Livingston.
Trapeze partners argue over a girl.

Miles Brewster and the Super Sex in *Cosmopolitan Magazine* (July 1921)
The Super-Sex
6 reels   sil.   b&w   1922
Dir and Adap: Lambert Hillyer. Prod: Frank R. Adams.
Cast: Robert Gordon, Charlotte Pierce.
Comedy. Miles Brewster Higgins is jealous when a salesman captures the attention of his sweetheart. He invests his money, becomes rich, and wins his girl back.

Proxies in *Cosmopolitan Magazine* (August 1920)
Proxies
7 reels   sil.   b&w   1921
Dir: George D. Baker. Prod: Cosmopolitan Pictures.
Cast: Norman Kerry, Zena Keefe.
Crook melodrama. A butler is recognized as a former convict by a visitor, who tries to embroil him in a fraudulent stock scheme.

Skin Deep in *Cosmopolitan Magazine*
Almost a Lady
5,702'   sil.   b&w   1926
Dir: E. Mason Hopper. Prod: Metropolitan Picture Corp.
Cast: Marie Prevost, Harrison Ford, George K. Arthur.
Romantic comedy. A young lady is introduced at a party as a famous writer. William, who's also an imposter, falls in love with her and she's forced to confess but all ends happily.

ADAMS, SAMUEL HOPKINS

Night Bus
  It Happened One Night
  105 min.   b&w   1934
  Dir: Frank Capra. Sp: Robert Riskin. Prod: Columbia. Dist: Budget, Modern,
    Swank.
  Cast: Clark Gable, Claudette Colbert.
Heiress, Colbert, forbidden by her millionaire father to marry a man she thinks
she loves, manages to flee her father's yacht. While her father and a squad of
detectives are searching the nation for her, she has joined forces in a journey across
the country with none other than Clark Gable, playing a wise-cracking reporter.

  You Can't Run Away from It
  95 min.   color   1956
  Dir: Dick Powell. Sp: Claude Binyon, Robert Riskin. Prod: Columbia Picture
    Corp.
  Cast: Jack Lemmon, June Allyson.
Musical comedy. A willful heiress escapes her father, who seeks to have her
marriage to a fortune hunter annulled. On route she falls for an unemployed
reporter.

The Perfect Specimen
  The Perfect Specimen
  10 reels   b&w   1937
  Dir: Michael Curtis. Sp: Norman Reilly Raine, Lawrence Riley, Brewster
    Morse, Fritz Falkenstein. Prod: Warner Brothers.
  Cast: Edward Everett Horton.
A man raised to be the "perfect specimen" discovers the outside world.

ADDINGTON, SARAH

Bless Their Hearts
  And So They Were Married
  74 min.   b&w   1936
  Dir: Elliott Nugent. Prod: Columbia.
  Cast: Simone Simon, James Ellison.
Screwball comedy about a girl who gives out too many keys to her apartment
during wartime. Re-issued in 1948 by Monogram.

ADE, GEORGE

Making the Grade in *Hearst's International Cosmopolitan*
    Making the Grade
    6 reels   sil.   b&w   1929
    Dir: Alfred E. Green. Prod: Fox Film.
    Cast: Edmund Lowe, Lois Moran, Lucien Littlefield.
    Social comedy-drama. Wealthy Herbert Dodsworth tries hard to prove himself as a man. Talking sequences and musical score.

AGEE, JAMES

A Mother's Tale
    A Mother's Tale
    18 min.   color   1977
    Dir: Rex Goff. Prod: Rex Goff. Dist: Learning Corp.
    A live-action film which features the off-screen voices of Maureen Stapleton and Orson Welles. The thought-provoking parable uses animals as the protagonists in an ironic commentary on human behavior. A mother cow relates to her children the story of a young bull who tried to warn the other cattle of the suffering they would endure at the hands of man, but met only skepticism. The young calves, like others before them, refuse to accept the story and resolve to discover the truth for themselves.

AIKEN, CONRAD

Silent Snow, Secret Snow
    Silent Snow, Secret Snow
    17 min.   1966
    Dir: Gene Kearney. Dist: Audio Brandon.
    A young boy gradually withdraws more and more completely into his own private world of fantasy.

ALBEE, GEORGE SOMNER

The Next Voice You Hear
    The Next Voice You Hear
    83 min.   1950
    Dir: William Wellman. Prod: M-G-M.
    Cast: James Whitmore, Nancy David, Gary Gray.
    Mysterious voice (perhaps God's) heard on a radio broadcast causes strange announcements all over the world.

ALEICHEM, SHOLOM

Mottele Peyse, the Cantor's Son
Laughter through Tears
82 min.   1933
Dir: G. Gritcher. Dist: Audio Brandon.
Cast: Michael Rosenberg, E. Kovenberg, S. J. Silberman.
Filmed in America and the U.S.S.R., Laughter through Tears recreates the color-ful life in Kozedayevka, a poor Jewish village in old Russia. In addition to playing the famous storyteller, Rosenberg speaks for all of the characters.

Fiddler on the Roof
Fiddler on the Roof
s.m. play by Joseph Stein, Sheldon Harnick, Jerry Bock and Jerome Robbins,
in turn based on story.
180 min.   color   1971
Dir: Norman Jewison. Sp: Joseph Stein. Prod: Norman Jewison.
Cast: Topol, Norma Crane, Leonard Frey, Mollie Picon.
Set in 1905 at the home of Tevye, a poor dairyman in a tiny Russian village. Elsewhere the Czar's cavalry is attacking young street revolutionaries.

ALEXANDER, ELIZABETH

Fifty-Two Weeks for Florette in *Prize Stories of 1921*
You Belong to Me
70 min.   b&w   1934
Dir: Alfred M. Werker. Sp: Walter DeLeon. Prod: Paramount. Dist: Universal.
Cast: Lee Tracy, Helen Morgan.
A six-year-old boy tries to protect his actress mother until she remarries and he ends up being shipped off to school.

The Self-Made Wife in *Saturday Evening Post* (Oct. 28-Nov. 18, 1922)
The Self-Made Wife
5 reels   sil.   b&w   1923
Dir: Jack Dillon. Prod: Universal.
Cast: Ethel Grey Terry, Crawford Kent, Virginia Ainsworth.
Melodrama. Lawyer Tim Godwin strikes it rich in oil and moves with his family to the city, but his wife is unhappy there.

ALLEN, FRANCIS K.

Murder Stole My Missing Hours
Road to Alcatraz
60 min.   b&w   1945
Dir: Nick Grinde. Prod: Republic Pictures. Dist: Ivy.

ALLEN, FRANCIS K. (cont'd)
Road to Alcatraz (cont'd)
Cast: Robert Lowery, Grant Withers.
A young attorney is haunted by the fear that he murdered his partner while sleep walking.

ALLEN, JANE

A Girl's Best Friend Is Wall Street
She Knew All the Answers
9 reels   b&w   1941
Dir: Richard Wallace. Sp: Harry Segall, Kenneth Earl, Curtis Kenyon. Prod:
Columbia.

ANDERSON, FREDERICK IRVING

Sophie Lang in several stories (Sophie was a charming thief, who reformed and appeared in many films)

The Return of Sophie Lang
7 reels   1936
Dir: George Archainbaud. Sp: Brian Marlow, Patterson McNott. Prod: Paramount.
Cast: Gertrude Michael, Sir Guy Standing.
A reformed Sophie is mixed up with the theft of a world-famous diamond.

Sophie Lang Goes West
6 reels   b&w   1937
Dir: Charles Riesner. Sp: Doris Anderson, Brian Marlowe, Robert Wyler. Prod:
Paramount.

ANDERSEN, HANS CHRISTIAN

The Shadow
The Shadow
27 min.   color   1976
Dir: Don Ham. Prod and Dist: LSB Productions.
A live action dramatization. A philosopher fantasizes that his shadow could slip inside rooms and discover the secrets within. His shadow does indeed enter the rooms, and years later returns to attempt to become the master of the man.

ANDERSON, SHERWOOD

I'm a Fool
  I'm a Fool
  38 min.   color   1977
  Dir: Noel Black. Sp: Ron Cowen. Dist: Perspective.
  A young person's job, his relationship with his co-workers, his desire to impress
those around him, motivate Andy, a "swipe" doing manual labor on the Ohio racetrack circuit in the early 1900s. When Andy meets a beautiful young woman at the
track, he tries to impress her by exaggerating his position in life.

ARLEN, MICHAEL

The Ace of Cads in *Everybody's Magazine* (June 1924)
  The Ace of Cads
  8 reels   b&w   sil.   1926
  Dir: Luther Reed. Prod: Famous Players—Lasky.
  Cast: Adelphne Menjou, Alice Joyce, Norman Trevor.
  Chappel Maturin and Basil De Gramercy are officers in the Guards and are in love
with the same girl. Basil betrays his friend and Maturin begins drinking. Twenty years
later Basil, who married Eleanor, is killed in the trenches and Maturin falls in love
with the daughter.

The Dancer of Paris in *The World's Best Short Stories of 1925*
  The Dancer of Paris
  7 reels   sil.   b&w   1926
  Dir: Alfred Santell. Prod: First National.
  Cast: Conway Tearle, Dorothy Mackaill.
  Drama. Consuelo Cox falls in love with Sir Roy Martel, a wealthy Englishman
and accepts his proposal, but she discovers his love is the basest kind and goes to Paris.

The Gay Falson in *To the Queen's Taste*, ed. by Ellery Queen
  The Gay Falcon (AKA A Date with the Falcon)*
  Dir: Irving Reis. Prod: RKO. Dist: Films Inc.
  Cast: George Sanders.
  The Falcon hunts down gem thieves. *Note: The Falcon, created by Arlen, was
a debonair troubleshooter. This character appeared in 16 mystery movies during the
1940s.

A Gentleman from America in *Great Ghost Stories of the World*, ed. by A. K. Laing.
  The Fatal Night (Br.)
  50 min.   color   1948
  Dir: Mario Zampi. Sp: Gerald Butler. Prod: Anglofilm.
  Cast: Lester Ferguson, Jean Short.
  Story of a haunted house.

ARMSTRONG, CHARLOTTE

The Enemy
    Talk about a Stranger
    65 min.   b&w   1952
    Dir: David Bradley. Prod: MGM. Dist: Films Inc.
    Cast: Nancy Davis, Billy Gray.
    A drama about a family's mysterious neighbors. The former title of the film was
The Enemy.

ASHWORTH, JOHN

High Diver
s.m. "The Gossamer World," by Faith Baldwin and "Horsie" by Dorothy Parker.
    Horsie
    107 min.   b&w   1951
    Sp: Seton Miller. Prod: United Artists. Dist: Ivy.
    Former title: Queen for a Day. Stories of the contestants of a radio show.

ASIMOV, ISAAC

The Ugly Little Boy
    The Ugly Little Boy
    26 min.   color
    Dir: Barry Morse, Don Thompson. Dist: Learning.
    Cast: Kate Reid, Barry Morse.
    Science versus morality. A group of scientists have brought a Neanderthal child up
through time to their futuristic world, 40,000 years advanced. To watch over him
they choose a nurse who has long eschewed emotional attachments. The laboratory
experiments begin—test after test—for the invaluable data they seek. In spite of herself, the dispassionate nurse sympathizes with the primitive creature's plight and tries
to surmount the communication barriers. But the scientists decide to return the boy
to make room for more advanced specimens. As they prepare to send him back in
time, the nurse makes a climactic decision. . . .

AUSTIN, FREDERICK BRITTEN

Buried Treasure in *On the Borderland* (Garden City, NY, 1923)
    Buried Treasure
    7 reels   sil.   b&w   1921
    Dir: George G. Baker. Prod: Cosmopolitan Prod.
    Cast: Marion Davies, Norman Kerry.
    A man in a trance recalls previous incarnations.

AVERY, STEPHEN MOREHOUSE

Head Over Heels
    Hard to Get

AVERY, STEPHEN MOREHOUSE (cont'd)

Hard to Get (cont'd)
s.m. the screen story was in turn based on this short story
80 min.　　b&w　　　　1938
Dir: Ray Enright. Prod: Warner Bros. Dist: United Artists.
Cast: Dick Powell, Olivia de Havilland.

AYERS, JOHN H.

Missing Men (jt. author Carol Bird)
Bureau of Missing Persons
73 min.　　b&w　　　　1933
Dir: Roy Del Ruth. Prod: First National Pictures. Dist: United Artists.
Cast: Bette Davis, Pat O'Brien, Louis Stone.
A murderess is trapped into attending a "mock-up" of her own funeral.

AYME, MARCEL

Walker through Walls (novelette) in *Across Paris and Other Stories* (New York, 1958)
Mr. Peek-a-Boo
74 min.　　1951
Dir: Jean Boyer. Sp: Michel Audiard and Jean Boyer. Prod: Arthur Sachson
　　Enterprises.
Government official discovers he can walk through walls. He catches a burglar,
and reforms a girl.

BAER, ARTHUR (BUGS)
s.m. "Rufftown Stories"
Battle Royal
2 reels　　　b&w　　　　1932
Dir: Harry Sweet. Sp: Ralph Ceder. Prod: RKO Radio Picture Corp.

BAER, THOMAS

Little Eva Ascends in *Saturday Evening Post* (April 9, 1921)
Little Eva Ascends
5 reels   sil.   b&w   1922
Dir: George D. Baker. Prod: Famous Players—Lasky.
Cast: Gareon Hughes, Eleanor Fields.
Comedy drama. The two sons of Blanche St. George play Uncle Tom and Little Eva in *Uncle Tom's Cabin* for her repertory company, but they yearn for a real home. They are finally reconciled with their father, whom Blanche left to pursue a career.

BAINES, JOHN V. see Dead of Night under BENSON, E. F.

BAKER, MELVILLE

Hundred Million Dollars (jt. author John S. Kirkland)
Mills of the Gods
7 reels   b&w   1934
Dir: Roy William Neill. Sp: Garrett Ford. Prod: Columbia.

BALDWIN, FAITH

Apartment for Jenny
Apartment for Peggy
99 min.   b&w   1948
Dir: George Seaton. Sp: George Seaton. Prod: Twentieth Century Fox. Dist:
Films Inc.
Cast: Jeanne Crain, William Holden.
"Excellent, warmly amusing comedy of young marrieds on post-war campus"
—*NY Times* (Feb. 19, 1978)

August Weekend
August Week-end
7 reels   b&w   1936
Dir: Charles Lamont. Sp: Paul Perez. Prod: Chesterfield Motion Pictures.
Cast: Valerie Hobson, G. J. Huntley, Jr.
A man's relentless struggle for power and social position.

Comet Over Broadway in *Cosmopolitan Magazine*
Comet Over Broadway
72 min.   b&w   1938
Dir: Busby Berkeley. Prod: First National Pictures. Dist: United Artists.
Cast: Kay Francis, Ian Hunter.

BALDWIN, FAITH (cont'd)

Comet Over Broadway (cont'd)
Prior movie title was Curtain Call. A self-abnegating actress gives up the theater and returns to her child and husband.

The Gossamer World see Horsie under ASHWORTH, JOHN

Wife Versus Secretary
Wife Versus Secretary
85 min.   b&w   1936
Dir: Clarence Brown. Sp: Norman Krasna, Alice Duer Miller, John Lee Mahin.
    Dist: Films Inc.
Cast: Jean Harlow, Clark Gable, Gay Robson.
A trite story in which a man's mother ignites the jealousy of his wife.

BALLARD, TODHUNTER (pseud.)

Red Horizon in *Esquire*
s.m. novel: *Two-Edged Vengeance* (Macmillan, 1951)
The Outcast
90 min.   color   1953
Dir: William Witney. Sp: John K. Butler, Richard Wormser. Prod: Republic
    Pictures. Dist: Ivy.
Cast: John Derek, Joan Evans.
Western: A young man hires nine gunmen to try to repossess his ranch, which was stolen by an unscrupulous uncle.

BALZAC, HONORE DE

Le Grande Breteche
La Grande Breteche
24 min.   color   1976
Prod: Twentieth Century Fox. Dist: Encyclopaedia Britannica.
Orson Welles introduction. This tale of revenge, set in France during the Napoleonic wars, begins as a love story involving a French countess, a Spanish prisoner of war and a jealous husband. On a visit to his wife's bedroom, the count tricks his devout wife into swearing the closet is empty, when he knows otherwise. Pretending to believe her, he calmly proceeds to have the closet sealed up behind an impenetrable brick wall while his wife looks on in horror.

The Maid of Thilouse
The Maid of Thilouse
15 min.   b&w   1955
Prod: Dynamic Films. Dist: Audio Brandon.
Cast: Monty Woolley.
An elderly Baron seeks the hand of a young peasant girl. When she rejects him, he decides to court her mother.

BALZAC, HONORE DE (cont'd)

La Peau de Chagrin
  The Dream Cheater
  sil.   1920
  Dir: Ernest C. Warde. Prod: Hodkinson.
  Cast: J. Warren Kerrigan.

La Peau de Chagrin
  10 min.   color
  Dir: Vlado Kristl, Ivo Urbanic. Dist: McGraw-Hill.
  A sardonic animated short story in which a gambler makes a pact with a croupier (the devil) for a magic skin which can fulfill his every wish. Ironically, with every wish granted, the skin grows smaller. Finally the hero dies with a cry of panic on his lips, and the skin, now a mere scrap of leather, is blown away by the wind.

Slave of Desire
  7 reels   sil.   1923
  Dir: George D. Baker. Adap: Alice D. G. Miller. Prod: Goldwyn.
  Cast: George Walsh, Bessie Love.
  Allegorical drama. Poet Raphael Valentin meets the vampish Countess Fedora, who makes him successful overnight and then leaves him. An antiquarian gives him a magical piece of leather that grants his every wish.

BANNING, MARGARET CULKEN

Enemy Territory
  Woman against Woman
  6 reels   1938
  Dir: Robert Sinclair. Sp: Edward Chodorov. Prod: M-G-M.
  Cast: Mary Astor, Virginia Bruce, Herbert Marshall.
  Pits wife number one against wife number two.

BARNETT, S. H.

A Place of Dragons*
  Father Goose
  115 min.   color   1964
  Dir: Ralph Nelson. Sp: Peter Stone, Frank Tarloff. Prod: Universal. Dist: Ivy.
  Cast: Cary Grant, Leslie Caron.
  Comedy. A WWII tale of a beach bum who watches a strategic South Seas isle where a French woman and seven girls are stranded. *Note: According to the AFI, publication of this story is uncertain; according to the Writers' Guild it was published.

BARRY, JEROME

Ice Storm
  Ice Storm
  25 min.   color   1976

BARRY, JEROME (cont'd)

Ice Storm (cont'd)
Prod: Twentieth Century Fox. Dist: Encyclopaedia Britannica.
Orson Welles narrates. A librarian-turned-detective must pit her wits against a ruthless killer of unknown identity. As the assistant to the owner of a priceless book collection, she finds herself alone in her employer's mansion during an impassable storm. Three visitors come to buy rare books. A phone call reveals that one is an imposter who will kill to get a share of the collection. By using her research skills, she unmasks the killer—just in time.

BARTEAU, MORTON (jt author) see Six Hours to Live under MORRIS, GORDON

BEACH, REX

Big Brother in *Big Brother and Other Stories* (NY, 1923)
Big Brother
7 reels   sil.   b&w   1923
Dir: Alan Dwan. Prod: Paramount.
Cast: Tom Moore, Edith Roberts, Raymond Hatton.
Crook melodrama. Gangster Jimmy Donovan is made guardian of 7-year-old Midge and he decides to reform.

The Crimson Gardenia in *Crimson Gardenia and Other Tales of Adventure*
The Crimson Gardenia
6 reels   sil.   b&w   1919
Dir: Reginald Barker. Prod: Goldwyn.

The Goose Woman in *The Goose Woman and Other Stories* (NY, 1925)
The Goose Woman
8 reels   sil.   b&w   1925
Dir: Clarence Brown. Prod: Universal. Dist: Cinema 8 (8mm)
Cast: Louise Dresser, Jack Pickford, Constance Bennett.
The tragic experiences of a proud opera star who falls from grace by drinking.

The Past of Mary Holmes
4 reels   b&w   1933
Dir: Harlan Thompson. Sp: Marion Dix, Edward Doherty. Prod: RKO Radio
    Picture Corp.

The Michigan Kid in *The Goose Woman and Other Stories* (NY, 1925)
The Michigan Kid
6 reels   sil.   b&w   1928
Dir: Irwin Willat. Prod: Universal Jewel. Dist: Cine Service Vintage Films.
Cast: Renée Adorée.

BEACH, REX (cont'd)

The Michigan Kid in *The Goose Woman and Other Stories* (NY, 1925)
    The Michigan Kid
    70 min.   color   1947
    Dir: Ray Taylor. Sp: Roy Chanslor. Prod: Universal. Dist: Universal.
    Cast: Jon Hall, Victor McLaglen.
    Western. A number of characters try to find the loot stolen from a stagecoach.
This film is far removed from the story though Universal used the title.

The Recoil in *Big Brother and Other Stories* (NY, 1923)
    The Recoil
    7 reels   sil.   b&w   1924
    Dir: T. Hayes Hunter. Prod: Goldwyn.
    Cast: Mahlon Hunter, Betty Blythe.
    Romantic melodrama. Gordon Kent's wife runs away with an admirer and he and
a detective pursue them.

Rope's End in *Cosmopolitan Magazine* (May 1913)
    A Sainted Devil
    9 reels   sil.   b&w   1924
    Dir: Joseph Henabery. Adap: Forest Halsey. Prod: Famous Players—Lasky.
    Melodrama. On her wedding eve, Julietta is kidnapped.

BEAHAN, CHARLES see also Murder by the Clock under KING, RUFUS

BEAHAN, CHARLES

Rose of the Ritz (jt author Garrett Ford)
    Naughty Baby
    7 reels   sd. effects and mus.   1929
    Dir: Mervyn LeRoy. Prod: First National Pictures.
    Cast: Alice White, Jack Mulhall.
    Comedy drama. Rosie McGill, a hat snatcher at a posh hotel, sets her cap for
wealthy Terry Vandeveer and goes to Long Beach where she poses as a society girl.

BEAUCHAMP, D. D.

A-Hunting We Will Go
    Father's Wild Game
    60 min.   b&w   1950
    Prod: Monogram.
    A father protests the inflation at a meat market by hunting wild game.

The Cruise of the Prairie Queen
    Leave It to Henry
    57 min.   b&w   1949
    Dir: Jean Yarbrough. Prod: Monogram.

BEAUCHAMP, D. D. (cont'd)

Leave It to Henry (cont'd)
Cast: Raymond Walburn, Walter Catlett.
Farce. A lawyer is accused of setting fire to a bridge.

Enough for Happiness
She Couldn't Say No
89 min.   b&w   1954
Dir: Lloyd Bacon. Sp: D. D. Beauchamp, William Bowers, Richard Flournoy.
    Prod: RKO Radio Picture Corp. Dist: Films Inc.
Cast: Robert Mitchum, Jean Simmons.
Comedy. A young oil heiress anonymously distributes gifts and money to the
inhabitants of a small Arkansas town and many difficulties result.

Journey at Sunrise
Father Makes Good
61 min.   b&w   1950
Prod: Monogram.
Father purchases a cow to show his contempt for the new milk tax.

The Wonderful Race with Rimrock in *Collier's Magazine* (March 8, 1946)
Feudin, Fussin and a-Fightin
78 min.   b&w   1948
Dir: George Sherman. Sp: D. D. Beauchamp. Prod: Universal.
Cast: Donald O'Connor, Marjorie Main.
Comedy. A fast-running salesman is captured by a whole town, which is planning
to race him in the annual footrace with a rival community.

BEAUMONT, GERALD

Betty's a Lady in *Redbook*
The Count of Ten
6 reels   sil.   b&w   1928
Dir: James Flood. Prod: Universal.
Cast: Charles Ray, James Gleason, Jobyna Ralston.
Melodrama. An ambitious prizefighter falls in love with Betty, a salesgirl.
He is ordered not to fight when he hurst his hand. Betty, now his wife, tells him she is
pregnant and he goes into the ring and loses.

The Blue Ribbon
s.m. "The Dove," play by Willard Mack, based on the story "The Blue Ribbon"
The Girl and the Gambler
7 reels   b&w   1939
Dir: Lew Landers. Sp: Joseph A. Fields, Clarence Upson Young. Prod: RKO
    Radio Picture Corp.

BEAUMONT, GERALD (cont'd)

The Girl and the Gambler (cont'd)
A Latin American cabellero bets he can woo and win a maiden's heart within 24 hours.

Dixie in *Redbook* (September 1924)
The Dixie Handicap
7 reels   sil.   b&w   1925
Dir: Reginald Barker. Adap: Waldemar Young. Prod: Metro-Goldwyn.
Cast: Claire Windsor, Frank Keenan.
Melodrama. Judge Roberts hides his true financial situation from his daughter. After major financial reverses, he is left with only a horse, which dies soon after foaling. However, the filly that is born turns out to be a champion.

Even Stephen in *Redbook* (October 1925)
Just Another Blonde
6 reels   sil.   b&w   1926
Dir: Alfred Santill. Prod: Rockett Prod.
Cast: Dorothy Mackaill. Jack Mulhall.
Romantic drama. Jimmy O'Connor and Scotty, his pal, share everything 50-50 until Scotty falls in love with Diana. Scotty arranges for Jimmy to meet another woman, Jeanne, but Jimmy is indifferent to her.

The Flower of Napoli in *Redbook* (March 1924)
The Man in Blue
6 reels   sil.   b&w   1925
Dir: Edward Laemmle. Prod: Universal.
Cast: Herbert Rawlinson, Madge Bellamy, Nick De Ruiz.
Melodrama. Tom Conlin falls in love with Tita Sartoni; she loves him but believes he is already married. Later when Tom rescues her from a man who kidnaps her, she discovers Tom is actually single.

Heavenbent in *Redbook*
The Rainmaker
6,055'   sil.   b&w   1926
Dir: Clarence Badger.
Cast: William Collier, Jr., Georgia Hale.
War wounds tell a jockey when rain is coming.

Jack O'Clubs in *Redbook* (December 1923)
Jack O'Clubs
5 reels   sil.   b&w   1924
Dir: Robert F. Hill (uncredited). Adap: Raymond L. Schrock. Prod: Universal.
Cast: Herbert Rawlinson, Ruth Dwyer, Eddie Gribbon.

BEAUMONT, GERALD (cont'd)

Jack O'Clubs (cont'd)
Action melodrama. Jack Foley, a tough cop, loses his nerve when he thinks he's hurt Tillie Miller, the girl he loves.

John McArdle, Referee in *Redbook* (July 1921)
The Referee
5 reels　　　　sil.　　　　　　b&w　　　　　1922
Dir: Ralph Ince. Prod: Selznick Pictures.
Cast: Conway Tearle, Anders Randolf.
Melodrama. An ex-boxer (McArdle) falls in love but the girl's father objects until he learns that McArdle is a man of character.

The Lady Who Played Fidele in *Redbook* (February 1925)
Scarlet Saint
7 reels　　　　sil.　　　　　　b&w　　　　　1925
Dir: George Archainbaud. Prod: First National Pictures.
Cast: Mary Astor, Lloyd Hughes.
Melodrama. Fidele, who is betrothed to Baron Badrew, loves Phillip. Phillip is wounded by the Baron in a duel and is sent to jail.

The Lord's Referee in *Redbook* (July 1923)
The Blue Eagle
7 reels　　　　sil.　　　　　　b&w　　　　　1926
Dir: John Ford. Prod: Fox
Cast: George O'Brien, Janet Gaynor, William Russell.
Melodrama. Rival leaders of neighborhood gangs become stokers and water-tenders on a U.S. battleship during WWI.

The Silk Hat Kid
6,250'　　　　b&w　　　　　1935
Dir: H. Bruce Humberstone. Sp: Edward Eliscu, Lou Breslow, Dore Schary.
　　Prod: Fox Film Corp.

The Making of O'Malley in *Redbook* (October 1924)
The Great O'Malley
71 min.　　　　b&w　　　　　1937
Dir: William Dieterle. Prod: Warner Brothers and Vitaphone. Dist: United
　　Artists.
Cast: Pat O'Brien, Ann Sheridan.
A re-make of The Making of O'Malley. A policeman who lived by the rulebook learns that tickets for misdemeanors may cost a life.

The Making of O'Malley
8 reels　　　　sil.　　　　　　b&w　　　　　1925
Dir: Lambert Hillyer. Prod: First National Pictures.
Cast: Milton Sills, Dorothy Mackerill.
Melodrama. O'Malley, a tough policeman, is assigned to duty as a traffic cop. He meets Lucille, a teacher, and discovers the hideout for a gang of bootleggers, but he doesn't arrest the leader when he discovers Lucille is engaged to him.

BEAUMONT, GERALD (cont'd)

The Money Rider in *Redbook* (September 1924)
   Down the Stretch
   7 reels   sil.   b&w   1927
   Dir: King Baggot. Adap: Curtis Benton. Prod: Universal.
   Cast: Robert Agnew, Marian Nixon.
   Melodrama. Jockey Marty Krugger falls in love with Katie. Marty is laid up by
an accident and when he returns to the track he's overweight. The strict diet he
is put on endangers his health.

The Rose of Kildare in *Redbook* (December 1922)
   The Rose of Kildare
   7 reels   sil.   b&w   1927
   Dir: Dallas M. Fitzgerald. Adap: Harold Shumate.
   Cast: Helene Chadwick, Pat O'Malley.
   Romantic melodrama. Bob Avery, owner of a dancehall in South Africa, loves
singer Eileen O'Moore, but she dreams of her former financé, who later turns up
married.

Said with Soap in *Redbook* (April 1925)
   Babe Comes Home
   6 reels   sil.   b&w   1927
   Dir: Ted Wilde. Prod: First National Pictures.
   The up and down courtship of Babe Dugan, a baseball player whose uniform is
always dirty, and his laundress, who tries to reform him.

The Sporting Venus in *Redbook* (June 1924)
   The Sporting Venus
   7 reels   sil.   b&w   1925
   Dir: Marshall Neilan. Prod: M-G-M.
   Cast: Blanche Sweet, Ronald Colman, Lew Cody.
   Romantic drama. Lady Gwen falls in love with a medical student far below her
station and her father opposes the match.

Thoroughbreds in Beaumont, G. *Riders Up* (NY, Appleton, 1922)
   Silks and Saddles
   6 reels   sil.   b&w   1929
   Dir: Robert F. Hill. Adap: Edward Clark, James Gruen. Prod: Universal Jewel.
      Dist: Mogull's.
   Cast: Richard Walling, Marion Nixon.
   Drama. Jockey Johnny Spencer loses his job with Mrs. Calhoun for throwing a
race. The film was originally released as Thoroughbreds.

Two Bells for Pegasus in *Redbook* (February 1922)
   The Victor
   5 reels   sil.   b&w   1923

BEAUMONT, GERALD (cont'd)

The Victor (cont'd)
Cast: Herbert Rawlinson, Dorothy Manners.
Dir: Edward Laemmle. Prod: Universal.

Romantic comedy. The Honorable Waring comes to America to marry a rich girl in order to save the family estate. Instead, he falls in love with Teddy, a poor actress.

United States Smith
Pride of the Marines
64 min.   b&w   1936
Prod: Columbia
Cast: Charles Bickford, Florence Rice.
A Marine adopts an orphan.

BECHDOLT, JACK

Fog Bound in *Argosy* (December 22, 1921)
Fog Bound
6 reels   sil.   b&w   1923
Dir: Irvin Willat. Prod: Famous Players—Lasky.
Cast: Dorothy Dalton, David Powell.
Melodrama. Roger Wainright is suspected of killing his friend Gale Brenton.

BEDFORD, JONES H.

Garden of the Moon in *Saturday Evening Post* (jt. author Barton Browne)
Garden of the Moon
94 min.   b&w   1938
Dir: Busby Berkeley. Prod: Warner Bros. Dist: United Artists.
Cast: Pat O'Brien, John Payne, Jimmy Fidler, Jerry Colonna.
Story of a cranky, objectionable nightclub owner.

BEHN, MARC (jt. author) see Charade under STONE, PETER

BELLAH, JAMES WARNER

The Big Hunt see She Wore a Yellow Ribbon under WAR PARTY

Command in *Saturday Evening Post* (June 8, 1946)
A Thunder of Drums
97 min.   color   1961
Dir: Joseph Newman. Sp: James Warner Bellah. Prod: M-G-M. Dist: Films Inc.
Cast: Richard Boone, George Hamilton.
U.S. Cavalry officers fighting Apaches when not fighting with each other.

Massacre
Fort Apache
127 min.   b&w   1948
Dir: John Ford. Prod: Argosy Pic., rel. RKO. Dist: Macmillan.
Cast: John Wayne, Henry Fonda.
Henry Fonda plays Colonel Owen Thursday, a West Point officer who assumes command of an isolated Western fort. His rigid adherence to Eastern military traditions and his failure to adjust to the particular demands of Indian fighting result in the massacre of his troop. John Wayne plays Captain York, an experienced frontier cavalryman, whose advice and warnings are rejected by Thursday.

Mission with No Record in *Saturday Evening Post* (September 27, 1947)
Rio Grande
105 min.   b&w   1950
Dir: John Ford. Prod: Republic. Dist: Ivy.
Cast: John Wayne, Maureen O'Hara.
A tough cavalry officer awaits orders to cross the river to engage in battle with the Indians.

War Party in *Saturday Evening Post* (June 19, 1948)
s.m. "The Big Hunt," in *Saturday Evening Post* (December 6, 1947)
She Wore a Yellow Ribbon
103 min.   color   1949
Dir: John Ford. Prod: Argosy Picture Corp., rel. RKO. Dist: Macmillan, Images.
Cast: John Wayne, Joanne Dru.
Ford has cast aside the glamour of the cavalry and leaves in its place human weakness as the Captain (Wayne) and his sergeant (McLaglen) near retirement age. The rules of the cavalry as a disappearing society are scrutinized and tested by Dru and Agar (the next generation).

BELLEM, ROBERT LESLIE

Stock Shot
Blackmail
71 min.   b&w   1947

BELLEM, ROBERT LESLIE (cont'd)

Blackmail (cont'd)
Dir: Lesley Selander. Sp: Royal K. Cole. Prod: Republic. Dist: Ivy.
Cast: William Marshal, Adele Mara.
A detective is called in to protect a rich playboy from blackmail.

BEMELMANS, LUDWIG (jt. author) see Yolanda and the Thief under
THERY, JACQUES

BENET, STEPHEN VINCENT

The Devil and Daniel Webster
All That Money Can Buy see The Devil and Daniel Webster
The Devil and Daniel Webster
109 min.   b&w   1952
Dir: William Dieterle. Prod: Astor Films Prod. Dist: Alba.
Cast: James Craig, Simone Simon, Walter Huston.
A reissue and retitle of All That Money Can Buy (1941). A man sells his soul
for riches.

Everybody Was Very Nice in *Saturday Evening Post* (September 5, 1936)
Love, Honor and Behave
7 reels   1938   b&w
Dir: Stanley Logan. Sp: Clements Ripley, Michel Jacoby, Robert Buckner,
Lawrence Kimble. Prod: Warner.
A young man grows up, still under his dominating mother's influence, but along
comes a pretty girl to help him straighten himself out.

Famous
Just for You
104 min.   color   1952
Dir: Elliott Nugent. Prod: Paramount. Dist: Films Inc.
Cast: Bing Crosby, Jane Wyman.
Comedy drama. A producer sets out to win the affection of his children after
years of concentrating on his career.

The Sobbin Women
Seven Brides for Seven Brothers
102 min.   color   1954
Dir: Stanley Donen. Prod: M-G-M. Dist: Films Inc.
Cast: Jane Powell, Howard Keel.
When the eldest of seven brothers in the Oregon Territory brings a wife home to
take care of the family and farm, the other six brothers want wives of their own.
They sneak into town and steal six girls they had met at a barn raising.

BENET, STEPHEN VINCENT (cont'd)

Uriah's Son
>The Necessary Evil
>7 reels   sil.   b&w   1925
>Dir: George Archainbaud. Prod: First National Pictures.
>Melodrama. On her deathbed Frances Jerome secures David Devanant's promise
to raise her son Frank, who grows into a wild young man. Frank is wrongly
accused of stealing, but Devanant pretends to believe he is guilty to send him to
the tropics, where he develops into manhood.

BENSON, EDWARD F.

The Bus Conductor see Dead of Night under The Room in the Tower

Mrs. Amworth
>Mrs. Amworth
>29 min.   color   1977
>Dir: Alvin Rakoff. Sp: Hugh Whitemore. Dist: Learning.
>Cast: Glynis Johns.
>Doctors ascribe the mysterious epidemic attacking the quiet village of Maxley to
the bite of venomous gnats. But they are puzzled by the disease which seems to drain
the body of blood. When David Benson arrives to visit his uncle, he is intrigued
by Mrs. Amworth's charms. She has captivated the townspeople—with one exception—
Francis Urcombe, former psysiology professor and student of the occult, who is
suspicious of her strange nocturnal appearances. David is stricken by the disease,
and Urcombe concludes it is the work of a vampire—Mrs. Amworth. A chain of
horrifying events leads him and David's uncle to decide that they must take drastic
steps to destroy the sinister presence . . . the glamorous and deadly Mrs. Amworth.
The film builds to a chilling climax.

The Room in the Tower
s.m. "The Bus Conductor"
>Dead of Night*
>104 min.   b&w   1945
>Dir: Alberto Cavalcanti, Charles Crichton, Basil Dearden, Robert Hamer. Prod:
>   Ealing Studios Ltd., rel. Universal. Dist: Janus.
>Cast: Mervyn Johns, Roland Culver.
>*This film consists of five sequences. Verification of whether or not they were
based on original stories or short stories was impossible at the time of publication.
1. The Hearse Driver Sequence, story by E. F. Benson. 2. The Christmas Party
Sequence, story by Angus MacPhail. 3. The Haunted Mirror Sequence, story by
John V. Baines. 4. The Ventriloquist's Dummy Sequence, story by John V. Baines.
5. The Golfing Story Sequence, story by H. G. Wells. An architect is invited to spend
a weekend at the country house of a client in order to survey the house and suggest
improvements. When the architect arrives, he finds a small house party in progress.
All the guests are total strangers to him, but he suddenly realizes that he has met them

BENSON, EDWARD F. (cont'd)

Dead of Night (cont'd)
all before in a recurring dream, and that a series of trivial incidents will lead to a
terrible disaster that weekend.

"The 5 ghost stories in the 1945 English production increase in intensity, until
the trap closes in the surrealist climax—the encompassing ghost story. Perhaps
because the people are matter of fact and contemporary and the settings are of
the reasonably sophisticated forties, the horror seems more shocking than if the
characters and settings were Gothic and Transylvanian"—Pauline Kael in *Kiss
Kiss Bang Bang.*

BENTHAM, JOSEPHINE

A Bride for Henry
    A Bride for Henry
    7 reels   1937
    Dir: William Nigh. Adap: Marion Orth. Prod: Monogram Picture Corp.
    Cast: Warren Hull, Anne Nagel.
    When the groom fails to show up at the wedding, the bride marries the best man.

BERCOVICI, KONRAD

The Bear Tamer's Daughter in *Ghitza and Other Romances of Gypsy Blood* (NY,
    1921)
    Revenge
    7 reels   mus. score, and sd. effects   b&w   1928
    Dir: Edwin Carewe. Prod: Edwin Carewe Prod.
    Cast: Dolores Del Rio, James Marcus.
    Rascha, the wild daughter of Costa, the Gypsy bear tamer, swears revenge on her
father's enemy.

BIALK, ELISA

The Sainted Sisters of Sandy Creek
    The Sainted Sisters
    s.m. unpublished play "The Sainted Sisters of Sandy Creek" by Elisa Bialk and
        Alden Nash
    90 min.   b&w   1948
    Dir: William Russell. Prod: Paramount. Dist: Universal.
    Cast: Veronica Lake, Joan Caulfield, Barry Fitzgerald.
    Two con girls are reformed.

BIERCE, AMBROSE

Boarded Window
    Boarded Window
    17½ min.   color   1973
    Dir: Alan W. Beattie. Dist: Perspective.

BIERCE, AMBROSE (cont'd)

Boarded Window (cont'd)

The cabin has only one window, and that window has been boarded over for many years. When the hunter shared the cabin with his young wife years before, the window was not boarded over and flowers grew in the window box. One day when the hunter returns from the woods, he finds that his wife has a high fever. That night she died. Grief stricken, he lovingly prepares her body for burial and digs the grave. During the night before her burial the forces of nature intervene to create a macabre ending.

Chickamauga
    Chickamauga
    33 min.   b&w   1961
    Dir: Robert Enrico. Sp: Robert Enrico. Dist: McGraw-Hill, Wholesome Film
        Center.
A symbolic world of the horrors of war, as a little boy wanders away from home, reaches a battlefield, plays soldier among the dead and dying, and returns home to find his house burned and his family slain.

The Man and the Snake
    The Man and the Snake
    26 min.   color   1975
    Dir: Sture Rydman. Sp: Brian Scobie, S. Rydman. Dist: Pyramid.
Loosely based on the above story, this is the story of the unsettling struggle between the common sense of the day and the eerie effects of nightfall.

The Mockingbird
    The Mockingbird
    39 min.   1966
    Dir: Robert Enrico. Dist: Audio Brandon.
A private in the Union Army, standing night guard, sees an indistinct figure, panics, and fires. The next day, troubled by his experience, he goes in search of his victim and finds the body of his twin brother in Confederate uniform. The shock causes the soldier to desert.

An Occurrence at Owl Creek Bridge
    An Occurrence at Owl Creek Bridge
    30 min.   b&w   1964
    Dir and Sp: Robert Enrico. Prod: Janus. Dist: McGraw-Hill.
    Cast: Roger Jacquet, Anne Cornaly, Anker Larsen.
Set during the Civil War, a spy is condemned to die by hanging. But, at the last minute, he may be saved by a near-miracle. Is it the final paroxysm of a mind hoping against death, or is the hero really going to escape the noose, the bullets . . . death by drowning in the swirling waters of Owl Creek?

BIERCE, AMBROSE (cont'd)

An Occurrence at Owl Creek Bridge (cont'd)
   The Spy
   1932
   Dir: Charles Vidor.
   Cast: Nicholas Bela.
   Drama. The instant before his death by hanging the spy imagines an elaborate
escape.

One of the Missing
   One of the Missing
   56 min.   color   1971
   Dist: Audio Brandon.
   Cast: Talmadge Armstrong, Gordon Baxter.
   A spellbinding tale of a Civil War sharpshooter, pinned down after an explosion,
with his own cocked rifle pointed at his face. Knowing that the slightest move will
set the gun off, the man cautiously tries to free himself, and at the same time recalls
the events of his life which have led to his present predicament.

   One of the Missing
   52 min.   color   1977
   Dist: Educational Communications.
   A chilling tale set during the Civil War of a bounty hunter caught in a cabin as
the roof is collapsing.

Parker Adderson, Philosopher
   Parker Adderson, Philosopher
   20 min.   color   1970
   Dist: Film Images. Prod: Ching Kuai.
   A literal rendering of this story of a Federal spy questioned by a Confederate
general.

   Parker Adderson, Philosopher
   38½ min.   color   1977
   Dir and Sp: Arthur Barron. Dist: Perspective Films.
   Drama. Captured behind enemy lines at the end of the Civil War, Parker Adderson confronts a weary Confederate General. The harsh reality of his impending
execution causes Adderson to undergo abrupt character changes. His bravado and
disdain for life arouse the general's instincts for sham. A vicious battle in the
general's tent ensues, leading to the death of an innocent man and wounding of the
general.

Unidentified story
   The Return
   s.m. a story by A. M. Burrage
   30 min.   color   1976

BIERCE, AMBROSE (cont'd)

The Return (cont'd)
Dir: Elizabeth McKay. Dist: Pyramid.
There are rumors a ghost inhabits a boarded-up mansion in Edwardian England.

BIGGERS, EARL DERR

Behind That Curtain in *Saturday Evening Post* (March 31, May 5, 1928)
Behind That Curtain
10 reels   sd.   b&w   1929
Dir: Irving Cummings. Prod: Fox.
Mystery melodrama. Eve Mannering, daughter of a wealthy Englishman, marries a fortune hunter who kills the investigator hired by her father.

Broadway Broke in *Saturday Evening Post* (October 7, 1922)
Broadway Broke
6 reels   sil.   b&w   1923
Dir: J. Searle Dawley. Prod: Murray W. Garrson.
Cast: Mary Carr, Percy Marmont.
Melodrama. Nellie Wayne, a retired theatrical star, saves her family from bankruptcy when she sells her plays.

The Deuce of Hearts
Take the Stand
9 reels   1934
Dir: Phil Rosen. Prod: Liberty Picture Corp.

The Girl Who Paid Dividends in *Saturday Evening Post* (April 23, 1921)
Her Face Value
5 reels   sil.   b&w   1921
Dir: Thomas N. Neffron. Prod: Realart Pictures.
Cast: Wanda Hawley, Lincoln Plummer.
Society melodrama. Chorus girl Peggy Malone, who supports her father and brother, marries press agent Jimmy Parsons. But Jimmy's health is jeopardized and she must go back to work. She becomes a star and must choose between her husband and a wealthy admirer.

Honeymoon Flats in *Saturday Evening Post* (July 2, 1927)
Honeymoon Flats
6 reels   sil.   b&w   1928
Dir: Millard Webb. Prod: Universal.
Cast: George Lewis, Dorothy Gulliver, Kathlyn Williams.
Comedy drama. Lila Garland marries Jim Clayton against her parent's wishes. Her mother's interference in the marriage almost causes it to end.

BIGGERS, EARL DERR (cont'd)

Idle Hands in *Earl Derr Biggers Tells Ten Stories*
  The Millionaire
  80 min.   b&w   1931
  Dir: John Adolfi. Prod: Warner Brothers. Dist: United Artists.
  Cast: George Arliss, James Cagney.
  Comedy. A millionaire takes a job incognito and lends a hand toward the
straightening-out of several people's affairs.

  That Way with Women
  84 min.   b&w   1947
  Dir: Frederick de Cordova. Prod: Warner Brothers. Dist: United Artists.
  Cast: Dane Clark, Sydney Greenstreet.
  Comedy of an irascible, benign old man.

John Henry and the Restless Sex in *Saturday Evening Post* (March 5, 1921)
  Too Much Business
  Dir: Jess Robbins. Prod: Vitagraph.
  Cast: Tully Marshall, Edward Everett Horton.
  The romance of a sales manager and his secretary, and the consolidation of their
company with a rival one.

The Ruling Passion in *Saturday Evening Post* (1922)
  The Ruling Passion
  7,000'   sil.   1922
  Dir: Harmon Weight. Prod: Distinctive Prod.
  Cast: George Arliss, Doris Kenyon.
  Comedy drama. James Alden—machinist, designer, inventor and millionaire—is
told by his daughter to retire. However, he can't remain idle and so he goes into
partnership with a young man in a garage.

Trouping with Ellen in *Saturday Evening Post* (April 8, 1922)
  Trouping with Ellen
  7 reels   sil.   b&w   1924
  Dir: T. Hayes Hunter. Prod: Eastern Prod.
  Cast: Helene Chadwick, Gary Thurman, Gaston Glass, Basil Rathbone.
  Romantic comedy. Ellen, a chorus girl, is frequently asked by the orchestra leader
to marry him, but she refuses.

BIRD, CAROL (jt. author) see AYERS, JOHN H. under Missing Men

BLOCH, ROBERT

The Cloak see The House That Dripped Blood under Method for Murder

BLOCH, ROBERT (cont'd)

Enoch
    Torture Garden
    s.m. "Terror Over Hollywood," "Mr. Steinway," "The Man Who Collected Poe"
    93 min.   color   1967
    Dir: Freddie Francis. Prod: Columbia Pictures Corp. Dist: Modern.
    Cast: Jack Palance, Peter Cushing, Burgess Meredith.
    Horror thriller. A unique sideshow is presided over by a sinister-looking man who
calls himself Dr. Diablo. Several persons see what is in store for them if they allow
the evil side of their nature to take over their lives.

Frozen Fear see Asylum under The Weird Taylor

Lucy Comes to Stay see Asylum under The Weird Taylor

The Man Who Collected Poe see Torture Garden under Enoch

Mannikins of Horror see also Asylum under The Weird Taylor

Mannikins of Horror
    The Mannikin
    28 min.   color   1977
    Dir: Don Thompson. Dist: Learning.
    Cast: Ronee Blakley, Keir Dullea.
    A beautiful New York singer finds little relief from oddly recurring back pains
after visits to her psychologist, a cynical young man who loves her. The pains dis-
appear only when she returns to her childhood home and the reclusive housekeeper
who helped raise her. Dragged again into the mysterious rituals she hated as a child,
the heroine sends her sweetheart away when he comes to find her. He goes, but
uneasy, and decides to drive back. The car gathers speed . . . and suddenly, lurking
evil manifests itself in a scene of shock and terror.

Method for Murder
    The House That Dripped Blood
    s.m. "Waxworks," "Sweets to the Sweet," "The Cloak"
    101 min.   color   1970
    Dir: Peter Duffell. Dist: Swank
    Cast: Christopher Lee, Peter Cushing.
    Four fascinating and suspenseful short stories set in an eerie country mansion.

Mr. Steinway see Torture Garden under Enoch

The Skull of the Marquis de Sade in *The Skull of the Marquis de Sade* (NY, 1965)
    The Skull
    85 min.   color   1965

BLOCH, ROBERT (cont'd)

The Skull (cont'd)
Dir: Freddie Francis. Prod: Paramount. Dist: Films Inc.
Cast: Peter Cushing, Christopher Lee, Nigel Green.
The skull of the infamous Marquis de Sade is purchased by a student of the super-natural even though he knows its diabolic history.

Sweets to the Sweet see The House That Dripped Blood under Method for Murder

Terror Over Hollywood see Torture Garden under Enoch

Waxworks see The House That Dripped Blood under Method for Murder

The Weird Taylor
Asylum
s.m. "Lucy Comes to Stay," "Frozen Fear," "Mannikins of Horror"
88 min.   color   1972
Dir: Roy Ward Baker. Prod: Cinerama Releasing. Dist: Swank.
Cast: Peter Cushing, Britt Ekland, Herbert Lom.
A spine-tingling tale by the author of Psycho, which takes place in a private asylum for the incurably insane and it wallows in tantilizing mystery and murder. Four short individual horror stories, told by inmates, fill out the main plot which involves a guessing game in search of the identify of the mad doctor at the asylum.

BLOCK, LIBBIE

Pin-Up Girl
Pin-Up Girl
7,450'   1944
Dir: Bruce Humberstone. Sp: Robert Ellis, Helen Logan. Prod: Twentieth Cen-
    tury Fox.
Cast: Betty Grable, Martha Raye, Joe E. Brown.
The romance of a sailor.

BLOCKMAN, LAWRENCE C.

Death from the Sanskrit
Quiet Please, Murder
70 min.   b&w   1942
Dir: John Larkin. Prod: Twentieth Century Fox. Dist: Films Inc.
Cast: George Sanders, Gail Patrick.
Offbeat yarn of a master forger who passes off his copies of original Shakespeare volumes he stole. Murder and romance are woven into the story.

BOCCACCIO

Decameron
Archangel Gabriel and Mother Goose
28 min.   color
Dir: Jiri Trnka. Dist: McGraw-Hill.

A free adaptation from a story in Boccaccio's Decameron, this film tells of a philandering monk who takes advantage of a beautiful lady's secret love for Archangel Gabriel. He decides that the best way to gain the lady's favors is to appear to her in the Archangel's form. To accomplish this, he creates an elaborate disguise, including large goose-feather wings and a golden halo. When he visits her that night, she submits to him in an ecstacy of religious zeal. But finally, the monk is proven a fraud, and he flees the city, leaving a foolish Mother Goose to reclaim her lost dignity. Puppet animation.

Decameron Nights
85 min.   1953
Dir: Hugo Fregonese. Prod: RKO.
Cast: Joan Fontaine, Louis Jourdan, Joan Collins

Costume adventure. Author Boccaccio tries to win the love of his lady by telling her two spicy tales.

BOLL, HEINRICH

Dr. Murke's Collected Silences
Dr. Murke's Collected Silences
23 min.   1971
Dir: Per Berglund. Dist: McGraw-Hill.

A sound editor who collects "silences" that he makes by cutting our phrases from the soundtracks of various radio programs. Especially furious this day is the need to delete the word "God" 26 times from a tape and replace it with an equivalent but pretentious-sounding phrase. As if this were a matter of earth-shaking importance, everyone at the station pursues it with him and with utmost solemnity and concern . . . even going as far as to try to record the replacement-phrase with deep emotion: No trespass into absurdity is forbidden. Boll is a winner of a Nobel Prize. Swedish dialogue with English sub-titles.

BOND, LEE

Homesteads of Hate
Land of the Open Range
60 min.   b&w   1942
Dir: Edward Killy. Sp: Morton Grant. Prod: RKO
Cast: Tim Holt

A man leaves his land to crooks who served two or more years in prison.

BOYD, THOMAS ALEXANDER

The Long Shot in *Points of Honor* (NY, 1925)
Blaze O'Glory

BOYD, THOMAS ALEXANDER (cont'd)

Blaze O'Glory (cont'd)
10 reels   sd.   b&w   1929
Dir: Renaud Hoffman, George J. Crone. Prod: Sono-Art Prod.
Cast: Eddie Dowling, Betty Compson.
Drama. On trial for murder, Eddie Williams tells his story.

BOYLE, JACK

An Answer in Grand Larceny see Missing Millions under A Problem in Grand
Larceny

Boston Blackie, a character created by Boyle, also appeared in After Midnight
with Boston Blackie, Alias Boston Blackie, Boston Blackie and the Law, Boston
Blackie Booked on Suspicion, Boston Blackie Goes to Hollywood, Boston Blackie
Goes to Washington, Boston Blackie's Chinese Venture, Boston Blackie's Rendezvous,
The Chance of a Lifetime, A Close Call for Boston Blackie, Trapped by Boston
Blackie.

Boston Blackie's Little Pal in *Redbook*
Boston Blackie's Little Pal
1918
Dir: E. Mason Hopper. Adap: Albert Shelby Le Vino. Prod: Metro Pictures Corp.

Boston Blackie's Mary
Blackie's Redemption
s.m. "Fred the Count"
5 reels   sd.   b&w   1919
Dir: John Ince. Prod: Metro Pictures Corp.

Debt of Dishonor in *Redbook*
Soiled
7 reels   sil.   b&w   1924
Dir: Fred Windemere. Prod: Phil Goldstone Prod.
Cast: Kenneth Harlan, Vivian Martin.
Melodrama. Wilbur Brown steals $2,500 from his employer and his sister is almost
forced to compromise herself in order to get the money to repay the company.

The Face in the Fog in *Cosmopolitan Magazine* (May 1920)
The Face in the Fog
7 reels   sil.   b&w   1922
Dir: Alan Crosland. Prod: Cosmopolitan Prod.
Cast: Lionel Barrymore, Seena Owen.
Mystery melodrama. Reformed crook Boston Blackie accidently comes into
possession of the Romanov jewels.

BOYLE, JACK (cont'd)

Fred the Count see Blackie's Redemption under Boston Blackie's Mary

A Problem in Grand Larceny in *Redbook* (December 1918-January 1919)
    Missing Millions
    s.m. "An Answer in Grand Larceny"
    6 reels   sil.   1922
    Dir: Joseph Henabery. Prod: Famous Players—Lasky.
    Cast: Alice Brady, David Powell.
    Crook drama. Mary Dawson is determined to repay Jim Franklin for sending her father to Sing Sing, after Franklin reneged on his promise to drop the charges against her father.

Unidentified story in *Cosmopolitan Magazine*
    The Return of Boston Blackie
    6 reels   sil.   b&w   1927
    Dir: Harry O. Holt. Adap: Leah Baird. Prod: Chadwick Pictures. Dist: Mogull's.
    Crook melodrama. Vowing to go straight now that he is out of jail, Boston Blackie tries to reform a pretty blonde who he thinks just stole a necklace. However, the jewels turn out to belong to the girl's mother.

BRACE, BLANCHE

The Adventures of a Ready Letter Writer in *Saturday Evening Post* (November 13, 1920)
    Don't Write Letters
    5 reels   sil.   b&w   1922
    Dir: George D. Baker. Prod: Famous Players—Lasky.
    Cast: Gareth Hughes, Bartine Burkett.
    Comedy drama. A small-statured Army man finds a letter from Anna May and begins a correspondence with her pretending he is a muscular, tall man. They are married by proxy, but finally the deception ends happily.

    A Letter for Evie
    9 reels   b&w   1945
    Dir: Jules Dassin. Sp: De Vallon Scott, Alan Friedman. Prod: M-G-M.
    Cast: Marsha Hunt, John Carroll, Hume Cronyn.
    A re-make of Don't Write Letters. A shy man writes to a girl, but he assumes the identify of his handsome buddy. She meets both of them.

BRACKETT, CHARLES WILLIAM

Interlocutory in *Saturday Evening Post* (March 14, 1924)
    Tomorrow's Love
    6 reels   sil.   b&w   1925
    Dir: Paul Bern. Sp: Howard Higgin. Prod: Famous Players—Lasky. Dist: Audio Brandon.

BRACKETT, CHARLES WILLIAM (cont'd)

Tomorrow's Love (cont'd)
Cast: Agnes Ayres, Pat O'Malley.
Comedy drama. Judith becomes annoyed by her husband's bad habits. When his car breaks down and an old girlfriend picks him up, his wife suspects the worst and asks for a divorce. They are later reconciled.

Pearls Before Cecily in *Saturday Evening Post* (February 17, 1923)
Risky Business
7 reels   sil.   b&w   1926
Dir: Alan Hale. Adap: Beulah Marie Dix. Prod: De Mille Pictures. Dist: Select
8 min.
Social drama. A pampered rich girl loves Ted Pyncheon, a struggling doctor, but her mother wants her to marry wealthy Coults-Browne.

BRADBURY, RAY

The Beast from 20,000 Fathoms in *Saturday Evening Post Stories, 1950-1953* (Random House)
The Beast from 20,000 Fathoms
80 min.   b&w   1953
Dir: Eugene Lourie. Sp: Lou Morheim, Fred Freiberger. Prod: Warner
      Brothers. Dist: Budget, Macmillan, Modern, Roa, Select, Twyman.
Cast: Paul Christian, Paula Raymond.
The prehistoric past and the nuclear future meet in this thrilling monster epic.

The Long Rain
The Illustrated Man
s.m. The Veldt and The Last Night of the World
103 min.   color   1969
Dir: Jack Smight. Prod: Warner Brothers.
Cast: Rod Steiger, Claire Bloom, Robert Drivas.
Three stories are tied together by the presence of a travelling performer whose strange tattoos come to life to act out lessons in human nature.

The Pedestrian
The Pedestrian
6 min.   1960
Prod: USC
In a repressive society of the future, a man who is out for a walk is stopped by incredulous police.

The Veldt see The Illustrated Man under The Long Rain

BRADSHAW, GEORGE

Memorial to a Bad Man
The Bad and the Beautiful

BRADSHAW, GEORGE (cont'd)

The Bad and the Beautiful (cont'd)
s.m. "Of Good and Evil"
118 min.   b&w   1952
Dir: Vincente Minelli. Sp: Charles Schnee. Prod: M-G-M. Dist: Films Inc.
Cast: Lana Turner, Kirk Douglas.
When producer Douglas finds his career almost finished, he calls upon three former associates to help him. Super-director Sullivan, super-writer Powell, and super-star Turner reflect on their past careers with venom directed at Douglas, who gave them their first break in Hollywood, but later tormented them with his own destructive personality.

Of Good and Evil see The Bad and the Beautiful under Memorial to a Bad Man

Shoestring
New Faces of 1937
12 reels   b&w   1937
Dir: Leigh Jason. Sp: Nat Perrin, Philip G. Epstein, Irving S. Brecher. Prod: RKO.
Cast: Joe Penner, Milton Berle.
The launching of a Broadway show.

Venus Rising in *Practise to Deceive*
How to Steal a Million
127 min.   color   1966
Dir: William Wyler. Prod: Twentieth Century Fox. Dist: Films Inc.
Cast: Audrey Hepburn, Peter O'Toole, Hugh Griffith, Eli Wallach.
Elegantly gowned Audrey enlists the aid of impeccably dressed burglar O'Toole to steal a Cellini statue which belongs to her art collector father, who had long been foisting fraudulent Old Masters on the art world.

BRANCH, HOUSTON

Congo Crossing
Congo Crossing
85 min.   color   1956
Dir: Joseph Pevney. Sp: Richard Alan Simmons. Prod and Dist: Universal.
A melodrama set in Africa. A young woman unjustly accused of murder evades a man who has been hired to kill her.

BRAND, MAX (pseud. of Frederick Faust)

Dr. Gillespie, a character created by Brand, appeared in several films including Calling Dr. Gillespie, Dr. Gillespie's Criminal Case, and Dr. Gillespie's New Assistant.

Dr. Kildare, a character also created by Brand, appeared in a number of films including Dr. Kildare Goes Home, Dr. Kildare's Crisis, Dr. Kildare's Strangest Case, Dr. Kildare's Victory, Dr. Kildare's Wedding Day, The People Versus Dr. Kildare, The Secret of Dr. Kildare, and Young Dr. Kildare.

BRAND, MAX (cont'd)

Alcatraz
  Just Tony
  5 reels   sil.   b&w   1922
  Dir: Lynn Edwards. Prod: Twentieth Century Fox.
  Cast: Tom Mix, Claire Adams, and a horse, Tony.
  A wild horse saved by the hero from a cruel captor later saves the cowboy's life.

Champion of Lost Causes in *Flynn's Magazine*
  Champion of Lost Causes
  5 reels   sil.   b&w   1925
  Dir: Chester Bennett. Prod: Fox
  Cast: Edmund Lowe, Barbara Bedford.
  Mystery melodrama. An author notices Joseph Wilbur at a gambling resort; Wilbur is acting strangely and is later murdered.

Children of the Night in *All Story Weekly Magazine*
  Children of the Night
  5 reels   sil.   b&w   1921
  Dir: Jack Dillon. Prod: Twentieth Century Fox.
  Cast: William Russell, Ruth Renick
  Fantasy melodrama. A clerk falls asleep in his office and dreams that he has an aggressive personality. When he awakens, he is aggressive.

Cuttle's Hired Man in *Western Story Magazine*
  Against All Odds
  5 reels   sil.   b&w   1924
  Dir: Edmund Mortimer. Prod: Fox.
  Cast: Charles "Buck" Jones, Dolores Rousse, Ben Hendricks, Jr., William Scott.
  Western melodrama. Chick Newton's friend Bill Warner is arrested for murdering his uncle, but he has been framed and his friend rescues him from lynching.

Hired Guns in *Western Story Magazine* (March 10, 1923)
  The Gunfighter
  5 reels   sil.   b&w   1923
  Dir: Lynn F. Reynolds. Prod: Fox.
  Cast: William Farnum, Doris May.
  Melodrama. A feud between the Benchleys and the Camps arises when Lew Camp learns that his daughter was kidnapped from her mother to replace a dead Benchley child.

The Secret of Dr. Kildare
  The Secret of Dr. Kildare
  9 reels   b&w   1939
  Dir: Harold Bucquet. Sp: Willis Goldbeck, Harry Ruskin. Prod: M-G-M. Dist:
      Classic Film Museum.

BRAND, MAX (cont'd)

The Secret of Dr. Kildare (cont'd)
Cast: Helen Gilbert, Lew Ayres, Lionel Barrymore.
Dr. Kildare and Dr. Gillespie keep secrets from each other, supposedly for the good of the other.

Señor Jingle Bells in *Argosy All-Story Weekly* (March 7, April 4, 1925)
The Best Bad Man
5 reels   sil.   b&w   1925
Dir: J. G. Blystone. Prod: Fox
Cast: Tom Mix, Buster Gardner.
Western comedy melodrama. An absentee ranchowner visits his property disguised as a peddler.

Who Am I? in *Argosy All-Story Weekly* (February 3, 1918)
Who Am I?
5 reels   sil.   b&w   1921
Dir: Henry Kolker. Prod: Selznick Pictures.
Cast: Claire Anderson, Gertrude Astor.
Melodrama. Ruth Burns didn't know her father was a professional gambler until after his death.

Unidentified story
Interns Can't Take Money
77 min.   b&w   1937
Dir: Alfred Santell. Prod: Paramount
Cast: Joel McCrea, Barbara Stanwyck.
The first Dr. Kildare movie. A woman sent to prison can be helped by one doctor—if he would.

BRANSTEN, RICHARD (jt. author) see Margie under McKENNEY, RUTH

BREN, J. ROBERT (jt. author) see The Band Plays On under STUHLDREHER, HARRY

BRENNAN, FREDERICK HAZLITT

The Matron's Report in *Cosmopolitan Magazine* (March 1928)
Blue Skies
6 reels   mus. score and sd. effects   1929
Dir: Alfred L. Werker. Prod: Fox
Cast: Carmencita Johnson, Freddie Frederick, Helen Twelvetrees, Frank
    Albertson.
Two children are eventually rescued from an orphanage. *Variety* said (July 17, 1929) that this film is "Fox's kid version of 'Over the Hill.' "

BRENNAN, FREDERICK HAZLITT (cont'd)

The Matron's Report (cont'd)
   Little Miss Nobody
   6,620'   b&w   1936
   Dir: John Blystone. Sp: Low Breslow, Paul Burger, Edward Eliscu. Prod: Fox.
   Cast: Jane Withers, Jane Darwell.
   A homeless harum-scarum with a heart so big she gives up her own happiness
for another.

Miss Pacific Fleet
   Miss Pacific Fleet
   76 min.   b&w   1935
   Dir: Ray Enright. Prod: Warner Brothers. Dist: United Artists.
   Cast: Joan Blondell, Glenda Farrell.
   Chorus girls trying to win popularity with the Navy.

Perfect Week End
   St. Louis Kid
   67 min.   b&w   1934
   Dir: Ray Enright. Prod: Warner Brothers. Dist: United Artists
   Cast: James Cagney, Patricia Ellis.
   A truck driver in the diary business fights crooked officials.

The Pumpkin Shell
   My Pal Wolf
   76 min.   b&w   1944
   Dir: Alfred M. Werker. Prod: RKO. Dist: Films Inc.
   Cast: Sharyn Moffett, Jill Esmond.
   A little girl deserted by her parents and cared for by a cruel governess befriends
a stray dog.

BRESLIN, HOWARD

Bad Times at Hondo
   Bad Day at Black Rock
   81 min.   b&w   1955
   Dir: John Sturges. Sp: Mildred Kaufman. Prod: M-G-M. Dist: Films Inc.
   Cast: Spencer Tracy, Robert Ryan.
   When a one-armed stranger gets off the train, he encounters hostile reactions
from the community's 37 inhabitants when he asks about a Japanese-American
farmer to whom he is delivering a war medal.

BRESLIN, HOWARD (cont'd)
Bad Times at Hondo (cont'd)
    Platinum High School
    93 min.   1960
    Dir: Charles Haas. Sp: Robert Smith. Prod: M-G-M.
    Cast: Dan Duryea, Mickey Rooney, Terry Moore.
    Melodrama. An unlikely drama of an academic Alcatraz for wealthy youths, and
a father investigating the death of his son.

BRODIE, JULIAN (jt. author) see Love on the Run under GREEN, ALAN

BROMFIELD, LOUIS

The Life of Vergie Winters
    The Life of Vergie Winters
    9 reels   b&w   1934
    Dir: Alfred Santell. Sp: Jane Murfin. Prod: RKO.

Single Night
    Night after Night
    75 min.   b&w   1932
    Dir: Archie Mayo. Prod: Paramount, Dist: Universal.
    Cast: Mae West, George Raft.
    The owner of a high-class speakeasy wants to become educated.

BROOKE, EDGAR see It's a Big Country under PETRACCA, JOSEPH

BROWN, FREDERIC

Madman's Holiday
    Crack-Up
    93 min.   b&w   1946
    Dir: Irving Reis. Prod: RKO
    Cast: Pat O'Brien, Claire Trevor.
    An art curator is tricked by art forgers into thinking he was in a train wreck.

BROWN, GEORGE CARLTON

The Holy Terror
    Big Punch
    80 min.   b&w   1948
    Dir: Sherry Shourds. Prod: Warner Brothers. Dist: United Artists.
    Cast: Wayne Morris, Gordon MacRae.
    Prizefight drama.

BROWN, JAMES

The Magic Garden
  Penny Whistle Blues
  b&w   1952
  Prod: Swan Film Co. Dist: Cinema Service/Vintage Films (listed as The Magic
    Garden)
  Comedy. A thief loses the loot he stole himself.

BROWN, KARL

The Creep in the Dark
  The Ape Man
  64 min.   b&w   1943
  Dir: William Beaudine. Prod: Monogram Pictures Corp. Dist. Budget,
    Macmillan, Universal.
  Cast: Bela Lugosi, Wallace Ford.
  A scientist experiments and becomes half-man and half-ape.

BROWN, WALTER C.

Prelude to Murder
  The House in the Woods
  62 min.   b&w   1957
  Dir: Maxwell Munden. Sp: Maxwell Munden. Prod: St. John's Woods Studios.
  Cast: Patricia Roc, Ronald Howard, Michael Gough.
  Ghost of murdered woman returns.

BROWNE, BARTON (jt. author) see Garden of the Moon under
BEDFORD-JONES, H.

BRUCE, GEORGE (jt. author) see Baby Face under OPPENHEIMER, GEORGE

BRUSH, KATHERINE

Free Woman in Brush, K. *This Man and This Woman* (NY, Blakiston, 1944)
  My Love Is Yours
  95 min.   b&w   1939
  Dir: Edward H. Griffith. Prod: Paramount.
  Cast: Fred MacMurray, Madeleine Carroll, Allan Jones.
  A romantic comedy about a cold, calculating career girl, who falls for a man.
Also known as the film Free Woman.

BRUSH, KATHERINE (cont'd)

Maid of Honor in *Other Women* (NY, Farrar, 1933)
    Lady of Secrets
    b&w   1936
    Dir: Marion Gering. Prod: Columbia.
    Cast: Ruth Chatterton, Otto Kruger, Lloyd Nolan.
    A woman's one love affair has made her live a life of seclusion.

BUCKLEY, FRANK R.

Peg Leg—The Kidnapper in *Western Story Magazine* (September 26, 1925)
    The Gentle Cyclone
    5 reels   sil.   b&w   1926
    Dir: William S. Van Dyke. Sp: Thomas Dixon, Jr. Prod: Fox.
    Cast: Buck Jones, Rose Blossom.
    Western farce. The uncles of orphan June feud when they learn she has inherited
valuable property between their lands.

BUCKNER, ROBERT

Moon Pilot
s.m. serialized story in *Saturday Evening Post* (March 19-April 2, 1960)
    The Moon-Spinners
    119 min.   color
    Dist: Macmillan, Roa's Films
    A search for valuable stolen jewels and the thief.

BUHLER, KITTY

Time Is a Memory
    China Doll
    88 min.   b&w   1958
    Dir: Frank Borzage. Prod: Romina Prod. Dist: United Artists
    Cast: Victor Mature, Lili Hau, Bob Mathias, Stuart Whitman.
    An Air Force captain in China during WWII combats aerial bombardment to protect his young bride.

BUNNER, HENRY C.

Zenobia's Infidelity
    Zenobia
    74 min.   b&w   1939
    Dir: Gordon Douglas. Sp: Carey Ford. Prod: Hal Roach. Dist: Mogull's, Select.
    Cast: Oliver Hardy, Harry Langdon.

BURKE, THOMAS

The Chink and the Child in *The Limehouse Nights*
  Broken Blossoms
  68 min.   b&w   1919
  Dir: D. W. Griffith. Sp: D. W. Griffith. Prod: United Artists.
  Cast: Lillian Gish, Richard Barthelmess, Donald Crisp.
  A gentle, contemplative Chinese youth (Barthelmess) arrives in the squalid Limehouse district of London hoping to spread his philosophy of peace and love. Quickly
disillusioned, he decides to remain in London and opens a small shop. One day,
Lucy (Gish), having suffered a beating by her father, falls unconscious outside the
door of his shop. The Chinaman takes her in and cares for her, and in his hidden love
shows her the first real kindness she has ever known. When Lucy's father, a sadistic
boxer named Battling Burrows (Crisp), discovers what has happened, he destroys
the Chinaman's shop and drags the girl back home. The anguished youth follows
after, and finding Lucy beaten to death, shoots the attacking boxer and carries the
girl's body back to his shop where he commits suicide.

  Broken Blossoms
  b&w   1936
  Dir: Hans Brahm.
  Cast: Emlyn Williams.

Gina of Chinatown in *The Limehouse Nights*
  Dream Street
  s.m. "The Lamp in the Window"
  102 min.   b&w   1921
  Dir and Sp: D. W. Griffith. Dist: Audio Brandon.
  Cast: Carol Dempster, Ralph Graves, Charles Emmett Mack.
  Love and romance powerfully affect the lives of three people living in the slums
of London. Gypsy Fair (Dempster) is a vivacious young dancer who cares for her
ailing, eccentric father, and loves to wander the streets. Spike McFadden (Graves)
is an aggressive Don Juan, who is smitten by Gypsy's charm. Billy (Mack), Spike's
brother, is a frail and gentle poet, who dotes on his strong, protective brother, and
secretly longs to possess Gypsy's heart. The two brothers are torn by their love for
the same girl, but in the end, as tragedy strikes, their lifelong devotion to each other
reasserts itself.

The Lamp in the Window see Dream Street under Gina of Chinatown

Twelve Golden Curls in *The Limehouse Nights*
  Curlytop
  5,828'   sil.   b&w   1924
  Dir: Maurice Elvey. Adap: Frederick Hatton, Fanny Hatton.

BURKE, THOMAS (cont'd)

Curlytop (cont'd)
Cast: Shirley Mason, Wallace MacDonald.
Romantic melodrama. Two girls love the same man.

BURNET, DANA

The Billings Spend His Dime in *Redbook* (June-August 1920)
The Billings Spends His Dime
6 reels   sil.   b&w   1923
Dir: Wesley Ruggles. Prod: Famous Players—Lasky.
Cast: Walter Hiers, Jacqueline Logan.
Comedy. Salesclerk John falls in love with Suzanna Juárez when he sees her picture on a cigar band. He later buys a cigar, obtains information, goes to Santo Dinero and wins Suzanna.

Private Pettigrew's Daughter
Pettigrew's Girl
b&w   1919
Dir: George Melford. Prod: Paramount.
Cast: Ethel Clayton.

The Shopworn Angel
The Shopworn Angel
8 reels   sd.   b&w   1928
Dir: Richard Wallace. Sp: Howard Estabrook, Alberty Shelby Le Vinn. Prod:
      Paramount Famous Players—Lasky.
Cast: Nancy Carroll, Gary Cooper, Paul Lukas.
Romantic drama. Daisy, a sophisticated New York chorus girl with a "guardian" falls in love with Bill, a naive Army private from Texas who has gone A.W.O.L. to be with her.

Shopworn Angel
8 reels   b&w   1938
Dir: H. C. Potter. Sp: Waldo Salt. Prod: M-G-M. Dist: Films Inc.
Cast: Margaret Sullavan, James Stewart.
A kept woman has a bittersweet love affair with a naive soldier.

Technic in *Saturday Evening Post* (May 16, 1925)
The Marriage Clause
8 reels   sil.   b&w   1926
Dir: Lois Weber. Prod: Universal—Jewel.
Cast: Francis X. Bushman, Billie Dove, Warner Oland.

BURNET, DANA (cont'd)

The Marriage Clause (cont'd)
Romantic drama. A shy, timid girl auditions for a role in a New York play and the director accuses her of stealing a purse. Her emotional outcry convinces him that she has potential as a star.

Those High Society Blues in *Saturday Evening Post* (May 23, 1925)
High Society Blues
10 reels   b&w   1930
Dir: David Butler. Adap: Howard J. Green. Prod: Fox.
Cast: Janet Gaynor, Charles Farrell.
Comedy-drama. Eli Granger and his family move to a wealthy area of Scarsdale after selling their business in Iowa. Their neighbors scorn these *nouveaux riches.*

Wandering Daughters in *Hearst's International Magazine* (July 1922)
Wandering Daughters
6 reels   sil.   b&w   1923
Dir and Sp: James Young. Prod: Sam E. Rork.
Cast: Marguerite De La Motte, William V. Mong.
Comedy drama. The daughter of straight-laced parents, Bessie Bowden finds fast set member Austin Trull more interesting than hard-working John.

BURNETT, WILLIAM RILEY

Across the Aisle
Thirty Six Hours to Kill
5,700'   b&w   1936
Dir: Eugene Forde. Sp: Lou Breslow, John Patrick. Prod: Twentieth Century
     Fox.

Dr. Socrates
Dr. Socrates
69 min.   b&w   1935
Dir: William Dieterle. Sp: Robert Lord. Prod: Warner Brothers.
Cast: Paul Muni, Ann Dvorak.
A doctor becomes involved with hoodlums after they break into his home. The town becomes suspicious and he eventually foils the gang by putting them to sleep.

King of the Underworld
69 min.   b&w   1939
Dir: Lewis Saler. Sp: George Bricker. Prod: Warner Brothers. Dist: United Artists.
Cast: Humphrey Bogart, Kay Francis, James Stephenson.
A distaff physician (Francis) was out for revenge against a hood who manipulated her husband.

BURNETT, WILLIAM RILEY (cont'd)

Jail Break
   The Whole Town's Talking
   86 min.   b&w   1935
   Dir: John Ford. Prod: Columbia Pictures Corp. Dist: Budget.
   Cast: Edward G. Robinson, Jean Arthur.
   A meek little white-collar worker who wouldn't hurt a fly has just one problem—he's a deadringer for the cold-blooded hoodlum who just happens to be Public Enemy No. 1. When the gang mistakes him for their chief, and the real gangster decides to use him for a fall guy, Robinson is in big trouble in this hilarious comedy. He is aided by pretty stenographer Jean Arthur.

BURR, JANE

I'll Tell My Husband in Burr, Jane. *The Queen Is Dead* (NY, Eliot Pub. Co., 1938)
   The Arnelo Affair
   87 min.   b&w   1947
   Dir: Arch Obooler. Prod: M-G-M.
   Cast: George Murphy, John Hodiak, Lowell Gilmore, Eve Arden.
   A murder web.

BURRAGE, A. M. see The Return under BIERCE, AMBROSE

BURT, KATHARINE NEWLIN

The Red-Headed Husband in *Cosmopolitan Magazine* (January 1926)
   The Silent Rider
   6 reels   sil.   b&w   1927
   Dir: Lynn Reynolds. Prod: Universal.
   Cast: Hoot Gibson, Blanche Mehaffey.
   Western melodrama. Marian Faer is hired to assist in cooking. She's very popular with all the men, but she wants a red-headed husband.

Summoned in *Ainslee's* (February 1923)
   The Way of a Girl
   Dir: Robert G. Vignola. Prod: M-G-M
   Cast: Eleanor Boardman, Matt Moore, William Russell.
   Social melodrama. Society girl Rosamond craves the excitement her staid financé won't provide.

BURTIS, THOMSON

War of the Wildcats
   In Old Oklahoma
   102 min.   b&w   1943

BURTIS, THOMSON (cont'd)

In Old Oklahoma (cont'd)
Dir: Albert S. Rogell. Prod: Republic. Dist: Ivy.
Cast: John Wayne, Marsha Scott.
Movie title changed from War of the Wildcats.

BUSCH, NIVEN (jt. author) see The Big Shakedown under ENGELS, S.

BYRNE, DONN

The Changelings in *Changeling and Other Stories* (NY, 1923)
His Captive Woman
8 reels   b&w   1929
Dir: George Fitzmaurice. Prod: First National Pictures.
Melodrama. Cabaret dancer Anna Janssen kills her sugardaddy and escapes to an island in the South Seas. A New York detective arrests her, but on the way back the ship sinks and they are stranded on a small island where they fall in love. When rescued, she is tried for her crime.

Destiny Bay
Wings of the Morning
87 min.   b&w   1937
Dir: Harold Schuster. Prod: Twentieth Century Fox. Dist: Budget.
Cast: Henry Fonda, Annabella, John McCormack.
A Canadian trains the horse of a princess to win the Derby. Featured is the only screen appearance of the famed Irish Tenor, John McCormack.

CAIN, JAMES M.

Baby in the Ice-Box
She Made Her Bed
8 reels   b&w   1934
Dir: Ralph Murphy. Sp: Casey Robinson, Frank R. Adams. Prod: Paramount.
Cast: Richard Arlen, Sally Eilers.
A two-timing husband meets disaster.

CALEF, NOEL

Rudolphe et le Revolver
  Tiger Boy
  105 min.   b&w   1959
  Dir: J. Lee Thompson. Prod: Continental Dist. Inc. Dist: Walter Reade 16.
  Cast: John Mills, Hayley Mills, Horst Buchholz.
  Hayley Mills makes her film debut as a little girl who witnesses a murder. A sailor
home on leave discovers that his girlfriend no longer loves him. In a blind rage, he
kills her. The child, Gillie, witnesses the crime through a mail slot. Thinking only of
playing cowboys and Indians, the girl steals the murder weapon; she is soon pursued by the killer, while a police inspector races against time to prevent another
killing.

CAMERSON, ANNE

Green Dice
  Mr. Skitch
  6,200'   b&w   1933
  Dir: James Cruze. Sp: Sonya Levien, Ralph Spence. Prod: Fox.
  Cast: Will Rogers, ZaSu Pitts, Rochelle Hudson.
  A family's adventures as they travel to California by car.

CAMP, WADSWORTH

The Black Cap in *Collier's* (January 24, 1920)
  A Daughter of the Law
  5 reels   sil.   b&w   1921
  Dir: Jack Conway. Prod: Universal.
  Cast: Carmel Myers, Jack O'Brien.
  Crook melodrama. The daughter of a police inspector tries to retrieve her brother
from an underworld gang.

Hate in *The Communicating Door* (Garden City, NY, 1923)
  Hate
  5,500'   sil.   b&w   1922
  Dir: Maxwell Karger. Adap: June Mathis.
  Cast: Alice Lake, Conrad Nagel.
  Crime melodrama. Ed Felton and Dave Hume, gamblers, are rivals for the love
of Babe Lennox, a chorus girl. Hume, who is ill, commits suicide and tries to make
it appear that Felton killed him.

CAMPBELL, EVELYN

Remorse in *Redbook*
  Masked Angel

CAMPBELL, EVELYN (cont'd)

Masked Angel (cont'd)
6 reels   sil.   b&w   1928
Dir: Frank O'Connor. Prod: Chadwick Prod.
Cast: Betty Compson, Erick Arnold.
Romantic drama. Unjustly accused of stealing, a fleeing cabaret hostess ducks
into a hospital and pretends to visit a blind, crippled soldier. Eventually they fall in
love.

Yesterday's Wife in *Snappy Stories* (May 1, 1920)
Yesterday's Wife
6 reels   sil.   b&w   1923
Dir: Edward J. LeSaint. Prod: Columbia Pictures Corp.
Cast: Irene Rich, Eileen Percy.
Romantic drama. A quarrel causes a divorce and the man re-marries, but when
his second wife is accidentally killed, he reconciles with his first wife.

CAMPBELL, JOHN W., JR.

Who Goes There? in *Seven Tales of Science Fiction* (Shasta, 1951).
The Thing
87 min.   b&w   1951
Dir: Christian Nyby. Prod: RKO.
Cast: James Arness, Margaret Sheridan, Kenneth Tobey, Robert Cornthwaite.
A U.S. Air Force research team, isolated in the Arctic region, is attacked by a
ferocious creature with the chemistry of a plant that lives on human blood and
multiplies a hundred-fold in a matter of hours.

CANFIELD, DOROTHY (pseud. of FISHER, D. F. C.)

Eternal Masculine (suggestion for)
Two Heads on a Pillar
8 reels   b&w   1934
Dir: William Nigh. Prod: Liberty Pictures.

CAPOTE, TRUMAN

Among the Paths to Eden
s.m. "A Christmas Memory," "Miriam"
Truman Capote's Trilogy
99 min.   color   1969
Dir: Frank Perry. Prod: Allied Artists. Dist: Hurlock.
Cast: Mildred Natwick in no. 1; Maureen Stapleton, Martin Balsam in no. 2;
    Geraldine Page in no. 3.

CAPOTE, TRUMAN (cont'd)

Truman Capote's Trilogy (cont'd)

No. 1: A lonely governess experiences a schizophrenic breakdown. Her delusions take the form of the child Miriam. No. 2: A spinster looks for a husband in the cemetery where widowers visit the graves of their dead wives. No. 3: A memory of Christmas in Alabama and of a distant cousin over 60 years of age.

A Christmas Memory see Truman Capote's Trilogy under Among the Paths to Eden

Miriam see Truman Capote's Trilogy under Among the Paths to Eden

CARLISLE, HELEN GRACE

Unidentified story
Live, Love and Learn
8 reels   b&w   1937
Dir: George Fitzmaurice. Sp: Charles Brackett, Cyril Hume, Richard Maibaun.
    Prod: M-G-M.
Cast: Robert Montgomery, Rosalind Russell, Robert Benchley, Monty Woolley,
    Helen Vinson, Mickey Rooney.
Comedy. A story about a struggling artist and his rich wife living in Greenwich Village.

CARPENTER, JOHN J.

The Reluctant Hangman
Good Day for a Hanging
85 min.   color   1959
Dir: Nathan Juran. Prod: Morningside. Dist: Argus, Modern
Cast: Fred MacMurray, Robert Vaughan
Ben Cutler watches as a smiling blue-eyed, baby-faced youth brutally guns down the town marshal in cold blood. Cutler testifies to the fact, but the townspeople, as well as his own daughter and the pretty widow he intends to marry, refuse to believe his story.

CARR, ALBERT H. Z.

Return from Limbo in *Saturday Evening Post* (February 22, 1936)
Women Are Like That
78 min.   b&w   1937
Dir: Stanley Logan. Prod: Warner Brothers. Dist: United Artists
Cast: Pat O'Brien, Kay Francis.
A long-winded marital drama.

CARR, ALBERT H. Z. (cont'd)

The Trial of Johnny Nobody in *Ellery Queen's Magazine* (November 1950)
Johnny Nobody
88 min.   b&w   1965
Dir: Noel Patrick. Sp: Patrick Kirwan. Prod: Viceroy Films.
Cast: Nigel Patrick, Yvonne Mitchell.
Mulcahy, a drunken writer living in a small Irish town, is killed in front of a church.

CARR, JOHN DICKSON

Gentlemen from Paris
The Man with a Cloak
81 min.   b&w   1951
Dir: Fletcher Markle. Prod: M-G-M. Dist: Films Inc.
Cast: Joseph Cotten, Barbara Stanwyck.
Set in 19th century New York. The hero's secret identity is Edgar Allan Poe.

CARROLL, SIDNEY

Who Is Mr. Dean?
Gambit
109 min.   color   1966
Dir: Ronald Neame. Prod: Universal. Dist: Universal.
Cast: Michael Caine, Shirley MacLaine, Herbert Lom, John Abbot, Roger C.
Carmel.
This comedy-thriller, loaded with gimmicks and set against the exotic backgrounds of Hong Kong and the Middle East, tells the story of a scoundrel and his Eurasian partner who attempt to pull the perfect heist on an invaluable statue.

CARSON, ROBERT

Aloha Means Goodbye
Across the Pacific
97 min.   b&w   1942
Dir: John Huston. Dist: United Artists.
Cast: Humphrey Bogart, Mary Astor, Sidney Greenstreet, Monte Blue.
Melodrama. A taut spy story of international intrigue about a secret service agent who pretends to sell out to the Japanese to foil a plot to blow up the Panama Canal.

Bedside Manner in *Saturday Evening Post*
Her Favorite Patient
90 min.   b&w   1945
Prod: United Artists. Dist: Roa's Films.

CARSON, ROBERT (cont'd)

Her Favorite Patient (cont'd)
Cast: Ruth Hussey, Charlie Ruggles, Ann Rutherford.
Can a woman physician with a charming "bedside manner" treat a handsome
test pilot? Former film title was Bedside Manner.

Come Be My Love
Once More, My Darling
94 min.   b&w   1949
Dir: Robert Montgomery. Prod: Universal International. Dist: Universal 16.
Cast: Robert Montgomery, Ann Blyth.
Comedy. A young lady sets her cap for a somewhat older film matinee idol who
is recalled to active duty in the Army.

The Reformer and the Redhead
The Reformer and the Redhead
90 min.   b&w   1950
Dir and Sp: Norman Panama, Norman Frank. Prod: M-G-M. Dist: Films Inc.
Cast: June Allyson, Dick Powell.
Powell is a candidate for mayor, Allyson a zoo-keeper's daughter with large pets.

Third Girl from the Right
Ain't Misbehavin'
81 min.   b&w   1955
Dir: Edward Buzzell. Sp: Edward Buzzell, Philip Rapp, Devery Freeman. Prod:
    Universal. Dist: Universal.
Cast: Rory Calhoun, Piper Laurie.
A chorus girl marries a wealthy tycoon.

You Gotta Stay Happy (serialized story)
You Gotta Stay Happy
100 min.   b&w   1948
Dir: H. C. Potter. Sp: Karl Tunberg. Prod: Universal. Dist: Universal.
Cast: Jean Fontaine, James Stewart, Eddie Albert, Roland Young.
Comedy. The richest girl in the world leaves her fiance at the altar and goes on a
cross-country adventure with two veterans who started their own airline.

CARY, LUCIAN

Johnny Gets His Gun
Straight from the Shoulder
7 reels   b&w   1936
Dir: Stuart Heisler. Sp: Madeleine Ruthven. Prod: Paramount.

CARY, LUCIAN (cont'd)

Straight from the Shoulder (cont'd)
Cast: Ralph Bellamy, Katharine Locke.
Drama of two people who witness a hold-up and murder.

White Flannels in *Saturday Evening Post* (June 27, 1925)
White Flannels
7 reels   sil.   b&w   1927
Dir: Lloyd Bacon. Prod: Warner Brothers.
Cast: Louise Dresser, Jason Robards.
Domestic melodrama. Mrs. Jacob Politz, whose husband is a coalminer, saves
for years to send her son to college. There a rumor starts that he's a nobleman. When
his friends learn the truth, they turn against him.

CASE, ROBERT ORMOND

Golden Portage in *Saturday Evening Post*
The Girl from Alaska
8 reels   b&w   1942
Dir: Nick Grinde. Sp: Edward T. Lowe. Prod: Republic. Dist: Ivy.
Cast: Ray Niddleton, Jean Parker.
Disappointed because he did not strike gold, a young man prepares to leave
Alaska. He accidentally shoots a law officer and falls in with a robber.

CASPARY, VERA

Gardenia
Blue Gardenia
90 min.   b&w   1953
Dir: Fritz Lang. Sp: Charles Hoffman. Prod: Warner Brothers.
Cast: Anne Baxter, Richard Conte.
A telephone operator implicated in a murder is cleared by a reporter who
discovers the real killer.

CHADWICK, JOSEPH

Phantom .45's Talk Loud
Rim of the Canyon
65 min.   b&w   1949
Dir: John English. Prod: Gene Autry Pictures. Dist: Budget, Roa's Films.
Cast: Gene Autry, Nan Leslie.
Autry gets the girl and the outlaws in this musical western.

CHAMBERLAIN, GEORGE AGNEW

The Phantom Filly in *Saturday Evening Post*
    April Love
    99 min.   color   1957
    Dir: Henry Levin. Prod: Fox.
    Cast: Pat Boone, Shirley Jones.
    Musical. A romance on the farm.

    Home in Indiana
    9,567'   b&w   1944
    Dir: Henry Hathaway. Sp: Winston Miller. Prod: Fox. Dist: Films Inc.
    Cast: Walter Brennan, Jeanne Crain, Lon McCallister.
    Story of a blind harness-racing filly.

CHAMBERLAIN, LUCIA

Blackmail in *Saturday Evening Post*
    Blackmail
    6 reels   sil.   b&w   1920
    Dir: Dallas M. Fitzgerald. Prod: Metro.

CHAMBERLAIN, WILLIAM

A Company of Cowards
    Advance to the Rear
    97 min.   color   1964
    Dir: George Marshall. Sp: Samuel Peeples, William Bowers. Prod: M-G-M. Dist:
        Films Inc.
    Cast: Melvyn Douglas, Glenn Ford, Joan Blondell.
    Comedy. Civil War officers in a troop of misfits are distracted from battle.

CHAMBERS, ROBERT W.

Pickets
    A Time Out of War
    22 min.   b&w   1954
    Dir: Denis and Terry Sanders. Dist: Pyramid.
    Two Union soldiers and a Confederate soldier form a tentative camaraderie
during a one-hour truce that reveals the dignity and tension of each participant.
Winner of an Academy Award for best short live action film.

Spy 13 (and other stories)
    Operator 13
    9 reels   b&w   1934
    Dir: Richard Boleslawski. Sp: Harvey Thew, Zelda Sears, Eve Green. Prod: M-G-M.

CHAMBERS, ROBERT W. (cont'd)

Operator 13 (cont'd)
Cast: Gary Cooper, Marion Davis, Marjorie Gateson.
Drama. Set during the Civil War, Marion Davis plays a Northern spy assigned to kill Southern officer Cooper, but they fall in love (of course!).

CHANSLOR, ROY

Hi, Nellie
Hi, Nellie
79 min.   b&w   1934
Dir: Mervyn LeRoy. Prod: Warner Brothers and Vitaphone
Cast: Paul Muni, Glenda Farrell.
A light-weight newspaper story.

The House across the Street
69 min.   b&w   1949
Dir: Richard Bare. Prod: Warner Brothers
Cast: Wayne Morris, Janis Paige.
Crime. A newspaper editor crusades against crime and solves a murder.

Love Is on the Air
61 min.   b&w   1937
Dir: Nick Grinde. Prod: Warner Brothers. Dist: United Artists.
Cast: Ronald Reagan, June Travis.
A radio commentator is forced to soft-pedal issues on the air when he exposes a racketeer.

You Can't Escape Forever
77 min.   b&w   1942
Dir: Jo Graham. Prod: Warner Brothers. Dist: United Artists.
Cast: George Brent, Brenda Marshall, Gene Lockhart, Don DeFore.

CHARTERIS, LESLIE

The Million Pound Day
Saint in London (Br.)
72 min.   b&w   1939
Dir: John Paddy Carstairs. Sp: Lynn Root, Frank Fenton. Prod: RKO.
Cast: George Sanders, Sally Gray.
The Saint picks up a wounded man on the road and is plunged into mysterious doings.

CHASE, BORDEN

Blue, White and Perfect
Blue, White and Perfect
s.m. the character Michael Shane, created by Brett Halliday
78 min.   b&w   1942

CHASE, BORDEN (cont'd)

Dir: Herbert I. Leeds. Prod: Fox. Dist: Films Inc.
Cast: Lloyd Nolan, Mary Beth Hughes.
Shane chases foreign agents, who are stealing industrial diamonds during the war.

Concerto in *American Magazine*
I've Always Loved You
95 min.   b&w   1946
Dir: Frank Borzage. Sp: Borden Chase. Prod: Republic.
Cast: Philip Dorn, Catherine McLeod, Maria Ouspenskaya, William Carter.

Myra Hassman (McLeod), a young pianist, becomes the prodigy of Leopold
Goronoff (Dorn), a famous conductor. At their first Carnegie Hall concert together,
Myra receives more applause than he does, and the outraged Goronoff abandons
her. In despair, Myra gives up her career, and marries a farmer (Carter), who has
adored her since childhood. Years later, her daughter Porgy has a romance with a
teacher, parallelling Myra's love for Goronoff. Myra must confront her master once
again, to find out whether she has truly gotten over the spell which he once exerted
over her.

Dr. Broadway
Dr. Broadway
60 min.   b&w   1942
Dir: Anthony Mann. Prod: Paramount. Dist: Universal
Cast: Macdonald Carey, Jean Phillips, J. Carrol Naish, Warren Hymer, Eduardo
    Cianelli.

A Runyonesque tale of a Times Square doctor with a motley assortment of
patients: gangsters, flower vendors, and newshawks. The doctor is persuaded to do a
last favor for a dying gunman and runs into complications with rival mobsters and
the police. Mann's first film.

Midnight Taxi
Midnight Taxi
6,610'   b&w   1937
Dir: Eugene Forde. Sp: Lou Breslow. Prod: 20th Century Fox.
Cast: Brian Donlevy, Frances Drake.

A federal man, disguised as a taxi driver, must run down a band of
counterfeiters.

Pay to Learn in *Saturday Evening Post* (January 14, 1939)
The Navy Comes Through
82 min.   b&w   1942
Dir: A. Edward Sutherland. Sp: Roy Chanslor, Aeneas MacKenzie. Prod: RKO.
Cast: Pat O'Brien, George Murphy, Jane Wyatt.
Merchant Marines in action during World War II.

CHASE, MARY COYLE

Chi House
> Sorority House
> 64 min.   b&w   1939
> Dir: John Farrow. Sp: Dalton Trumbo. Prod: RKO.

CHEAVANS, MARTHA

Penny Serenade
> Penny Serenade
> 124 min.   b&w   1941
> Dir: George Stevens. Sp: Morkie Ryskind. Prod: Columbia Pictures. Corp. Dist:
> Ivy, Macmillan.
> Cast: Cary Grant, Irene Dunne.

Romance. Told in flashbacks, Julie (Dunne) is on the verge of breaking up with her husband, Roger (Grant). She listens to phonograph records, each of which brings back a memory in their tragedy-filled life. After heart-breaking struggles, the couple is finally united.

Unidentified story
> Sunday Dinner for a Soldier
> 86 min.   b&w   1944
> Dir: Lloyd Bacon. Sp: Wanda Tuchock, Melvin Levy. Prod: 20th Century Fox.
> Dist: Films Inc.
> Cast: Anne Baxter, John Hodiak.

A family invites a soldier for dinner and are repaid for their kindness.

CHEEVER, JOHN

The Swimmer in *New Yorker Magazine*
> The Swimmer
> 94 min.   color   1968
> Dir: Frank Perry. Sp: Frank and Eleanor Perry. Prod: Columbia Pictures Corp.
> Cast: Burt Lancaster, Janet Landgard, Janice Rule, Marge Champion, Diana
> VanDerVlis, Kim Hunter, Cornelia Otis Skinner, Charles Drake, Joan Rivers,
> Diana Muldaur.

An advertising man in his forties one day finds himself eight miles from home, dressed in swimming trunks. He decides to "swim home" via the pools that cover the county from one end to the other. As Ned moves from one pool to another, he encounters the whole spectrum of Eastern suburbia, and begins to understand that he has continually misjudged himself and others. At one poolside, supposed friends make cruel remarks about his wife and daughters; another leads him into a lavish party; at another he meets his ex-mistress (Rule), and reveals that he has no memory of their final bitter scene years before. Each sequence sheds new light on his character, and the total picture is of a compulsively youthful, sexual, and

CHEEVER, JOHN (cont'd)

The Swimmer (cont'd)
self-deluded individual, an aging adolescent who is jolted into a realization that time is passing quickly.

CHEKHOV, ANTON

The Bass Fiddle
  The Bass Fiddle
  28 min.   b&w   1962
  Dir: M. Fasquel (France). Dist: McGraw-Hill.
  A lighthearted and frolicsome tale of how a young man and woman face a most improbable and embarrassing situation when they discover that their clothes have been stolen while they were swimming.

The Bet
  The Bet
  24 min.   color   1969
  Dir: Ron Waller. Dist: Pyramid.
  An updated version of the Chekhov story, capturing the boredom, panic, hysteria and near-madness experienced by a young man who bets a wealthy friend that he can isolate himself in a single room for five years.

The Boarding House
  The Boarding House
  27 min.   b&w   1977
  Dist: Macmillan.
  Narrated by John Gielgud. Love turns out to be an expensive proposition for a penniless young artist. He answers a notice for a room in a boarding house and is pleasantly surprised when the landlady turns out to be an attractive young widow. The rent is also gratifyingly low. Infatuated by the widow's charms, the young man pursues and "seduces" her, only to receive at his departure, a stiff bill for her amorous services. Trapped, he must go into debt to pay the bill.

The Boor
  The Boor
  15 min.   b&w   1955
  Prod: Dynamic Films. Dist: Audio Brandon.
  Cast: Monty Woolley.
  A merry tenant farmer comes to collect a debt and matches wits with an attractive widow.

CHEKHOV, ANTON (cont'd)

Desire to Sleep
    Desire to Sleep
    14 min.   b&w   rel. 1977
    Dist: Macmillan.
    Narrated by John Gielgud. Domestic bliss turns to tragedy when an overwrought
servant veers out of control. A young serving girl and babysitter is rendered sleep-
less by her mistress's demands and the constant crying of the child. Insomnia drives
her to the point of exhaustion and she begins to hallucinate. Caught up in the
vortex of madness, she suffocates the child to gain a brief moment of peace.

The Drop of Water
    Black Sabbath
    s.m. "The Telephone Call," "The Wurdlak"
    99 min.   color   1964
    Dir: Mario Bava. Sp: Mario Bava, Marcello Fannato, Alberto Bevilacqua. Dist:
        Audio Brandon, Macmillan, Roa's Films, Select.
    Cast: Boris Karloff, Mark Damon, Michele Mercier.
    Black Sabbath consists of three separate episodes, each involving a return from
the dead. In The Drop of Water, a nurse steals a diamond ring from the hand of a
slain clairvoyant; she is later murdered by the clairvoyant's ghost. In The Telephone
Call, a prostitute kills a man who has threatened her life, and shortly afterwards
receives a phone call from the same man. In the final episode, The Wurdlak, a young
nobleman falls in love with a girl whose father (Karloff) is a vampire, thirsting for
the blood of all his relatives.

An Event, or Proisshestviye in *Best Known Works*
    An Event (Yugoslavia)
    93 min.   color   1970
    Dir: Vatroslav Mimica. Prod: Jadran Film. Dist: Walter Reade 16.
    Cast: Paule Vujisic, Serdjo Mimica.
    On their return from a fair, a boy and his grandfather are pursued by a
gamekeeper.

The Fugitive
    The Fugitive
    15 min.   b&w   rel. 1977
    Prod: Macmillan.
    Narrated by John Gielgud. Terror turns to compassion as a small boy learns to
cope with some of the harsh realities of life. A boy of seven living in a remote
village takes ill. He is brought to a hospital where, for the first time, he encounters
aged and moribund patients. Frightened and revolted by the death of a patient, he
runs away. After a dreadful night in the woods a search party finally locates him.

CHEKHOV, ANTON (cont'd)

The Fugitive (cont'd)
Upon his return to the hospital, a kindly doctor's concern reverses the boy's attitudes toward the hospital and life.

Grief
    The Father
    28 min.   b&w
    Dir: Mark Fine. Dist: New Line Cinema.
    Cast: Burgess Meredith.
    Meredith plays the driver of a horse-drawn cab in New York, trying to explain
to his fares about the death of his son.

The Lady with the Dog
    The Lady with the Dog (Russian with English subtitles)
    86 min.   b&w   1960
    Dir: Joseph Heifitz. Sp: Joseph Heifitz.
    Cast: Iya Savvina, Alexei Batalov, Alla Chostakova.
    The bittersweet, nostalgic story opens in Yalta at the beginning of the century.
While vacationing, Dmitri Gurov (Batalov), a middle-aged bank official, encounters
a beautiful young woman named Anna (Savvina), who each day walks her small dog
along the promenade. They drift into an affair, then part and return to their respective homes and unhappy marriages. Once back in Moscow, however, Dmitri is
haunted by the memory of Anna. Eventually he invents a reason for visiting her in
provincial Leningrad. They arrange clandestine meetings in Moscow and their affair
lasts for years. Although they realize that they are doomed to a life of brief, secret
encounters, they are not strong enough to reach any other solution.

Revenge
    Revenge
    26 min.   b&w   1977
    Dist: Macmillan.
    Narrated by John Gielgud. A jealous husband decides to avenge himself on his
unfaithful wife by shooting her lover. He goes to a gunsmith to buy a weapon. As
the gunsmith eloquently describes the murderous qualities of a Smith and Wesson
revolver, the husband has second thoughts. While he's in jail, his wife would be free
to marry again. Not a very satisfying vengeance! Embarrassed, he rejects the gun but
buys a small item to avoid ridicule.

Rothschild's Violin
    Rothschild's Violin
    23 min.   b&w   rel. 1977
    Dist: Macmillan

CHEKHOV, ANTON (cont'd)

Rothschild's Violin (cont'd)

Narrated by John Gielgud. A miserly coffinmaker is the meanest man in the village. Although he plays the violin at social events, he also abuses his wife, and is especially vicious to a fellow musician named Rothschild. One day the coffinmaker's wife dies and his grief turns to bitter regret at the way he has treated those closest to him. At his death, he leaves his violin to Rothschild who plays mournful, nostalgic melodies upon it.

The Telephone Call see Black Sabbath under The Drop of Water

Volodya
  Volodya
  25 min.   b&w   rel. 1977
  Dist: Macmillan.
  Narrated by John Gielgud. Seventeen-year-old Volodya broods over his father's suicide brought on by an extravagant wife. He, in turn, falls in love with a flirtatious young married woman, only to be led on and then cruely rejected. Humiliated and despairing, Volodya takes his own life just as his father did before him.

A Work of Art
  A Work of Art; Satirical Shorts (Russian with English subtitles)
  10 min.   b&w   1960
  Dir and Sp: M. Kovalyov. Dist: Macmillan.
  An inhibited provincial doctor receives a nude statue from one of his patients.

The Wurdlak see Black Sabbath under The Drop of Water

CHESTER, GEORGE RANDOLPH

The Head of the Family in *Saturday Evening Post* (December 26, 1912)
  The Head of the Family
  7 reels   sil.   b&w   1928
  Dir: Joseph C. Boyle. Sp: Peter Milne. Prod: Gotham Prod.
  Cast: William Russell, Mickey Bennett.
  Henpecked Daniel Sullivan goes for a health cure and leaves Eddie, the plumber, in charge of his nagging wife. Eddie tames Alice, but they fall in love.

CHESTERTON, GILBERT KEITH

Father Brown Stories
  The Detective
  92 min.   b&w   1954

CHESTERTON, GILBERT KEITH (cont'd)

The Detective (cont'd)
Dir: Robert Hamer. Prod: Facet Prod. London. Dist: Budget, Macmillan, Roa's
    Films, Twyman Films.
Cast: Alec Guinness, Joyce Greenwood, Peter Finch, Cecil Parker, Bernard Lee,
    Gerard Oury.
The Roman cleric as a hobby, applies transcendental logic to solving puzzling
crimes. Original title was Father Brown.

Father Brown, Detective
67 min.   b&w   1935
Dir: Edward Sedgwick. Prod: Paramount.
Cast: Walter Connolly, Gertrude Michael.
International crook Flambeau announces the time and date he will steal a famous
jewel.

CHILD, RICHARD WASHBURN

The Game of Light in *Everybody's* (July 1914)
The Live Wire
8 reels   sil.   b&w   1925
Dir: Charles Hines. Dist: Em Gee Film Library, Mogull's.
Cast: Johnny Hines, Edmund Breese.
Comedy. The great Maranelli is forced to quit the circus and takes to the open
road. He meets Dorothy Langdon, the daughter of a power company president, and
goes to work for her father. The father has opened an amusement center and is
having problems. Maranelli solves them and wins the girl.

Here's How in *Fresh Waters and Other Stories* (New York, 1924)
The Mad Whirl
7 reels   sil.   b&w   1925
Dir: William A. Seiter. Adap: Frederic Hatton, Fanny Hatton. Prod: Universal.
    Dist: Griggs-Moviedrome.
Social melodrama. John and Mary Herrington try to keep pace with their son
Jack on an endless round of parties. Jack falls in love with a childhood friend, but
the girl's father objects to their romance.

Whiff of Heliotrope in *Famous Story Magazine* (December 1925)
Forgotten Faces
7,640'   sil.   b&w   1928
Dir: Victor Schertzinger. Prod: Paramount.
Cast: Clive Brook.
Harry finds his wife cheated on him and kills her lover. Before surrendering to
the police, he leaves his daughter on the steps of a wealthy couple's home.

CHILD, RICHARD WASHBURN (cont'd)

Forgotten Faces
8 reels b&w   1936
Dir: E. A. Dupont. Sp: Marguerite Roberts, Robert Yost, Brian Marlow. Prod:
 Paramount.
Cast: Clive Brook, Mary Brian, William Powell, Baclanova.
Melodrama. Harry Harlow finds his wife cheated on him and kills her lover. He
goes to prison but leaves his daughter on the doorstep of a wealthy couple who
raise her.

Gentleman after Dark
77 min. b&w   1942
Dir: Edward L. Marin. Prod: Small. Dist: Walter Reade 16.
Cast: Brian Donlevy, Miriam Hopkins, Preston Foster.
Re-make of Forgotten Faces.

Heliotrope
b&w   1920
Dir: George D. Baker. Prod: Cosmopolitan.
Cast: Fred Burton.

CHRISTIE, AGATHA

Philomel Cottage
 Love from a Stranger
 s.m. the play "Love from a Stranger," by Frank Vosper, which was based on
  Christie's short story
 9 reels b&w   1937
 Dir: Rowland V. Lee. Sp: Frances Marion. Prod: United Artists. Dist: Classic
  Film Museum.
 Cast: Basil Rathbone.

 Love from a Stranger (Br.)
 81 min. b&w   1947
 Dir: Richard Whorf. Prod: Eagle Lion Films. Dist: Ivy.
 Cast: John Hodiak, Sylvia Sidney.
 After marriage a woman suspects her husband to be a mad strangler.

Witness for the Prosecution
 Witness for the Prosecution
 s.m. written in story and play form
 114 min. b&w   1957
 Dir: Billy Wilder. Prod: United Artists. Dist: United Artists.

CHRISTIE, AGATHA (cont'd)

Witness for the Prosecution (cont'd)
Cast: Tyrone Power, Marlene Dietrich, Charles Luaghton.
A sensational London murder trial.

CHURCHILL, ROBERT B.

Hell on Wheels
Born to Speed
61 min.   b&w   1947
Dir: Edward L. Cahn. Prod: Releasing Corp. Dist: Ivy, Lewis Film Service.
Cast: Johnny Sands, Terry Austin.
Tale of auto racing men.

CLARK, KENNETH B.

The Girl Who Wasn't Wanted in *Munsey's Magazine* (April 1928)
Rough Romance
6 reels   b&w   1930
Dir: A. F. Erickson. Prod: Fox.
Cast: George O'Brien, Helen Chandler.
The life and death struggle between two men.

CLARK, WALTER VAN TILBURG

The Portable Phonograph
The Portable Phonograph
24 min.   color   1977
Prod: Encyclopaedia Britannica. Dist: Encyclopaedia Britannica.
A desolate landscape—the wind howls—faintly, a human voice reads from
Shakespeare's The Tempest. Four survivors of a devastating war gather in a dugout
built by soldiers. They have come to hear the portable phonograph one of them has
saved. In Story into Film (11 min.), the director discusses adapting the story for
film.

CLARKE, ARTHUR

The Sentinel*
2001: A Space Odyssey
139 min.   color   1968
Dir and Sp: Stanley Kubrick, Arthur C. Clarke. Prod: M-G-M. Dist: Films Inc.
Cast: Keir Dullea, Gary Lockwood, Douglas Rain, William Sylvester.
In the year 2001 a strange monolith, throwing off unexplained rays, is found
at the bottom of a moon excavation and points the way to something more foreign
and distant than man can imagine. Exploring the dynamics of space travel while

CLARKE, ARTHUR (cont'd)

2001: A Space Odyssey (cont'd)
tracing the technological history of mankind, man is shown to have an inability to cope with the new and the strange from the beginning of time up to an age where he is controlled by computers. *Note: The novel was published after the film was released.

CLAUSEN, CARL

The Perfect Crime in *Saturday Evening Post* (September 25, 1920)
    The Perfect Crime
    5 reels   sil.   b&w   1921
    Dir: Allan Dwan. Prod: Allan Dwan Prod.
    Cast: Monte Blue, Jacqueline Logan.
    Drama. Wally Griggs, a timid bank messenger, lives another life as a dashing young sport.

Poker Face
    Killer at Large
    6 reels   b&w   1936
    Dir: David selman. Sp: Harold Shumate. Prod: Columbia. Dist: Ivy, Mogull's.
    Cast: Robert Lowery, Annabel Shaw.

CLIFFORD, W. K.

Eve's Lover in *Eve's Lover and Other Stories* (New York, 1924)
    Eve's Lover
    7 reels   sil.   b&w   1925
    Dir: Roy Del Ruth. Adap: Darryl Francis Zanuck. Prod: Warner Brothers.
    Cast: Irene Rich, Bert Lytell, Clara Bow.
    Melodrama. A business rival coveting Eve's steel mill, convinces an impoverished count to marry her, but the count falls in love with her and won't deceive her.

CLIFT, DENISON

Room 40, O.B.
    Secrets of Scotland Yard
    7 reels   b&w   1944
    Dir: George Blair. Sp: Denison Clift. Prod: Republic.
    Cast: Edgar Barrier, Lionel Atwill, Stephanie Bachelor.
    A twin is killed after deciphering a Nazi secret code message and the other twin becomes part of the British communications staff.

COBB, IRVIN SHREWSBURY

Boys Will Be Boys in *Saturday Evening Post*
    Boys Will Be Boys
    s.m. play "Boys Will Be Boys," by Charles O'Brien
    5 reels   sil.   b&w   1921
    Dir: Clarence G. Badger. Prod: M-G-M
    Cast: Will Rogers, Irene Rich.
    Comedy drama. Peep O'Day, an orphan, falls heir to a small fortune.

Brer Fox and the Brier Patch see Judge Priest under A Tree Full of Hoot Owls

The Lord Provides see The Sun Shines Bright

Mob from Massac see The Sun Shines Bright

The Sun Shines Bright*
    The Sun Shines Bright
    s.m. "Mob from Massac," "The Lord Provides"
    92 min.   b&w   1953
    Dir: John Ford. Prod: Republic. Dist: Ivy
    Cast: Charles Winninger, Arlene Whelan.
    A small-town judge has a hard time running for re-election. *Note: Supposedly a re-make of Judge Priest, though the reference sources consulted indicate each film is based on different short stories.

A Tree Full of Hoot Owls
    Judge Priest
    s.m. "Brer Fox and the Brier Patch," "Words and Music"
    80 min.   b&w   1934
    Dir: John Ford. Prod: Fox. Dist: Films Inc.
    Cast: Will Rogers, Anita Louise.

Words and Music see Judge Priest under A Tree Full of Hoot Owls

The Young Nuts of America in *Irvin Cobb At His Best* (Garden, 1923)
    The New School Teacher
    6 reels   sil.   b&w   1924
    Dir: Gregory La Cava. Prod: Burr Pictures.
    Cast: Doris Kenyon, Charles "Chic" Sale.
    Comedy drama. A country school teacher's pupils play pranks on him until he wins their respect by saving a young boy from a burning schoolhouse.

COBURN, WALT

Black K. Rides Tonight
  Return of Wild Bill
  6 reels   b&w   1940
  Dir: Joseph H. Lewis. Sp: Robert Lee Johnson, Fred K. Myton. Prod: Columbia Pictures Corp.
  Cast: Iris Meredith, Bill Elliot.

Burnt Ranch
  The Westerner
  6 reels   b&w   1934
  Dir: David Selman. Sp: Harold Shumate. Prod: Columbia Pictures Corp.
  A man, out West, must be quick on the draw.

COCKRELL, EUSTACE

Count Pete
  Walking on Air
  8 reels   b&w   1936
  Dir: Joseph Santley. Sp: Bert Kalmar, Harry Ruby, Viola Brothers Shore, Rian James. Prod: RKO.
  Cast: Gene Raymond, Ann Sothern.
  Comedy. A young heiress falls for a scamp.

The Lord in His Corner
  Tennessee Champ
  73 min.   b&w   1954
  Dir: Fred M. Wilcox. Sp: Art Cohn. Prod: M-G-M. Dist: Films Inc.
  Cast: Dewey Martin, Shelley Winters.
  A prizefight drama mixed with religion.

Rocky's Rose
  Fast Company
  68 min.   b&w   1953
  Dir: John Sturges. Sp: William Roberts. Prod: M-G-M. Dist: Films Inc.
  Cast: Howard Keel, Polly Bergen.
  Comedy melodrama. A scheming horse trainer tries to buy a race horse at a fraction of its value.

COE, CHARLES FRANCIS

Ransom
  Nancy Steele Is Missing
  7,819'   b&w   1937

COE, CHARLES FRANCIS (cont'd)

Nancy Steele Is Missing (cont'd)
Dir: George Marshall. Sp: Hal Long, Gene Fowler. Prod: Fox.

Repeal (suggestion for)
The Gay Bride
9 reels   b&w   1934
Dir: Jack Conway. Sp: Bella and Samuel Spewack. Prod: M-G-M.
Cast: Carole Lombard, Chester Morris.
Comedy. A chiseling showgirl meets her match in a gangster.

COFFE, LENORE

Miss Aesop Butters Her Bread (jt. author William Joyce)
Good Girls Go to Paris
80 min.   b&w   1939
Dir: Alexander Hall. Prod: Columbia.
Cast: Joan Blondell, Melvyn Douglas.
Comedy. A waitress who wants to go to Paris tries her wiles on a scion of a wealthy family.

COHEN, ROY OCTAVIUS

Marco Himself in *Hearst's International Magazine* (September 1929)
The Social Lion
7 reels   b&w   1930
Dir: A. Edward Sutherland. Adap: Joseph L. Mankiewicz. Prod: Paramount.
Cast: Jack Oakie, Mary Brian.
Marco, a ham prizefighter, sets his sights on Gloria, a selfish society girl who leads him on for laughs.

Two Cents Worth of Humaneness in *Saturday Evening Post*
Dollars and Sense
5 reels   b&w   1920
Dir: Harry Beaumont. Prod: Goldwyn.

COLLINS, RICHARD (jt. author) see Thousands Cheer under JARRICO, PAUL

COLLINS, WILKIE

The Terribly Strange Bed
The Terribly Strange Bed
15 min.   b&w   1955
Prod: Dynamic Films

COLLINS, WILKIE (cont'd)

The Terribly Strange Bed (cont'd)
Cast: Monty Woolley.
A visitor at an inn wins money at gambling and then routs a pair of murderous scoundrels.

A Terribly Strange Bed
24 min.   b&w   1976
Prod: 20th Century Fox. Dist: Encyclopaedia Britannica.
A reckless young man-about-town patronizes a sleazy gambling house looking for excitement. He wins big money, but he also drinks too much. A kindly stranger suggests the gambler stay for the night rather than risk being robbed . . . he even puts him to bed. The bed is an ingenious death trap. Although the brash young hero escapes, he learns a very sobering lesson.

COLLISON, WILSON

Blondie Baby
Three Wise Girls
7 reels   b&w   1931
Dir: William Beaudine. Adap: Agnes Christine Johnston. Prod: Columbia Pictures Corp.
Cast: Jean Harlow, Loretta Young.

There's Always a Woman
There's Always a Woman
8 reels   b&w   1938
Sp: Gladys Lehman. Prod: Columbia.
Cast: Joan Blondell, Melvyn Douglas.
A private eye and a D.A., who are husband and wife, are working on the same case.

COLTER, ELI

Something to Brag About
The Untamed Breed
79 min.   b&w   1948
Dir: Charles Lamont. Prod: Sage Western Pictures. Dist: Newman Film Library.
Cast: Sonny Tufts, Barbara Britton.
The story deals with routine trials and tribulations of breeding cattle in old Texas.

COLTON, JOHN

Heat
   Wild Orchids
   11 reels   mus. score and sd. effects.   b&w   1928
   Dir: Sidney Franklin. Sp: Willis Golbeck. Prod: M-G-M. Dist: Films Inc.
   Cast: Greta Garbo, Lewis Stone, Nils Asther.
   A plantation owner and his wife visit Java, where she has an affair with a native
prince.

CONDON, FRANK

Speed But No Control in *Saturday Evening Post* (June 21, 1924)
   No Control
   6 reels   sil.   b&w   1927
   Dir: Scott Sidney, E. J. Babille. Prod: Metro Picture Corp.
   Cast: Harrison Ford, Phyllis Haver.
   Farce. Nancy Flood takes on a business job to help her father's floundering one-
ring circus. The boss's son flirts with her, his father fires her, but together they win
enough money by racing a dancing horse to save the circus.

CONNELL, RICHARD

Brother Orchid
   Brother Orchid
   91 min.   b&w   1940
   Dir: Lloyd Bacon. Prod: Warner Brothers. Dist: United Artists.
   Cast: Humphrey Bogart, Edward G. Robinson, Ann Sothern, Donald Crisp,
        Ralph Bellamy, Allen Jenkins.
   An ex-convict takes refuge in a monastery. He returns to the outside world to
clean up the rackets and, after overcoming obstacles, succeeds and then returns to
the monastery.

A Friend of Napoleon in *Saturday Evening Post* (June 30, 1923)
   Seven Faces
   9 reels   b&w   1929
   Dir: Berthold Viertel. Prod: Fox.
   Cast: Paul Muni, Marguerite Churchill.
   Youthful lovers Georges and Helene secretly meet. When her father discovers their
love for each other, he sends Helene away.

If I Was Alone with You in *Collier's* (November 30, 1929)
   Cheer Up and Smile
   7 reels   b&w   1930
   Dir: Sidney Lanfield. Adap: Howard J. Green. Prod: Fox.

CONNELL, RICHARD (cont'd)

Cheer Up and Smile (cont'd)
Cast: Dixie Lee, Arthur Lake.
Musical comedy. As his fraternity initiation, Eddie must kick the first man he meets and kiss the first female.

Isles of Romance in *Saturday Evening Post* (April 12, 1924)
No Place to Go
7 reels   sil.   b&w   1927
Dir: Mervyn Le Roy. Prod: Henry Hobart Prod.
Cast: Mary Astor, Lloyd Hughes.
Romantic comedy. Sally Montgomery yearns for exotic romance so she convinces her boyfriend to go to the South Seas, where they visit an island of cannibals.

A Little Bit of Broadway in *Liberty Magazine* (September 6-27, 1924)
Bright Lights
72 min.   b&w   1931
Dir: Michael Curtiz.
Cast: Dorothy Mackaill, Frank Fay, Noah Berry.
Romantic comedy. Cabaret girl Patsy goes home to her mother. Her sweetheart tries to imitate the style of her former cabaret friends with disasterous results, until she straightens him out.

The Most Dangerous Game
A Game of Death
72 min.   b&w   1946
Dir: Robert Wise. Sp: Norman Houston. Prod: RKO. Dist: Ivy.
Cast: John Loder, Edgar Barriel.
A hunter living on an island makes shipwrecked victims his prey.

The Hunt
30 min.   color   1970
Dir: David Deverell. Prod: David Deverell.
Two men on a hunting trip find their weekend going sour when one of them, new to the sport, discovers that he doesn't enjoy shooting animals. His companion, an avid huntsman, leaves him in disgust, wandering off to more than he bargained for. He meets an older hunter so jaded with killing that the only prize he yearns to stalk is human prey. The chilling pursuit that follows is a cliff-hanger until the very end when the victim escapes—a shaken but wiser man.

CONNELL, RICHARD (cont'd)

The Most Dangerous Game (cont'd)
  The Most Dangerous Game
  The Hounds of Zaroff (Br. title)
  65 min.   b&w   1932
  Dir: Ernest B. Shoedsack, Irving Pichel. Sp: James Ashmore Creelman. Prod:
      RKO. Dist: Classic Film Museum, Em Gee Film Library, Images Motion Pic-
      ture Rental Library, Janus Films.
  Cast: Joel McCrea, Fay Wray.
  Count Zaroff, an eccentric Russian lives in isolation so he can pursue delights
that would not be tolerated in civilized communities. He is a big game hunter, but
has wearied of big game since they are far too easy to catch. Looking for something
to hunt that will really offer a challenge, he decides to hunt men.

$100 in *Hearst's International Magazine* (August 1928)
  New Year's Eve
  7 reels   sil. or sd. effects, music   b&w   1929
  Dir: Henry Lehrman. Prod: Fox.
  Cast: Mary Astor, Charles Morton.
  Melodrama. A young woman, who has to care for her younger brother, puts
aside her scruples and goes to see a gambler who lusts after her. She finds the gamb-
ler dead, and she is put on trial for his murder.

The Solid Gold Article in *Collier's* (May 11, 1929)
  Not Damaged
  7 reels   b&w   1930
  Dir: Chandler Sprague. Adap: Frank Gay. Prod: Fox.
  Cast: Lois Moran, Walter Byron.
  Romantic comedy drama. A young lady, though engaged, loves wealthy Kirk
Randolph and goes to his apartment for a wild time.

The Swamp Angel in *Collier's* (February 10-March 10, 1923)
  Painted People
  7 reels   sil.   b&w   1924
  Dir: Clarence Badger. Prod: Associated First National.
  Cast: Colleen Moore, Ben Lyon.
  Comedy drama. Ellie and Don want to marry wealthy people, but when they each
become successful, they realize how much they mean to each other.

Tropic of Capricorn in *The Sins of Monsieur Pettipon and Other Humorous Tales*
(New York, 1922)
  East of Broadway
  6 reels   sil.   b&w   1924

CONNELL, RICHARD (cont'd)

East of Broadway (cont'd)
Dir: William K. Howard. Adap: Paul Schofield. Prod: Encore Pictures.
Cast: Owen Moore, Marguerite De La Motte.
Comedy melodrama. The son of Irish immigrants dreams of becoming a police-
man, but he is rejected from service because he is not tall enough. Later he earns a
badge by preventing a robbery.

CONNOLLY, MYLES

Lady Smith
Palm Springs
8 reels   b&w   1936
Dir: Aubrey Scotto. Sp: Joseph Fields. Prod: Paramount.
Cast: Frances Langford, Sir Guy Standing, David Niven.
A nobleman becomes a gambler to pay for his daughter's expensive school.

CONRAD, JOSEPH

Bride Comes to Yellow Sky (no. 2)
Face to Face (Composite Film)*
s.m. The Secret Sharer (no. 1)
90 min.   b&w   1952
Dir: John Brahm, Bretaigne Windust. Sp: No. 1—Aeneas MacKenzie, No. 2—James
    Agee. Prod: Theasquare Prod.
No. 1—A young ship's captain, on his first command, comes to the aid of
another ship. No. 2—A sheriff returning from his honeymoon must cope with a
gunman who has terrorized the town in his absence. *Note: A composite film
consists of separate films spliced together on one reel.

The Secret Sharer see also Face to Face under The Bride Comes to Yellow Sky

The Secret Sharer
The Secret Sharer
30 min.   color   1969
Dist: Encyclopaedia Britannica.
Haunting tale of a young sea captain whose inner conflicts pit his conscience
against the safety of the ship he commands and the men he leads—a struggle
caused by the "secret sharer" of his cabin.

COOK, WILLIAM WALLACE

'49–'17
The Old West Per Contract in *Argosy Magazine*
50/75 min.   sil.   b&w   1917

COOK, WILLIAM WALLACE (cont'd)

The Old West Per Contract (cont'd)
Dir and Sp: Ruth Ann Baldwin. Dist: Kit Parker.
Cast: Joseph Girard, Leo Pierson, Jean Hersholt, Mrs. Witting, Donna Drew.
An action western.

COOPER, COURTNEY RYLEY

Christmas Eve in Pilot Butte in *Redbook* (January 1921)
Desperate Trails
5 reels   sil.   b&w   1921
Dir: Jack Ford. Prod: Universal.
Cast: Harry Carey, Irene Rich.
Western melodrama. Bart Carson accepts the guilt for a crime committed by his girlfriend's "brother," and later learns the "brother" is really her lover.

Desperate Trails
60 min.   b&w   1939
Dir: Albert Ray. Sp: Andrew Bennison. Prod: Universal.
Cast: Johnny Mack Brown, Frances Robinson.

CORT, VAN

Mail-Order . . . in *Saturday Evening Post* (August 11, 1951)
Mail Order Bride
83 min.   color   1964
Dir and Sp: Burt Kennedy. Prod: M-G-M. Dist: Films Inc.
Cast: Lois Nettleson, Keir Dullea, Buddy Ebsen.
Comedy western. A hell-raising friend is in need of a wife.

COWARD, NOEL

Pretty Polly Barlow in *Pretty Polly Barlow and Other Stories* (London, 1964)
A Matter of Innocence
102 min.   color   1968
Dir: Guy Green. Sp: Keith Waterhouse, Willis Hall. Prod and Dist: Universal.
Drama. A lonely girl meets a gigolo while they are on a cruise to Singapore.

COXE, GEORGE H.

Return Engagement
Here's Flash Casey
6 reels   b&w   1937
Dir: Lynn Shores. Sp: John Krafft. Prod: Grand National Films.
Cast: Eric Linden, Boots Mallory.
A crime photographer solves a mystery.

COXE, GEORGE H. (cont'd)

The Shadow in The Shadow series
 The Shadow Strikes*
 65 min.   b&w   1937
 Dir: Lynn Shores. Prod: Grand National Films. Dist: Budget.
 A murder mystery. *Note: Reviews show the source as a magazine story en-
titled The Ghost of the Manor by Maxwell Grant.

Women Are Trouble
 Women Are Trouble
 6 reels   b&w   1936
 Dir: Errol Taggart. Sp: Michael Fessier. Prod: M-G-M.
 Cast: Florence Rice, Stuart Erwin, Paul Kelly.
 Crime thriller. A B-grade picture.

COZZEN, JAMES GOULD

S.S. San Pedro in *Scribner's Magazine* (August 28, 1930)
 S. S. San Pedro
 1932
 Rel.: Universal.

CRAM, MILDRED

The Feeder in *Redbook* (May 1926)
 Behind the Make-Up
 8 reels   b&w   1930
 Dir: Robert Milton. Adap: George Manker Watters, Howard Estabrook. Prod:
     Paramount Famous Players—Lasky Corp.
 Cast: Hal Skelly, William Powell, Fay Wray.
 Hap Brown, an easygoing, happy-go-lucky actor, falls in love with Marie, a
waitress in the French Quarter of New Orleans and befriends Gardoni, a fallen
actor with whom he becomes partners. They soon have a disagreement.

Navy Born
 Mariners of the Sky
 8 reels   b&w   1936
 Dir: Nate Watt. Sp: Albert De Mard, Olive Cooper. Prod: Republic.
 Cast: Claire Dodd, William Gargan, Douglas Fowley.
 A navy pilot raises an orphan. Prior movie title was Navy Born.

Sadie of the Desert in *Redbook* (October 1925)
 Subway Sadie
 7 reels   sil.   b&w   1926

CRAM, MILDRED (cont'd)

Subway Sadie (cont'd)
Dir: Alfred Santell. Sp: Adele Commandini, Paul Schofield. Prod: Al Rockett Prod.
Cast: Dorothy Mackaill, Jack Mulhall.
Comedy drama. Sadie Hermann dreams of going to Paris, but her big chance to go there as a buyer is lost when her fiance is hospitalized on the day she is to depart.

Thin Air
Stars Over Broadway
89 min.   b&w   1935
Dir: William Keighley. Prod: Warner Brothers. Dist: United Artists.
Cast: James Melton, Jane Froman.
A spoof of grand opera.

Wings Over Honolulu in *Redbook*
Wings Over Honolulu
78 min.   b&w   1937
Dir: H. C. Potter. Sp: Isabel Dawn, Boyce de Gaw. Prod: Universal.
Cast: Wendy Barrie, Ray Milland, William Gargan.
Adventure drama. A navy pilot involved in a romantic triangle.

CRANE, STEPHEN

The Blue Hotel
The Blue Hotel
54½ min.   color   1977
Dir: Jan Kadar. Sp: Harry M. Petrakis. Dist: Perspective Films.
A young Swede arrives at the hotel of a moody, frontier Nebraska town during the 1880s. He anticipates the wild West of dime novels, and parlays that anticipation into his own death.

The Monster in *The Monster and Other Stories* (Harper Brothers, 1899)
Face of Fire
80 min.   b&w   1959
Dir: Albert Band. Prod: Allied Artists. Dist: Hurlock Cine-World.
Cast: Cameron Mitchell, James Whitmore.
Disfigured in a fire, the local handyman becomes a social outcast.

Three Miraculous Soldiers
Three Miraculous Soldiers
17½ min.   color   1977
Dir: Bernard Selling Film. Dist: BFA Educational Media.

CRANE, STEPHEN (cont'd)

Three Miraculous Soldiers (cont'd)
A young girl is forced to recognize the humanity of both Confederate and Union soldiers.

The Upturned Face
The Upturned Face
10 min.   color   1972
Prod: Changeling Prod. Dist: Pyramid.
A young officer is killed in the Civil War, and buried by his two hesitant comrades.

CRANSTON, CLAUDIA see It's a Big Country under PETRACCA, JOSEPH

CUMMINS, RALPH

The Badge of Fighting Hearts in *Short Stories* (July 1921)
The Fire Eater
5 reels   sil.   b&w   1923
Dir: Reaves Eason. Sp: Harvey Gates. Prod: Universal.
Cast: Hoot Gibson, Louise Lorraine.
Western melodrama. Smilin' Bob Corey and his partner, Jim O'Neil, are forest rangers, who are sent to make a peaceful expedition to Paradise Valley, slated for a national park.

Cherub of Seven Bar in *Short Stories* (December 16, 1921)
The Loaded Door
5 reels   sil.   b&w   1922
Dir: Harry A. Pollard. Prod: Universal.
Cast: Hoot Gibson, Gertrude Olmstead, Bill Ryno.
Western melodrama. Bert Lyons returns to the Grainger spread and finds his former employer dead and the ranch in the hands of a dope smuggler. He rescues the ranch and the girl named Molly.

Rattler Rock in *Ace High Magazine* (August 18, 1923)
Rarin' to Go
5 reels   sil.   b&w   1924
Dir: Richard Thorpe.
Cast: Buffalo Bill, Jr., Olin Francis.
Western melodrama. Bill's friendship with Dorothy Harper helps resolve the irrigation difficulties of his employers.

CUNNINGHAM, JOHN M.

Raiders Die Hard
  Day of the Badman
  81 min.   color   1958
  Dir: Harry Keller. Sp: Lawrence Roman. Prod: Universal. Dist: Universal 16.
  Cast: Fred MacMurray, Joan Weldon.
  Western. A judge is confronted by the brother of a man he sentenced to die.

The Tin Star
  High Noon
  85 min.   b&w   1952
  Dir: Fred Zinnemann. Prod: Stanley Kramer Prod. Dist: Clem Williams Films,
    Ivy.
  Cast: Gary Cooper, Grace Kelly, Thomas Mitchell, Lloyd Bridges.
  In one short hour, in the hot and dusty little western town of Hadleyville in
1870, three gunmen await the arrival of the 12:00 o'clock train. Their leader is
returning from prison where he was sent by Marshal Cooper, whom they plan to
kill. As the Marshal endeavors to enlist decent citizens to be his deputies, he is
deserted.

CURWOOD, JAMES OLIVER

Back to God's Country in *Back to God's Country & Other Stories* (New York,
  1920)
  Back to God's Country
  6 reels   sil.   b&w   1927
  Dir: Irvin Willat. Prod: Universal—International.
  Adventure melodrama. Detained in Canada by an unscrupulous trader, a
schooner captain and his wife try to escape by dogsled.

  Back to God's Country
  78 min.   color   1953
  Dir: Joseph Pevney. Sp: Tom Reed. Prod and Dist: Universal.
  Cast: Rock Hudson, Marcia Henderson, Steve Cochran, Hugh O'Brian.
  Drama. A sea captain and his wife battle man and nature for their fur cargo.

Footprints
  The Fighting Trooper
  6 reels   b&w   1934
  Dir: Ray Taylor. Sp: Forrest Sheldon. Prod: Ambassador Pictures Inc.
  Cast: Kermit Maynard.
  Mounties bring law to the Northwest.

CURWOOD, JAMES OLIVER (cont'd)

Four Minutes Late
  Northern Frontier
  6 reels   b&w   1935
  Dir: Sam Newfield. Adap: Barry Barringer. Prod: Ambassador Pictures.
  Cast: Kermit Maynard.
  Story of a Mountie.

Hell's Gulch
  Timber War
  6 reels   b&w   1936
  Dir: Sam Newfield. Adap: Joseph O'Donnell, Barry Barringer. Prod: Ambassador Pictures.

In the Tentacles of the North in *Blue Book* (January 1915)
  Tentacles of the North
  6 reels   sil.   b&w   1926
  Dir: Louis Chaudet. Adap: Leslie Curtis. Prod: Ben Wilson Prod. Dist: Sylvan
    Films (8mm)
  Drama. Two vessels are stuck in the ice: on one is a crewman, on the other a
girl, who is the lone survivor. The crewman brings the girl back to civilization.

Jacqueline or Blazing Barriers in *Good Housekeeping Magazine* (August 1918)
  Jacqueline, or Blazing Barriers
  7 reels   sil.   b&w   1923
  Dir: Dell Henderson. Adap: Thomas F. Fallon, Dorothy Farnum. Prod: Pine
    Tree Pictures.
  Cast: Marguerite Courtot, Helen Rowland, Gus Weinberg.
  Melodrama. Jacqueline Roland, loved by Raoul Radon, meets Henri Dubois.
Dubois convinces Raoul that Jacqueline loves him instead of Raoul, though she
really does love Raoul.

The Other Man's Wife in *Back to God's Country & Other Stories* (New York, 1920)
  My Neighbor's Wife
  6 reels   sil.   b&w   1925
  Dir: Clarence Geldert. Prod: Clifford S. Elfelt Prod.
  Comedy. The son of a millionaire wants to make it on his own. He puts his last
dime into a film, hires Eric von Greed to shoot it, and to everyone's surprise it is a
success.

Peter God in *Back to God's Country & Other Stories* (New York, 1920)
  The Destroyers
  5 reels   b&w   1916
  Dir: Ralph Ince. Prod: Vitagraph

CURWOOD, JAMES OLIVER (cont'd)

The Poetic Justice of Uko San in *Outing* (June 1910)
I Am the Law
7 reels   sil.   b&w   1922
Dir: Edwin Carewe. Prod: Edwin Carewe Prod.
Cast: Alice Lake, Kenneth Harlan.
Northwest melodrama. A Royal Mounted Policeman rescues a young lady, who then falls in love with his brother.

Retribution
Timber Fury
63 min.   b&w   1950
Dir: Bernard B. Ray. Prod: Jack Schwarz Prod. Dist: Budget, Lewis Film
     Service, "The" Film Center
Cast: David Bruce, Laura Lee.
Outdoor adventure among the giant trees.

The Speck on the Wall
Law of the Timber
70 min.   b&w   1941
Dir: Bernard B. Ray. Prod: Producers Releasing Corp. Dist: Mogull's.
Cast: Marjorie Reynolds, Monte Blue.

Wapi, the Walrus
Back to God's Country
6 reels   b&w   1919
Dir: David M. Hartford. Prod: First National.
Cast: Nell Shipman.

When the Door Opened in *Leslie's Weekly* (November 13, 1920)
When the Door Opened
7 reels   sil.   b&w   1925
Dir: Reginald Barker. Prod: Fox.
Cast: Jacqueline Logan, Walter McGrail.
Northwest melodrama. Clive Grenfal returns home unannounced and finds his wife in the arms of Henry Morgan, whom he shoots. Believing Morgan dead, Clive hides in the Canadian North woods.

Yukon Manhunt
Yukon Manhunt
60 min.   b&w   1960
Prod: Monogram Picture Corp. Dist: Modern.
Cast: Kirby Grant, Chinook (dog)

CURWOOD, JAMES OLIVER (cont'd)

Yukon Manhunt (cont'd)
Corporal Webb of the Mounties sets out after the criminals behind a series of payroll robberies, and finds himself surrounded by danger on all sides.

DAHL, ROALD

Beware of the Dog in *Harper's* (October 1944)
    36 Hours
    s.m. TV play and unpublished stories by Carl K. Hittleman and Lois H. Vance.
    115 min.   b&w   1965
    Dir: George Seaton. Prod: M-G-M.
    Cast: James Garner, Rod Taylor, Eva Marie Saint.
    Thirty-six hours before D-Day in 1944, an American intelligence officer is drugged and kidnapped by the Nazis who hope to learn vital invasion plans from him. When he awakens, the Germans make him think it is 1950, and the war is over.

DANE, CLEMENCE

St. Martin's Lane
    Sidewalks of London (Br.; Br. rel. title St. Martin's Lane)
    86 min.   b&w   1940
    Dir: Tim Whelan. Prod: Pommer–Laughton–Mayflower. Dist: Budget, Mogull's
    Cast: Charles Laughton, Vivien Leigh.
    Vintage thirties melodrama with great stars. A sidewalk entertainer takes in a homeless waif and helps her to become a famous personality.

DAUDET, ALPHONSE

The Elixir of Father Gaucher
    Letters from My Windmill (with subtitles)
    s.m. "The Three Low Masses," "The Secret of Master Cornilie"
    116 min.   b&w   1955
    Dir and Sp: Marcel Pagnol. Prod: Marcel Pagnol.
    Cast: Henri Vilbert.

DAUDET, ALPHONSE (cont'd)

The Secret of Master Cornilie see Letters from My Windmill under The Elixir of Father Gaucher

The Three Low Masses see Letters from My Windmill under The Elixir of Father Gaucher

DAVID, CHARLES

Fairy Tale Murder* (jt. author Hugh Gray)
  River Gang
  60 min.   b&w   1945
  Dir: Charles David. Sp: Lester Charteris. Prod: Universal.
  Mystery. The only clue to a murder is a violin. *Note: According to Who Wrote the Movie, Fairy Tale Murder was a screen play.

DAVIS, CHARLES BELMONT

The Octopus in *Her Own Sort and Others* (New York, 1917)
  Mother O'Mine
  7 reels   sil.   b&w   1921
  Dir: Fred Niblo. Adap: C. Gardner Sullivan. Prod: Thomas H. Ince Prod.
  Melodrama. His mother's letter of introduction gets Robert a job with financier Thatcher, who is really his father. Theatcher uses him to cheat another banker. When Robert finds out, he struggles with Thatcher, who is accidentally killed. Robert is tried and only at the last minute is he saved from the electric chair.

When Johnny Comes Marching Home in *Metropolitan Magazine* (October 1914)
  The Home Stretch
  5 reels   b&w   sil.   1921
  Dir: Jack Nelson. Prod: Thomas H. Ince. Dist: Blackhawk (super 8)
  Cast: Douglas MacLean, Beatrice Burnham.
  Johnny Hardwick inherits a thoroughbred and stakes his bankroll on the horse.

DAVIS, ELMER

The Old Timer
  My American Wife
  8 reels   b&w   1936
  Dir: Harold Young. Sp: Virginia Van Upp. Prod: Paramount
  Cast: Francis Lederer, Fred Stone, Ann Sothern, Billy Burke.
  A crisis develops when a count wants to live on a ranch, but his wife wants to live in New York.

DAVIS, FREDERICK C.

The Devil Is Yellow
  Double Alibi
  60 min.   b&w   1940
  Dir: Philip Rosen. Sp: Harold Buckman, Charles Grayson. Prod: Universal.
  Cast: Wayne Morris, Margaret Lindsay.
  Murder mystery. A woman's ex-husband is the prime suspect in her death.

DAVIS, MAURICE

Twisted Road (suggestion for)
  Race Street
  79 min.   b&w   1948
  Dir: Edward L. Martin. Sp: Martin Rackin. Prod: RKO.
  Cast: George Raft, William Bendix, Marilyn Maxwell.
  Melodrama. When bookie Dan Gannin falls in love he decides to go straight,
but his friend is killed by a gang, and he vows revenge.

DAVIS, MEREDITH

When Smith Meets Smith
  Beyond the Border
  5 reels   sil.   b&w   1925
  Dir: Scott R. Dunlap. Adap: Harvey Gates. Prod: Rogstrom Prod. Dist: Select.
  Cast: Harry Carey, Mildred Harris.
  Western melodrama. When Sheriff Bob Smith catches a man accused, but inno-
cent of murder, he discovers the man is his sweetheart's brother.

DAVIS, NORBERT

A Gunsmoke Case for Major Cain
  Hands across the Rockies
  6 reels   b&w   1941
  Dir: Lambert Hillyer. Sp: Paul Franklin. Prod: Columbia Pictures Corp.
  Cast: William Elliot.
  Action western.

DAVIS, RICHARD HARDING

The Adventures of the Scarlet Car in *Collier's* (December 15, 1906; March 23, 1907;
      June 14, 1907)
  The Scarlet Car
  5 reels   sil.   b&w   1923
  Dir: Stuart Paton. Prod: Universal
  Cast: Herbert Rawlinson, Claire Adams.

DAVIS, RICHARD HARDING (cont'd)

The Scarlet Car (cont'd)
Melodrama. Billy Winthrop loves Beatrice, who is engaged to Peabody, a reform candidate for mayor. Winthrop exposes Peabody's plans to double-cross everyone.

The Adventures of Van Bibber
The Kiss Doctor
2 reels   sil.   b&w   1928
Prod: Fox
Note: Earlier films were also based on the character Van Bibber.

The Bar Sinister
Almost Human
6 reels   sil.   b&w   1927
Dir: Frank Urson. Sp: Clara Beranger. Prod: Pathé.
Cast: Vera Reynolds, Kenneth Thomson.
Re-made as It's a Dog's Life. Maggie, a mongrel, lures champion Regent Royal to the barn. Later a puppy, Pal, is born. Maggie leaves to find her owner.

It's a Dog's Life
87 min.   color   1955
Dir: Herman Hoffman. Sp: John Michael Hayes. Prod: M-G-M.
Cast: Edmund Gwenn, Dean Jagger, Jeff Richards.
Saga of a bull terrier from the Bowery that ends up in a classy dog show.

The Exiles in *The Exiles and Other Stories* (New York, 1894)
The Exiles
5 reels   sil.   b&w   1923
Dir: Edmund Mortimer. Adap: John Russell. Prod: Fox.
Cast: John Gilbert, Betty Bouton.
Melodrama. Alice, accused of murder, flies to Tangiers where the District Attorney finds her, but he learns she is innocent.

Fugitives
6 reels   b&w   sd. music   1929
Dir: William Beaudine. Prod: Fox
Melodrama. Alice's innocence in a murder case is not proven until she escapes from Sing Sing.

Gallegher
Gallegher
79 min.   color   1969

DAVIS, RICHARD HARDING (cont'd)

Gallegher (cont'd)
Prod: Walt Disney Prod. Dist: Modern.
Cast: Roger Mobley, Edmond O'Brien, Ray Teal, Harvey Korman.

Gallegher, an energetic newspaper copyboy noses his way into the hottest news breaks in town to solve a backstage murder, expose a confidence ring, and uncover graft. Set in 1899, this humorous and suspenseful story is packed with the flavor of the horse and buggy era.

Gallegher: A Newspaper Story in *Gallegher, & Other Stories*
Let 'er Go Gallegher
6 reels   sil.   b&w   1928
Dir: Elmer Clifton. Adap: Elliott Clawson. Prod: DeMille Pictures Corp.
Cast: Junior Coghlan, Harrison Ford.

Crime melodrama. A street urchin tips off Gallegher that a murder by Four Fingers, a notorious criminal, has been witnessed. A 1910 Edison production was also based on this story.

The Grand Cross of the Desert in *From "Gallegher" to "The Deserter"* (New York, 1927)
Stephen Steps Out
6 reels   sil.   b&w   1923
Dir: Joseph Henabery. Prod: Famous Players–Lasky.
Cast: Douglas Fairbanks, Jr., Theodore Roberts, Noah Beery.

Comedy. When Stephen Harlow, Jr., fails a course in the history of Turkey, his father sends him there.

The Men of Zanzibar in *The Lost Road* (New York, 1913)
The Men of Zanzibar
5 reels   sil.   b&w   1922
Dir: Rowland V. Lee. Adap: Edward J. Le Saint. Prod: Fox.
Cast: William Russell, Ruth Renick.

Mystery melodrama. The American consul in Zanzibar receives notice that a fugitive is headed there.

DAWSON, PETER
Long Gone in *Branded West*
Face of a Fugitive
81 min.   color   1959
Prod: Morningside.
Cast: Fred MacMurray, James Coburn.

Western. Man falsely accused of murder moves to a new town under a new name, but his past catches up with him.

DAY, LILLIAN

Living Up to Lizzie in *Saturday Evening Post* (December 8, 1934)
    Personal Maid's Secret
    58 min.   b&w   1935
    Dir: Arthur G. Collins. Prod: Warner Brothers and Vitaphone. Dist: United
       Artists.
    Cast: Margaret Lindsay, Warren Hull.
    A maid guides her employers to personal and financial success.

DELL, ETHEL MAY

Her Own Free Will in *The Odds and Other Stories*
    Her Own Free Will
    6 reels   sil.   b&w   1924
    Dir: Paul Scardon. Prod: Eastern Prod.
    Cast: Helene Chadwick, Holmes Herbert.
    Society drama. To save her father from bankruptcy, Nan Everard marries a
wealthy man and goes with him reluctantly to South America. On the way she is
injured and returns home where she renews an old friendship, but her husband
refuses to divorce her.

DELMAR, VINA

Angie in *Loose Ladies*
    Uptown New York
    85 min.   b&w   1932
    Dir: Victor Schertzinger. Prod: E. W. Hammons. Dist: Thunderbird.
    Cast: Jack Oakie, Raymond Hatton, Shirley Grey. Alexander Carr, Lee Moran.
    Shirley Grey, a young girl, loses the man she loves because his parents have arranged
for him to marry into a wealthy family. Shortly after, through an embarrassing incident,
Shirley meets Jack Oakie and their courtship leads to marriage. But then the other
man, now a famous surgeon, re-enters the scene, while Jack and Shirley, on the
poverty borderline, are trying to make their marriage work.

Bad Boy
    Bad Boy
    5,030'   b&w   1936
    Dir: John Blystone. Sp: Allen Rivkin. Prod: 20th Century Fox.
    Cast: James Dunn, Louise Fazenda.
    The hero warns the girl he loves that he is bad, but she won't give him up.

Dance Hall in *Liberty Magazine* (March 16, 1929)
    Dance Hall
    7 reels   b&w   sd. or sil.   1929
    Dir: Melville Brown. Sp: Jane Murfin, J. Walter Ruben. Prod: RKO.

DELMAR, VINA (cont'd)

Dance Hall (cont'd)
Cast: Olive Borden, Arthur Lake.
Melodrama. Tommy loves Gracie, but she loves Ted, who is not interested in her.

The Human Side
The Great Man's Lady
90 min.   b&w   1942
Dir: William A. Wellman. Sp: W. L. River. Prod: Paramount. Dist: Universal.
Cast: Barbara Stanwyck, Joel McCrea, Brian Donlevy.
Saga of the West in which McCrea dreams of oil wells and Donlevy steals his girl.

Playing Dead in *Metropolitan Magazine* (March 1915)
Restless Souls
4080'   b&w   sil.   1922
Dir: Robert Ensminger. Prod: Vitaphone.
Cast: Earle Williams, Francelia Billington.
Melodrama. James Parkington's wife is so attracted by a neosymbolist lecturer that he resolves to fake a suicide.

Pretty Sadie McKee (magazine fiction)
Sadie McKee
88 min.   b&w   1934
Dir: Clarence Brown. Sp: John Meehan. Prod: M-G-M. Dist: Films Inc.
Cast: Joan Crawford, Franchet Love, Edward Arnold, Gene Raymond.
A poor girl must choose between a rich alcoholic and her true love.

DEMING, RICHARD

The Careful Man (suggestion for)
Arrivederci, Baby
105 min.   color   1966
Dir: Ken Hughes. Sp: Ken Hughes, Ronald Harwood. Prod: Paramount. Dist: Films Inc.
Cast: Tony Curtis, Rosanna Schiaffino, Lionel Jeffries, Zsa Zsa Gabor.
Con-artist does away with his adoptive mother and her suitor, his chatterbox first wife, and his too-energetic second wife. But when he meets and weds the gorgeous, scheming wealthy widow, getting rid of her turns out to be a major problem.

DENEVI, MARCO

Secret Ceremony
Secret Ceremony

DENEVI, MARCO (cont'd)

Secret Ceremony (cont'd)
109 min.   b&w   1968
Dir: Joseph Losey. Sp: George Tabori. Prod: Universal. Dist: Twyman,
   Universal.
Drama. An aged prostitute meets a wealthy, but deranged girl, who insists that
the woman is her mother.

DETZER, KARL

Car Ninety-Nine in *Saturday Evening Post*
Car Ninety-Nine
70 min.   b&w   1935
Dir: Charles Barton. Prod: Paramount.
Cast: Fred MacMurray, Ann Sheridan.
A rookie trooper lets the bank robbers get away.

DICKENS, CHARLES

A Christmas Carol
Earlier filmed versions of his story include A Christmas Carol (Essaynay, 1908);
A Christmas Carol (Edison, 1910); A Christmas Carol (Great Britain, 1914).

A Christmas Carol
68 min.   b&w   1938
Dir: Edwin L. Marin. Prod: M-G-M. Dist: Films Inc.
Cast: Reginald Owen, Terry Kilburn.
Reformation of an old miser takes place through the influence of the ghosts of
Christmas Past, Present, and Future, and deceased business partner, Marley. A
faithful rendering of the Yuletide classic.

A Christmas Carol
54 min.   b&w   1954
Prod: United Films. Dist: Carousel.
Cast: Frederic March, Basil Rathbone, Ray Middleton.
Charles Dickens' classic in the first musical adaptation, score by Bernard
Herman, and a libretto by Maxwell Anderson. The miserly Scrooge is reformed in
one Christmas Eve by the ghosts of Christmas.

Mr. Magoo's Christmas Carol
60 min.   color   1964
Dir: Abe Levitow. Prod: UPA. Dist: Audio Brandon.
Voices: Jim Backus, Morey Amsterdam, Jack Cassidy, Royal Dano.
Mr. Magoo is superb in his portrayal of Ebenezer Scrooge. Original music by
Jule Styne and Bob Merril.

DICKENS, CHARLES (cont'd)

A Christmas Carol (cont'd)
Scrooge
67 min.   b&w   1935
Dir: Henry Edwards. Prod: Paramount. Dist: Buchan Pictures, Budget, Select,
  "The" Film Center.
Cast: Sir Seymour Hicks, Donald Calthrop.
The story of Ebenezer Scrooge, the miser who was reformed by the ghosts of
Christmas.

Scrooge
111 min.   color   1970
Dir: Ronald Neame. Prod: National General. Dist: Swank.
Cast: Albert Finney, Alec Guiness.
Music and lyrics by Leslie Bricusse. Lively and lavish musical version of the time-
less story of Ebenezer Scrooge.

Cricket on the Hearth

Biograph made two versions of this, one in 1909, and the other in 1914.

Cricket on the Hearth
7 reels   b&w   sil.   1923
Dir: Lorimer Johnston. Prod: Paul Gerson Pictures. Dist: Blackhawk (8mm or
  16mm)
Cast: Josef Swickard, Fritz Ridgeway.
In a small village in England, John Perrybingle, the mail carrier, courts and
marries Dot. Their trust in each other is shaken, but finally restored, by a cricket
that sings on the hearth.

Cricket on the Hearth
45 min.   color   1968
Prod: UPA. Dist: "The" Film Center.
Cast: Voices of Danny Thomas, Marlo Thomas, Ed Ames, Hans Conreid, Abbe
  Lane, Roddy McDowall, and the Norman Luboff Choir.
Animated. A cheerful little cricket gradually unravels all the troubles of a blind
girl, who regains her sight in time for a happy Christmas Day, when she and her
financé are reunited.

The Signalman
The Signalman
15 min.   b&w   1955
Prod: Dynamic Films. Dist: Audio Brandon
Cast: Monty Woolley.
A haunting tale of the vision of a lonely railroad signalman which foretells
disaster and his own death.

DINNEEN, JOSEPH F.

They Stole $2,500,000—and Got Away with It
  Six Bridges to Cross
  96 min.   b&w   1955
  Dir: Joseph Pevney. Sp: Sydney Beehm. Prod: Universal. Dist: Universal.
  Cast: Tony Curtis, Julie Adams.
  Drama. A rookie cop befriends a young hoodlum shot by a policeman during a
robbery.

DINELLI, MEL

Beware My Lovely
s.m. The Man, a play
  Beware My Lovely
  77 min.   b&w   1952
  Dir: Harry Horner. Prod: RKO. Dist: Ivy.
  Cast: Ida Lupino, Robert Ryan.
  A young war widow is menaced by a sinister handyman.

DINESEN, ISAK

The Immortal Story
s.m. original title "Une Histoire Immortelle," in *Anecdotes of Destiny*
  The Immortal Story
  63 min.   color   1968
  Dir and Sp: Orson Welles. Dist: Audio Brandon.
  Cast: Orson Welles, Jeanne Moreau, Roger Coggio, Norman Ashley.
  Welles plays Mr. Clay, an aging and wealthy merchant, living in Macao at the
turn of the century. A man of facts, disliking prophecies and fiction, he insists on
making reality out of a legend which has been related by sailors for many years;
he wants one sailor to be able to tell the story from his own experience. According
to the tale, a rich old man pays a handsome sailor to sleep with his beautiful young
wife, in order to provide an heir. Clay, who has no wife, instructs his clerk (Roger
Coggio) to find a woman who can play the role. The clerk hires a no-longer-young
woman (Jeanne Moreau); Clay finds a young sailor. The two spend the night
together and make love, while Clay, delighted with his power, waits outside. As the
sailor leaves the next morning, the clerk tells him that he can now tell the story to
others, as it happened to him. The sailor, who has been moved by his encounter
with the woman, replies that he would never repeat the tale, since no one would
believe it. Meanwhile, the old man has died.

DOSTOYEVSKY, FYODOR

The Crocodile
　The Crocodile
　29 min.　　color　　　1969
　Green and slimy, the crocodile stretches its mammoth jaws and—gulp!—swallows
Ivan Matveyevitch. What is more, Ivan refuses to come out. "This is utopia!," he
cries from within his cozy spot in the creature's belly. "I always thought this
would happen to him" remarks Ivan's superior.

The Gambler in *The Gambler & Other Stories* (N.Y., Macmillan, 1931)
　The Great Sinner
　110 min.　　b&w　　　1949
　Dir: Robert Siodmak. Prod: M-G-M. Dist: Films Inc.
　Cast: Gregory Peck, Ava Gardner.
　A story about people whose gambling fever almost ruins their lives.

The Gentle Woman (novella) in *Letters from the Underworld*
　Une Femme Douce
　87 min.　　color　　　1969
　Dir: Robert Bresson. Dist: New Yorker.
　Cast: Dominique Sanda.
　A gentle wife dies, a suicide. Her husband, an antique pawnbroker, sits by the bed
on which her body lies and reconstructs the past, in an attempt to retrace the paths
which led his wife to this end.

DOYLE, ARTHUR CONAN

　Sherlock Holmes, a character created by Doyle, appeared in many short stories
and novels. Below are the popular films released in the United States, based on
actual stories.
　Scores of films were made abroad based on the Holmes character. For complete
information consult *Sherlock Holmes on the Screen* by Robert W. Pohle, Jr., and
Douglas C. Hart (A. S. Barnes, Cranbury, N.J., 1977).
　Several original screenplays were also written based on the character of Holmes,
including The Private Life of Sherlock Holmes, Pursuit to Algiers, Scarlet Claw, The
Seven Per Cent Solution, Sherlock Holmes, Sherlock Holmes in Washington, Terror
by Night, and The Woman in Green.

The Adventure of Charles Augustus Milverton
　The Strange Case of the Missing Rembrandt (Br.)
　84 min.　　b&w　　　1932
　Dir: Leslie S. Hiscott. Sp: Cyril Twyford, H. Fowler Mear, Arthur Wontner. Prod:
　　First Division Films.
　Cast: Arthur Wontner, Jane Welsh.

DOYLE, ARTHUR CONAN (cont'd)

The Strange Case of the Missing Rembrandt (cont'd)
An unscrupulous American millionaire forces an opium addict to steal a Rembrandt from the Louvre.

The Adventure of the Beryl Coronet (Br.)
   The Adventures of Sherlock Holmes (a series of fifteen films)
   33-43 min.   b&w   sil.   1921
   Dir: Maurice Elvey. Sp: William J. Elliot. Prod: Stoll Picture Prod.
   Cast: Eille Norwood, Hubert Willis.
   The titles include (in brief form): The Dying Detective, The Devil's Foot, A
Case of Identity, The Yellow Face, The Red-Headed League, The Resident Patient,
A Scandal in Bohemia, The Man with the Twisted Lip, The Beryl Coronet, The
Noble Bachelor, Copper Beeches, The Empty House, The Tiger of San Pedro, The
Priory School, The Solitary Cyclist.

The Adventure of the Copper Beeches see The Adventures of Sherlock Holmes
   under The Adventure of the Beryl Coronet

The Adventure of the Dancing Men
   Sherlock Holmes and the Secret Weapon
   68 min.   b&w   1942
   Dir: Roy William Neill. Sp: Edward T. Lowe, W. Scott Darling, Edmond L.
      Hartmann. Prod: Universal. Dist: Audio Brandon, Wholesome.
   Cast: Basil Rathbone.
   Holmes and Watson are hot on the trail of Nazi agents who are planning to steal
a newly invented bombsight and its Swiss inventor. The unflappable Holmes contends with a mysterious cipher, as well as his traditional adversary, Professor
Moriarty.

The Adventure of the Devil's Foot see The Adventures of Sherlock Holmes under
   The Adventure of the Beryl Coronet

The Adventure of the Dying Detective
   The Return of Sherlock Holmes
   s.m. "His Last Bow"
   79 min.   b&w   sd.   1929
   Dir: Basil Dean, Clive Brook. Sp: Basil Dean, Garrett Ford. Prod: Paramount
      Famous Players—Lasky.
   Cast: Clive Brook, H. Reeves-Smith.
   Holmes attends the wedding of Watson's daughter, Mary, at which the father of
the groom is poisoned.

DOYLE, ARTHUR CONAN (cont'd)

The Adventure of the Empty House see also The Adventures of Sherlock Holmes
   under The Adventure of the Beryl Coronet; Sherlock Holmes' Fatal Hour
   under The Final Problem

The Adventure of the Empty House
   The Woman in Green
   68 min.   b&w   1945
   Dir: Roy William Neill. Sp: Bertram Millhauser. Prod: Universal. Dist: Audio
      Brandon, Kit Parker.
   Cast: Basil Rathbone, Nigel Bruce, Henry Daniell, Hillary Brooke.
   Freely adapted. Holmes hunts for the missing link in a series of bizarre murders.
The trail leads straight to the fiendish Professor Moriarty, who has one or two
surprises in store for Holmes.

The Adventure of the Five Orange Pips
   The House of Fear
   69 min.   b&w   1945
   Dir: Roy William Neill. Sp: Roy Chanslor. Prod and Dist: Universal.
   Cast: Basil Rathbone, Nigel Bruce, Paul Cavanagh, Dennis Hoey.
   One after another, the members of the Good Comrades Club are murdered in
a gloomy mansion off the Scottish coast until only two members and Watson
remain alone in the hazardous house. Holmes determines the method of the killer's
madness when someone is murdered out of turn.

The Adventure of the Noble Bachelor see The Adventures of Sherlock Holmes
   under The Adventure of the Beryl Coronet

The Adventure of the Priory School see The Adventures of Sherlock Holmes under
   The Adventure of the Beryl Coronet

The Adventure of the Six Napoleons (suggestion for)
   Pearl of Death
   69 min.   b&w   1944
   Dir: Roy William Neill. Sp: Bertram Millhauser. Prod: Universal. Dist: Audio
      Brandon.
   Cast: Basil Rathbone, Nigel Bruce, Evelyn Ankers.
   Holmes discovers a series of mysterious killings while stalking the stolen Borgia
pearl. The murders are all committed in the same manner and share a single baffling
clue.

DOYLE, ARTHUR CONAN (cont'd)

The Adventure of the Solitary Cyclist see The Adventures of Sherlock Holmes
under The Adventure of the Beryl Coronet

The Adventure of the Speckled Band
The Speckled Band
s.m. play "The Speckled Band"
90 min.   b&w   1931
Dir: Jack Raymond. Prod: First Division Pictures. Dist: Thunderbird.
Cast: Raymond Massey, Athole Stewart.
Dr. Rylott murders one of his stepdaughters by a unique plan and plans to murder
the other, but Holmes foils him. *Note: Earlier versions were produced in Great
Britain in 1912 and 1923.

The Adventure of Wisteria Lodge (film title: The Tiger of San Pedro) see The
Adventures of Sherlock Holmes under The Adventure of the Beryl Coronet

Brigadier Gerard Stories*
The Adventures of Gerard
91 min.   color   1970
Dir: Jerzy Skolinowski. Prod: United Artists.
Cast: Peter McEnery, Eli Wallach, Jack Hawkins, Claudia Cardinale.
The encounters of a British soldier with war and women. *Note: Earlier silent
versions were produced in Great Britain in 1915 and 1916.

The Fighting Eagle
9 reels   b&w   sil.   1927
Dir: Donald Crisp. Prod: De Mille Pictures.

A Case of Identity see The Adventures of Sherlock Holmes under The Adventure of
the Beryl Coronet

The Final Problem (Br.)
Sherlock Holmes' Fatal Hour
s.m. "The Empty House"
84 min.   b&w   1931
Dir: Leslie S. Hiscott. Sp: Cyril Twyford, H. Fowler Mear, Leslie S. Hiscott,
    Arthur Wontner. Prod: First Division Pictures.
Cast: Arthur Wontner, Ian Fleming.
A complex plot involving a young woman concerned about her brother's gambling
and Holmes's inevitable clash with Moriarty.

DOYLE, ARTHUR CONAN (cont'd)

The Final Problem (cont'd)
The Triumph of Sherlock Holmes
s.m. Valley of Fear (novel)
84 min.   b&w   1935
Dir: Leslie S. Hiscott. Prod: Real Art Prod.
Cast: Arthur Wontner, Lyn Harding, Ian Fleming.
Holmes investigates the murder of a Pinkerton detective.

His Last Bow see also The Return of Sherlock Holmes under The Adventure of the
Dying Detective

His Last Bow
Sherlock Holmes and the Voice of Terror
65 min.   b&w   ˙ 1942
Dir: John Rawlins. Sp: Lynn Riggs, John Bright. Dist: Audio Brandon.
Cast: Basil Rathbone, Nigel Bruce, Henry Daniell.
In this story, loosely based on His Last Bow, Holmes and Watson comb wartime
London for Nazi agents who are broadcasting accounts of successful espionage
activities.

The Lost Special in *Black Doctor & Other Tales of Terror & Mystery*
The Lost Special (serial in 12 chapters)
b&w   1932
Dir: Henry McRae. Sp: Ella O'Neill, George Plympton, Basil Dickey, George
Morgan. Prod: Universal.
Two college students and a girl reporter search for the Gold Special, a train
that disappears without a trace. Holmes is not in this film.

The Man with the Twisted Lip see The Adventures of Sherlock Holmes under
The Adventure of the Beryl Coronet

The Musgrave Ritual
Sherlock Holmes Faces Death
68 min.   b&w   1943
Dir: Roy William Neill. Sp: Bertram Millhauser. Prod: Universal. Dist: Audio
Brandon.
Cast: Basil Rathbone, Nigel Bruce, Hillary Brooke, Milburn Stone.
One of the most bizarre Holmes tales, the film is haunted throughout by howling
winds, an underground crypt (first used as a set in Dracula), a clock that strikes
thirteen before a murder, and a giant chessboard with an intelligence all its own.

DOYLE, ARTHUR CONAN (cont'd)

The Red-Headed League see The Adventures of Sherlock Holmes under The Adventure of the Beryl Coronet

The Resident Patient see The Adventures of Sherlock Holmes under The Adventure of the Beryl Coronet

A Scandal in Bohemia see The Adventures of Sherlock Holmes under The Adventure of the Beryl Coronet

Silver Blaze
    Silver Blaze
    s.m. The Hound of the Baskervilles (novel)
    66 min.   b&w   1941
    Dir: Thomas Bentley. Sp: Arthur Macrae, H. Fowler Mear, Arthur Wontner.
      Prod: Astor Pictures Corp. Dist: Select.
    Cast. Lyn Harding, Arthur Wontner, Ian Fleming.
    Holmes investigates the disappearance of Colonel Russ' horse, Silver Blaze.

    Silver Blaze
    31 min.   color   1977
    Dir: John Davies. Adap: Julian Bond. Dist: Learning.
    Cast: Christopher Plummer, Thorley Walters
    "The favorite [racehorse] for the Wessex Cup has disappeared," says Holmes, turning to the faithful Watson, "and his trainer has been foully murdered." Called in to solve the baffling case of the famous racehorse, Silver Blaze, Holmes and Watson arrive at the village of Tavistock to discover that the police have already arrested a stranger who had been lurking around the stables. But the great detective's keen powers uncover discrepancies.

Unidentified Story
    Dressed to Kill (Br. title: Sherlock Holmes and the Secret Code)
    72 min.   b&w   1946
    Dir: Roy William Neill. Prod: Universal. Dist: Budget, Kit Parker, Macmillan.
    Cast: Basil Rathbone, Nigel Bruce, Patricia Morison.
    In this film, the Bank of England's engraving plates are stolen. While hot on the trail, Holmes is captured and left hanging by his hands in an abandoned garage, as poison gas begins to fill the room.

The Yellow Face see The Adventures of Sherlock Holmes under The Adventure of the Beryl Coronet

DOYLE, LAIRD

The Heir Chaser
    Jimmy the Gent (jt. author Ray Nazarro)
    67 min.   b&w   1934
    Dir: Michael Curtiz. Prod: Warner Brothers. Dist: United Artists.
    Cast: James Cagney, Bette Davis.
    An enterprising businessman locates phony "missing" heirs to large fortunes.

DRAWBELL, J. W.

Love Story
    A Lady Surrenders (Br.)
    90 min.   b&w   1947
    Dir: Leslie Arliss. Prod: Gainsborough Studios, London.
    Cast: Margaret Lockwood, Stewart Granger.
    A war-time love story about a concert pianist and an RAF pilot, each of whom conceals an unhappy secret: her secret—that she will die soon, and his secret—that he will go blind. Original title Love Story.

DREISER, THEODORE

The Prince Who Was a Thief in *Best Short Stories*
    The Prince Who Was a Thief
    83 min.   color   1951
    Dir: Rudolph Mate. Prod and Dist: Universal.
    Cast: Tony Curtis, Piper Laurie, Everett Sloane.
    An adventure. An Arabian Nights' fantasy of a prince raised by thieves and the beautiful street urchin who loves him.

DU MAURIER, DAPHNE

The Birds in *Kiss Me Again, Stranger* (Garden City, N.Y., Doubleday, 1952)
    The Birds
    119 min.   color   1963
    Dir: Alfred Hitchcock. Prod: Universal. Dist: Swank, Twyman.
    Cast: Rod Taylor, Suzanne Pleschette, Tippi Hedren.
    Hundreds of people are victims of a mysterious mass attack by fierce birds.

Don't Look Now in *Don't Look Now*
    Don't Look Now
    110 min.   color   1973
    Dir: Nicholas Roeg. Sp: Alan Scott, Chris Bryant. Prod: British Lion.
    Cast: Donald Sutherland, Julie Christie.
    Mystery thriller. Set in Venice, a young couple's daughter drowns. The town is beseiged by a series of bizarre murders.

DUNCAN, DAVID

The Lost Treasure of the Andes
    Jivarro
    91 min.   b&w   1954
    Dir: Edward Ludwig. Prod: Paramount. Dist: Westcoast Films.
    Cast: Fernando Lamas, Rhonda Fleming.
    Two adventurers seek treasure in the jungle territory of head-hunters.

DUNN, ELIZABETH

Candy Takes a Job
    Meet the Stewarts
    8 reels   b&w   1942
    Dir: Alfred E. Green. Sp: Karen De Wolf. Prod: Columbia Pictures Corp.
    Cast: William Holden, Frances Dee.
    Comedy. An heiress marries a white collar worker and tries to live on a budget.

DUNN, J. ALLEN

The Mascotte of the Three Star in *Short Stories*
    Action
    5 reels   sil.   b&w   1921
    Dir: Jack Ford. Prod: Universal.
    Cast: Hoot Gibson, Francis Ford.
    Western melodrama. Molly (an orphan), heir to a ranch and mine, falls under
the influence of saloon-owner Plimsoll, who tries to get her inheritance.

DURLAM, ARTHUR

State Trooper
    Young Dynamite
    60 min.   b&w   1937
    Dir: Leslie Goodwins. Prod: Maurice Conn. Dist: Film Classics Exchange.
    Cast: Frankie Darro.

DWYER, JAMES

Maryland, My Maryland in *Collier's* (March 20, 1920)
    Bride of the Storm
    7 reels   b&w   sil.   1926
    Dir: J. Stuart Blackton. Adap: Marian Constance. Prod: Vitagraph.
    Cast: Dolores Costello, John Harron.
    Melodrama. An American ship is wrecked off the coast of the Dutch East Indies
and a little girl and her mother are washed ashore.

EBERHART, MIGNON

Dead Yesterday
   The Great Hospital Mystery
   5,250'   b&w   1937
   Dir: James Tinling. Sp: Bess Meredyth, William Conselman, Jerry Cady.
      Prod: 20th Century Fox.
   Cast: Jane Darwell, Sig Rumann.
   The mystery concerns a corpse that has been shot after already being dead.

EDGELOW, THOMAS

It Isn't Being Done This Season in *Breezy Stories* (August 1918)
   It Isn't Being Done This Season
   5 reels   sil.   b&w   1921
   Dir: George L. Sargent. Prod: Vitagraph.
   Cast: Corinne Griffith, Sally Crute, Webster Campbell.
   Society melodrama. Marcia Ventnor (Corinne Griffith) marries for money
instead of love. After her husband's death she agrees to marry her former poor
sweetheart if he obtains the contract from an   Oriental rugmaker.

EDGINTON, MAY (pseud. Helen Marion Edgington)

The Heart Is Young
   The False Madonna
   6,062'   b&w   1932
   Dir: Arthur Kober (pseud. of Stuart Walker). Prod: Paramount Publix.
   Cast: William Boyd, Conway Tearle.
   Story of two couples who are card sharps and blackmailers.

The Joy Girl in *Saturday Evening Post* (November 13-December 18, 1926)
   The Joy Girl
   7 reels   sil.   b&w   1927
   Dir: Allan Dwan. Adap: Adele Camondini. Prod: Fox.
   Cast: Olive Borden, Neil Hamilton, Marie Dressler.
   Society comedy. Jewel Courage marries for wealth, but later learns her husband
is really a chauffeur posing as a millionaire.

EDGINTON, MAY (cont'd)

Judgment in *Saturday Evening Post* (August 1924)
> Her Husband's Secret
> 7 reels   sil.   b&w   1925
> Dir: Frank Lloyd. Adap: J. G. Hawks. Prod: Frank Lloyd.
> Cast: Antonio Moreno, Patsy Ruth Miller.

Melodrama. To relieve his boredom, Leon Kent throws a wild party and his wife goes to the home of a sympathetic neighbor. When he finds his wife has spent the night at the home of another man, Kent divorces her. He takes his son with him and the boy and his mother do not meet until 25 years later under awkward circumstances.

Purple and Fine Linen in *The Bedside Book of Famous British Stories* (New York, 1940)
> Adventure in Manhattan
> 8 reels   b&w   1936
> Dir: Edward Ludwig. Prod: Columbia.
> Cast: Jean Arthur.

A re-make of Three Hours. A newspaper man sets out to capture a thief.

> Three Hours
> 6 reels   sil.   b&w   1927
> Dir: James Flood. Sp: Paul Bern. Prod: Corinne Griffith.
> Cast: Corinne Griffith, John Bowers.

Melodrama. Madeline Durkin, once married to a wealthy man, is reduced to poverty. She steals a wallet to give her enough money to see her child, which is in the custody of her former husband.

ELLIN, STANLEY

The Best of Everything in *Ellery Queen's Magazine* (November 1952)
> Nothing But the Best
> 98 min.   color   1964
> Dir: Clive Donner. Sp: Frederic Raphael. Prod: David Deutsch.
> Dist: Audio Brandon, Cine-Craft Co., Contemporary/McGraw, Modern.
> Cast: Alan Bates, Denholm Elliott, Harry Andrews, Millicent Martin, Nigel
> Stock, Peter Madden.

The game of one-upmanship as played by a cheeky young real-estate salesman. The man on the make is Jimmy Brewster (Bates). His first major step up the ladder to the top and the boss's daughter is to hire an upperclass reject, Charlie Prince (Elliott), for a crash course in manners and immorals. Poor Charlie ends up strangled by his own Etonian tie.

ELLSTON, ALLAN VAUGHAN

The Belled Palm
   Paradise Isle
   8 reels   b&w   1937
   Dir: Arthur Greville Collins. Adap: Marion Orth. Prod: Monogram Picture Corp.
   Cast: Movita, Warren Hull.
   A white man who is blind and seeking a doctor, loves a South Seas native.

EMERY, STEUART M.

The Wild, Wild Child in *Liberty Magazine* (January 31, 1925)
   Wild, Wild Susan
   6 reels   sil.   b&w   1925
   Dir: Edward Sutherland. Prod: Famous Players–Lasky.
   Cast: Bebe Daniels, Rod La Rocque.
   Comedy. An affluent New York girl in search of thrills goes to work in a detective agency.

ENGELS, S.

Cut Rate
   The Big Shakedown (jt. author Niven Busch)
   7 reels   b&w   1933
   Dir: John Francis Dillon. Sp: Niven Busch, Rian James. Prod: First National
      Pictures.

ENGLISH, RICHARD

Follow the Band in *Collier's*
   Follow the Band
   61 min.   b&w   1943
   Dir: Jean Yarbrough. Sp: Warren Wilson, Dorothy Bennett. Prod: Universal.
   Romantic mix-ups ensue when a Vermont boy gets a job in New York as a
trombone player.

No Place to Go in *Saturday Evening Post*
   Leather Gloves
   75 min.   b&w   1948
   Dir: Richard Quine, William Asher. Sp: Brown Holmes. Prod: Columbia Pictures
      Corp.
   A down-and-out boxer regains his self-respect.

ENTERS, ANGNA

Tenth Ave. Angel
   Tenth Ave. Angel
   s.m. Miracle at Midnight, radio sketch by Craig Rice
   74 min.   b&w   1948
   Dir: Roy Rowland. Sp: Harry Ruskin, Eleanore Griffin. Prod: M-G-M. Dist:
     Films Inc.
   Cast: Margaret O'Brien.
   A young girl living in a tenement influences everyone by her faith.

ERICKSON, CARL

Competition
   Stranger in Town
   66 min.   b&w   1932
   Dir: Eric C. Kenton. Sp: Carl Erickson. Prod: Warner Brothers. Dist: United
     Artists.
   Cast: Chic Sale, Ann Dvorak, Noah Beery.
   Story of a small town grandfather and his general store.

ERNST, PAUL

The Old Gang in *Saturday Evening Post* (July 11, 1942)
   Kid Dynamite
   70 min.   b&w   1943
   Dir: Wallace Fox. Prod: Monogram Picture Corp. Dist: Budget, Ivy.
   Cast: The Bowery Boys.
   Friction develops between two members of a gang.

When We Were Twenty-One
   Truth about Youth
   68 min.   b&w   1930
   Dir: William A. Seiter. Prod: First National Pictures. Dist: United Artists.
   Cast: Loretta Young, Myrna Loy.
   Romantic drama of crossed love affairs.

ERSKINE, LAURIE YORK

Renfrew of the Royal Mounted
   Sky Bandits
   b&w   1940
   Prod: Monogram Picture Corp.
   Cast: James Newill, Dave O'Brien.
   Mounties uncover the mystery of a disappearing plane carrying gold from a Yukon
mine.

EVANS, LARRY

Judgment of the Hills in *Cosmopolitan*
    Judgment of the Hills
    6 reels   sil.   b&w   1927
    Dir: James Leo Meehan. Adap: Dorothy Yost. Prod: R-C Pictures.
    Cast: Virginia Valli, Frankie Darro.
    Rural drama. Brant, an alcoholic, refuses to go to war until the sheriff finds him and sends him to boot camp. He returns home a hero, but still an alcoholic. He decides to reform when a child reproves him.

The Painted Lady in *Saturday Evening Post* (November 1912)
    The Painted Lady
    7 reels   sil.   b&w   1924
    Dir: Chester Bennett. Prod: Fox.
    Cast: George O'Brien, Dorothy Mackaill.
    Melodrama. Violet, released from prison after being convicted of a crime committed by her sister, is forced to become a woman of easy virtue. On an excursion she meets Luther Smith, but she feels unworthy of his love. There is also a 1917 version.

    Pursued
    6,175'   sd.   b&w   1934
    Dir: Louis King. Sp: Lester Cole, Stuart Anthony. Prod: Fox.

EVERSON, RONALD

Scare
s.m. "The Red Shadow Scare," and the radio show Street and Smith's Detective
    Story Magazine Hour
    The Red Shadow
    20 min.   b&w   1932
    Dir: Kurt Newmann. Sp: Frank Bowers. Prod: Universal.
    Mystery. A Shadow-Detective series short.

FAIRMAN, PAUL see JORGENSON, IVAR

FARAGO, SANDOR

The Boy, The Girl, and The Dog (jt. author Alexander G. Kenedi)
    Marry the Boss' Daughter
    5,282'   b&w   1941
    Dir: Thornton Freeland. Sp: Jack Andrews. Prod: 20th Century Fox.

FAST, HOWARD M.

Rachel
    Rachel and the Stranger
    92 min.   b&w   1948
    Dir: Norman Foster. Prod: RKO. Dist: Films Inc.
    Cast: William Holden, Loretta Young.
    Western. A man's love for his wife is aroused when a stranger visits their home.

FAULKNER, WILLIAM

The Barn Burning
    The Long Hot Summer
    s.m. "The Spotted Horses," *The Hamlet* (novel)
    115 min.   color   1958
    Dir: Martin Ritt. Sp: Jerry Wald. Prod: 20th Century Fox. Dist: Films Inc.
    Cast: Orson Welles, Paul Newman, Joanne Woodward, Lee Remick, Tony
       Franciosa.
Turbulent relationships exist between a wealthy, aggressive father and his two
grown children—one a frustrated, unmarried young woman, and the other a
weakling, married son.

The Spotted Horses see The Long Hot Summer under The Barn Burning

Tomorrow in *Knight's Gambit* (Random, 1949)
    Tomorrow
    102 min.   color   1972
    Dir: Joseph Anthony. Sp: Horton Foote.
A young Mississippi farmer nurses a pregnant woman abandoned by her husband,
marries her on her deathbed, and raises her son.

Turn About
    Today We Live
    110 min.   b&w   1933
    Dir: Howard Hawks. Prod: M-G-M.
    Cast: Joan Crawford, Gary Cooper.
    A war story filled with heroism and sacrifice.

FAUST, FREDERICK see BRAND, MAX

FAY, WILLIAM

The Disappearance of Dolan in *Saturday Evening Post*
Champ for a Day
90 min.   b&w   1953
Dir: Irving Shulman, Prod: Republic. Dist: Ivy.
Cast: Audrey Totter, Alex Nichol.
Melodrama. Investigating the disappearance of his manager, a young prize-fighter is indirectly responsible for breaking up a gambling syndicate.

The Man Who Sank the Navy in *Saturday Evening Post*
The Guy Who Came Back
91 min.   b&w   1951
Dir: Joseph Newman. Prod: 20th Century Fox. Dist: Ivy.
Cast: Paul Douglas, Joan Bennett.
Soap opera. A football hero can't seem to make it after his career is halted by an injury.

FERBER, EDNA

Classified in *Mother Knows Best* (Garden City, N.Y., 1927)
Classified
7 reels   sil.   b&w   1925
Dir: Alfred Santell. Sp: June Mathis. Prod: Corinne Griffith.
Cast: Corinne Griffith, Jack Mulhall.
Comedy. A girl who works in the classified advertising section of a newspaper flirts with every wealthy man she meets. But she falls in love with Lloyd, a garage owner.

Hard to Get
8 reels   sd. or sil.   b&w   1929
Prod: First National Pictures.
Cast: Dorothy Mackaill, Charles Delaney.
Comedy drama. A millionaire philanderer and an automobile mechanic are rivals for Bobby Martin, a mannequin in a fashionable shop.

Glamour
Glamour
75 min.   b&w   1934
Dir: William Wyler. Prod: Universal. Dist: Universal 16.
Cast: Paul Lukas, Constance Cummings.
A chorus girl who is married and a mother falls in love with a composer.

FERBER, EDNA (cont'd)

Mother Knows Best in *Mother Knows Best* (Garden City, N.Y., 1927)
  Mother Knows Best
  9 reels   sd., mus. score, sd. effects   b&w   1928
  Dir: John Blystone. Prod: Fox.
  Cast: Madge Bellamy, Louise Dresser.
  A domineering mother controls her daughter's successful show business career
until the daughter suffers a nervous breakdown.

Not a Day Over Twenty-One
  Summer Resort
  1932
  Prod: Worldwide.

Old Man Minick in *One Basket: 31 Short Stories*
  The Expert
  69 min.   b&w   1932
  Dir: Archie Mayo. Prod: Warner Brothers and Vitaphone. Dist: United Artists.
  Cast: Chic Sale. Lois Wilson.
  A neglected old man befriends a newspaper boy.

FESSIER, MICHAEL

The Sheriff Was Scared
  The Boy from Oklahoma
  88 min.   color   1953
  Dir: Michael Curtiz. Sp: Frank Davis. Prod: Warner Brothers.
  Western. A home-spun sheriff restores law and order to a crime-ridden town,
using a lariat as a weapon.

The Woman They Almost Lynched in *Saturday Evening Post* (June 1, 1951)
  The Woman They Almost Lynched
  90 min.   b&w   1953
  Dir: Allan Dwan. Prod: Republic. Dist: Ivy.
  Cast: Joan Leslie, Brian Donlevy.
  Western. A young Yankee girl is involved with a Confederate guerilla leader, his
unscrupulous wife, and a rebel spy.

FIELD, JULIAN

Tempermental Lady
  Setting of the Moon
  54 min.   b&w   1936
  Dir: Ralph Staub. Prod: Republic. Dist: Ivy.

FIELD, JULIAN (cont'd)

Setting of the Moon (cont'd)
Cast: Roger Pryor, Grace Bradley.
A composer helps a vocalist. His ex-girl friend turns up and calls herself his wife.

FINDLEY, FERGUSON

The Waterfront
The Mob
87 min.   b&w   1951
Dir: Robert Parrish. Sp: William Bowers. Prod: Columbia.
Cast: Broderick Crawford, Betty Buehler, Richard Kiley.
An undercover agent is sent back to the waterfront to catch a top mobster
after failing the first time.

FINKEL, ABEN (jt. author) see The Deceiver under MUNI, BELLE

FINNEY, JACK

Five Against the House in *Good Housekeeping*
Five Against the House
84 min.   b&w   1955
Dir: Phil Karlson. Sp: Sterling Silliphant, William Bowers, John Barnwell. Prod:
     Dayle Prod.
Melodrama. The prankish scheme of four college boys and a songstress to rob a
casino in Reno ends in a grim clash with the law.

House of Numbers in *Cosmopolitan* (July 1956)
House of Numbers
92 min.   b&w   1957
Dir: Russell Rouse. Prod: M-G-M. Dist: Films Inc.
Cast: Jack Palance, Barbara Lang.
A clever plan for a murderer's escape from prison.

FISHER, DOROTHY F. C. see CANFIELD, DOROTHY

FISHER, STEVE

If You Break My Heart in *Liberty Magazine*
Nurse from Brooklyn
65 min.   b&w   1938
Dir: S. Sylvan Simon. Sp: Roy Chanslor. Prod: Universal.
Cast: Sally Eilers, Paul Kelly.
Drama. The wounded detective who allegedly shot a nurse's brother is brought
to the hospital where she works.

FISHER, STEVE

The Sea Nymph
    September Storm (AKA The Girl in the Red Bikini)
    99 min.   b&w   1961
    Dir: Byron Haskin. Prod: Fox. Dist: Willoughby-Peerless, Warner Brothers.
    Cast: Joanne Dru, Mark Stevens.
    Melodrama. A model joins adventurers trying to recover a fortune in sunken
Spanish gold.

Shore Leave
    Navy Secrets
    7 reels   b&w   1939
    Dir: Howard Bretherton. Sp: Harvey Gates. Prod: Monogram Pictures.
    Cast: Fay Wray, Craig Reynolds.
    Daring girls versus a spy ring.

FITCH, GEORGE

Siwash Stories
    Those Were the Days
    8 reels   b&w   1940
    Dir: Jay Theodore Reed. Sp: Don Hartman. Prod: Paramount.
    Cast: Bill Holden, Bonita Granville.
    Comedy. College during the horse and buggy days is the setting for this story.

FITZGERALD, F. SCOTT

Babylon Revisited
    The Last Time I Saw Paris
    116 min.   color   1954
    Dir: Richard Brooks. Prod: M-G-M. Dist: Films Inc.
    Cast: Elizabeth Taylor, Van Johnson, Walter Pidgeon, Donna Reed, Eva Gabor.
    A war correspondent married during the WWI victory celebration in Paris, lives
happily ever after until he is unable to sell his novels, and falls into debt and extra-
marital affairs.

Bernice Bobs Her Hair
    Bernice Bobs Her Hair
    47½ min.   color   1977
    Dir and Sp: Joan Micklin Silver. Prod: Perspective.
    Cast: Shelley Duvall, Veronica Cartwright.
    "Ugly duckling" Bernice is transformed by her cousin into a sought-after vamp in
this story of flappers. Bernice becomes so adroit using the social cliches and conven-
tions that she wins the hearts of her cousin Marjorie's suitors. Shown at the New
York Film Festival, 1977.

FITZGERALD, F. SCOTT (cont'd)

Head and Shoulders
  The Chorus Girl's Romance
  6 reels   b&w   1920
  Dir: William C. Dowlan. Prod: Metro Pictures Corp.

Offshore Pirate in *Saturday Evening Post* (May 29, 1920)
  The Off-Shore Pirate
  6 reels   sil.   b&w   1921
  Dir: Dallas M. Fitzgerald. Adap: Waldemar Young. Prod: Metro Pictures Corp.
  Cast: Viola Dana, Jack Mulhall.
  Romantic comedy. Society girl Ardita Farnam is held up in her roadster and
rescued by a Russian in search of a rich wife.

FLEMING, BRANDON

The Pillory
  Eleventh Commandment
  8 reels   b&w   1933
  Dir: George Melford. Sp: Adele Buffington. Prod: Allied Pictures Corp.
  Cast: Allan Hale, Marian March.
  A step-father opposes his daughter's lover and tries to break up the romance.

FLEMING-ROBERTS, G. T.

Blackmail with Feathers
  Find the Blackmailer
  55 min.   b&w   1943
  Dir: Ross Lalerman. Prod: Warner Brothers. Dist: United Artists.
  Cast: Faye Emerson, Jerome Cowan.
  Comedy mystery. A detective is hired by a man who has been blackmailed by a
talking blackbird.

FLYNN, THOMAS T.

The Man from Laramie
  The Man from Laramie
  104 min.   color   1955
  Dir: Anthony Mann. Prod: Columbia Pictures Corp. Dist: Budget, Macmillan,
      Modern, Newman Film Library, Westcoast Films.
  Cast: James Stewart, Arthur Kennedy, Cathy O'Donnell.
  Western. James Stewart stars as a man hunting the cowboy responsible for his
brother's death in this taut psychological western. His mission pits him against a
group of vicious ranch-hands and a ruthless double-crosser, running guns to hostile
Indians.

FOOTE, JOHN TAINTOR

The Song of the Dragon in *The Song of the Dragon*
  The Convoy
  8 reels   b&w   sil.   1921
  Dir: Joseph C. Boyle. Prod: First National Pictures Corp.
  Cast: Lowell Sherman, Dorothy Mackaill.
  War melodrama. Sylvia tries to help her brother, who is a secret service operator, find information about one of her admirers, who is a German spy. In so doing she gets into trouble.

FOOTNER, HULBERT

A New Girl in Town in *Argosy All-Story Magazine* (September 30-October 28, 1922)
  The Dangerous Blonde
  5 reels   b&w   sil.   1924
  Dir: Robert F. Hill. Prod: Universal.
  Cast: Laura LaPlante, Edward Hearn.
  Romantic comedy. Colonel Faraday asks his daughter Diana to recover some letters that he once wrote to an adventuress.

FORD, COREY

College Hero
  Start Cheering
  8 reels   b&w   1938
  Dir: Albert S. Rogell. Sp: Eugene Solow, Richard E. Wormser, Phillip Rapp.
    Prod: Columbia.
  Cast: Jimmy Durante, Gertrude Niesen.
  An ambitious movie idol, leaving for college, finds that his ex-staff is trying to get him expelled.

Echoes That Old Refrain
  Winter Carnival
  105 min.   b&w   1939
  Dir: Charles Reisner. Prod: Walter Wanger Prod. Dist: Institutional Cinema
    Service, Mogull's.
  Cast: Ann Sheridan, Richard Carlson, Helen Parrish, Robert Armstrong.
  Winter Carnival is a parade of sports, thrills, romance, action and hilarity. Dartmouth's dizzy, the campus is in an uproar, the college is agog as youth rides high in one big grand and glorious snow frolic.

FORD, SEWELL

Tessie and the Little Sap in *Saturday Evening Post* (March 28, 1925)
    Tessie
    7 reels   b&w   sil.   1925
    Dir: Dallas M. Fitzgerald. Prod: Arrow Pictures.
    Cast: May McAvoy, Bobby Agnew.
    Comedy drama. A triangle involving an older woman.

FORESTER, CECIL SCOTT

The Commandos in *Cosmopolitan*
    Commandoes Strike at Dawn
    10 reels   b&w   1943
    Dir: John Farrow. Sp: Irwin Shaw. Prod: Columbia Pictures Corp.
    Cast: Paul Muni.
    The people of Norway resist the Nazis and pave the way for a commando strike.

Eagle Squadron in *Cosmopolitan*
    Eagle Squadron
    109 min.   b&w   1942
    Dir: Arthur Lubin. Sp: Norman Reilly Raine. Prod: Universal.
    Cast: Robert Stack, Diana Barrymore.
    An American in the RAF falls in love with an English girl.

FORNEY, PAULINE

Boarding House Blues (jt. author Dudley Murphy)
    Jazz Heaven
    7 reels   b&w   1929
    Dir: Melville Brown. Prod: RKO.
    Cast: John Mack Brown, Sally O'Neil.
    Comedy drama. A young woman who works in a music publishing house helps a
struggling song writer.

FORRESTER, IZOLA

The Gray Path in *Ainslee's* (September 1922)
    Youth for Sale
    6 reels   sil.   b&w   1924
    Dir: William Christy Cabanne. Prod: C. C. Burr Pictures.
    Cast: May Allison, Sigrid Holmquist.
    Society drama. Molly is blinded by her first drink of alcohol.

FORT, GARRETT (jt. author) see The Prince of Headwaiters under SHORE, VIOLA BROTHERS

FOSTER, BENNETT

The Outlaws Are in Town in *Saturday Evening Post* (May 28, 1949)
> The Desparados Are in Town
> 78 min.   b&w   1956
> Dir: Kurt Neuman. Prod: Regal Film's Inc., rel. 20th Century Fox.
> Cast: Rex Reason, Kathy Nolan.

Western. A penitent young man who was once involved with outlaws in Texas, goes home. His old acquaintances have arrived in town.

Trail Town Fever
> Flame of the West
> 55 min.   b&w   1945
> Dir: Lambert Hillyer. Prod: Monogram Pictures Corp.
> Cast: Johnny Mack Brown.

A doctor helps clean up a small Western town.

FOSTER, MAXIMILLAN

The Silent Partner in *Harper's Monthly* (May 1908)
> The Silent Partner
> 6 reels   sil.   b&w   1923
> Dir: Charles Maigne. Adap: Sada Cowan. Prod: Famous Players—Lasky.
> Cast: Beatrice Joy, Owen Moore.

Melodrama. Lisa Coburn becomes a "silent partner" for her husband in his Wall Street financial speculation.

FOX, PAUL HARVEY

Goddess
> The Stars Are Singing
> 99 min.   b&w   1953
> Dir: Norman Taurog. Prod: Paramount. Dist: Films Inc.
> Cast: Rosemary Clooney, Lauritz Melchoir.

Musical comedy. A broken-down opera singer, a struggling singer, a vaudeville entertainer, and an unemployed dancer aid a Polish sporano in legal difficulties.

Masterpiece
> Gentleman at Heart
> 66 min.   b&w   1942
> Dir: Ray McCarey. Prod: 20th Century Fox.
> Cast: Cesar Romero, Milton Berle.

Comedy. A racketeer goes into the art business.

FOX, PAUL HARVEY (cont'd)

Masterpiece (cont'd)
  Tall, Dark and Handsome
  78 min.   b&w   1941
  Dir: Bruce Humberstone. Dist: Films Inc.
  Cast: Cesar Romero.
  Comedy. A story about a soft-hearted gangster and an orphan.

FRANCE, ANATOLE

Boudu: Sauve Des Eaux
  Boudu: Saved from Drowning (Fr., English subtitles)
  87 min.   b&w   1932
  Dir: Jean Renoir.
  Cast: Michel Simon, Charles Grandval.
  "It's about time that someone of our class did something heroic," remarks a
bystander as Lestingois pulls Boudu from the Seine. A thousand people who
miraculously appear on the bridge over the troubled waters nod their agreement;
of course they have no intention of pushing their "class" forward to the point of
being helpful.

Juggler of Notre Dame
  Juggler of Notre Dame
  30 min.   color   1968
  Prod: Craven/Dimka. Dist: Pyramid.
  An adaptation of Anatole France's tale about a kind-hearted little juggler. Using
puppet-like animated figures, the film follows the juggler's travels from town to
town in medieval France and tells of his experience in a monastery where he takes
shelter.

FRANCIS, OWEN

Big
  The Magnificent Brute
  77 min.   b&w   1936
  Dir: John G. Blystone. Sp: Lewis R. Foster, Bertram Millhouse, Owen Francis.
    Prod: Universal.
  Cast: Victor McLaglen, Binnie Barnes, William Hall.
  A blast furnace boss becomes involved in a romantic triangle and stolen money.

FRANKEN, ROSE

Twenty-Two
  The Secret Heart
  s.m. Holiday, a play

FRANKEN, ROSE (cont'd)

The Secret Heart (cont'd)
97 min.   b&w   1946
Dir: Robert Z. Leonard. Sp: Whitfield Cook, Anne M. Chopin. Prod: M-G-M.
Cast: Patricia Medina, June Allyson, Marshall Thompson.
Love triangles.

FRANKLIN, EDGAR

Poker Faces in *Argosy All-Story Weekly* (August 18-September 25, 1923)
Poker Faces
8 reels   sil.   b&w   1926
Dir: Harry A. Pollard. Adap: Melville W. Brown. Prod: Universal.
Cast: Edward Everett Horton, Laura LaPlante.
A struggling office worker is given a big chance to land an important contract,
but complications ensue.

Protecting Prue in *Argosy All-Story Weekly* (August 16-September 13, 1924)
My Lady of Whims
7 reels   b&w   sil.   1925
Dir: Dallas M. Fitzgerald. Dist: Cinema Eight, Cinema Service, ESO-S Pictures.
Cast: Clara Bow, Donald Keith.
Society melodrama. A young man is hired to keep an eye on the Bohemian
daughter of a wealthy man. They fall in love.

Stay Home in *Argosy All-Story Weekly* (November-December 1921)
I Can Explain
5 reels   sil.   b&w   1922
Dir: George D. Baker. Adap: Edgar Franklin. Prod: Famous Players—Lasky.
Cast: Gareth Hughes, Bartine Burkett.
Comedy-melodrama. The boss' wife confides in a junior partner that she is
planning to open a rival business in South America. They are often seen together,
which makes her husband and the partner's fiancée jealous.

Whatever She Wants in *Argosy All-Story Weekly* (June 11—July 9, 1921)
The Idle Rich
s.m. White Collars, play based on the story by Edgar Franklin
9 reels   b&w   1929
Dir: William DeMille. Prod: M-G-M.
Cast: Conrad Nagel, Leila Hyams.
A typists' family refuses to share her husband's money until he offers to give it
to charity.

FRANKLIN, EDGAR (cont'd)

Whatever She Wants (cont'd)
    Rich Man, Poor Girl
    s.m. White Collars, play by Edith Ellis, based on story by Edgar Franklin
    8 reels   b&w   1938
    Sp: Joseph Fields, Jerome Chodorov. Prod: M-G-M. Dist: Time-Life Multimedia.
    Cast: Lew Ayres, Ruth Hussey, Robert Young.
    Re-make of The Idle Rich. A rich man carries off one of the daughters of
a middle class family.

    Whatever She Wants
    5 reels   sil.   b&w   1921
    Dir: C. R. Wallace. Prod: Fox.
    Cast: Eileen Percy, Herbert Fortier.
    Enid secretly gets a job in the office of the manufacturing company owned by
her fiancé.

Where Was I? in *Argosy All-Story Weekly* (November 1-22, 1924)
    Where Was I?
    7 reels   sil.   b&w   1925
    Dir: William A. Seiter. Prod: Universal—Jewel.
    Cast: Reginald Denny, Marion Nixon.
    Farce. A successful young businessman becomes engaged to the daughter of his
rival.

FRANKLIN, GEORGE CORY

Into the Crimson West
    Prairie Schooners
    6 reels   b&w   1940
    Dir: Sam Nelson. Sp: Fred Myton, Robert Lee Johnson. Prod: Columbia
        Pictures Corp.

FRAZEE, STEVE

Death Rides This Trail
    Wild Heritage
    78 min.   color   1958
    Dir: Charles Haas. Sp: Paul King, Joseph Stone. Prod: Universal. Dist: Univeral.
    Cast: Will Rogers, Jr., Maureen O'Sullivan.
    Western drama. Two pioneer families meet while traveling West.

FRAZEE, STEVE (cont'd)

Many Rivers to Cross
  Many Rivers to Cross
  92 min.   color   1955
  Dir: Roy Rowland. Prod: M-G-M. Dist: Films Inc.
  Cast: Robert Taylor, Eleanor Parker, Victor McLaglen, Russ Tamblyn.
  A good-natured spoof on the customs of a husband-hunting tomboy and a
frontiersman.

My Brother Down There
  Running Target
  83 min.   color   1956
  Dir: Marvin R. Weinstein. Prod: United Artists. Dist: United Artists.
  Cast: Arthur Franz, Doris Dowling, Richard Reeves, Myron Healey.
  A trigger-happy marksman joins a posse on the getaway trail of four escaped con-
victs through the Rocky Mountains.

FREEMAN, EVERETT

$1,000 a Minute in *Saturday Evening Post* (January 26, 1925)
  One Thousand Dollars a Minute
  54 min.   b&w   1935
  Dir: Aubrey Scott. Prod: Republic. Dist: Ivy.
  Cast: Edgar Kennedy, Edward Brophy.
  A reporter wins romance by proving to two crooks he can spend $1,000 a
minute for 12 hours.

FRIEDMAN, BRUCE JAY

A Change of Plan in *Black Angels*
  The Heartbreak Kid
  104 min.   color   1973
  Dir: Elaine May. Prod: 20th Century Fox. Dist: Films Inc.
  Cast: Charles Grodin, Cybill Shepherd, Jeannie Berlin, Eddie Albert.
  The story of a Jewish boy from New York City who falls in love with Cybill
Shepherd, the perfect shicksa, during his honeymoon in Miami, while his new wife
is suffering from sunburn.

GABINEAU, ARTHUR

Adelaide
Adelaide (English subtitles)
86 min.   color   1968
Dir: Jean-Daniel Simon. Sp: Jean-Pierre Petrolacci. Dist: Audio Brandon.
Cast: Ingrid Thulin, Jean Sorel, Sylvie Fennec.
Elisabeth marries a research engineer, Frederic, ten years her junior, following the death of her husband. Her daughter, Adelaide (Fennec), has also fallen in love with Frederic (Sorel), and continues to have an affair with him. Mother and daughter realize that they must share their lover. They dismiss their servant, shutter all the windows, and seal themselves and Frederic off from the outside world. The tense menage à trois ends violently.

GABY, ALEX

Fifty-Two Miles to Terror in *Saturday Evening Post* (January 14, 1956)
Hot Rods to Hell
92 min.   b&w   1967
Dir: John Brahm. Sp: Robert E. Kent. Prod: M-G-M. Dist: Films Inc.
Cast: Jeanne Crain, Laurie Mock, Dana Andrews.
Melodrama. A family is menaced on the road.

GADDIS, PEGGY

The Part Time Wife in *Snappy Stories Magazine* (August 1925)
The Part-Time Wife
6 reels   sil.   b&w   1925
Dir: Henry McCarty. Prod: Gotham Prod.
Cast: Alice Calhoun, Robert Ellis.
Melodrama. Poor newspaperman Kenneth Scott marries a screen star whose success hurts his pride.

GALE, ZONA

The Way
When Strangers Meet
8 reels   b&w   1934
Dir: William Christy Cabanne. Prod: Liberty Pictures Corp.

GALLAND, VICTORIA

The Golden Gallows in *Snappy Stories* (October 1, 1921)
  The Golden Gallows
  5 reels   sil.   b&w   1922
  Dir: Paul Scardon. Prod: Universal.
  Cast: Miss Du Pont, Edwin Stevens.
  Society melodrama. Leander Sills, impressed by a chorus girl's resistance to his offers of wealth, leaves her his fortune; this makes her boyfriend suspicious and jealous.

GALLICO, PAUL

The Adventure of Joe Smith, American in *Cosmopolitan*
  Joe Smith, American
  63 min.   b&w   1942
  Sp: Allen Rivkin. Prod: M-G-M. Dist: Films Inc.
  Cast: Robert Young, Marsha Hunt.
  A story of a munitions factory worker and his unglamorous wife.

  The Big Operator
  91 min.   b&w   1959
  Dir: Charles Haas. Sp: Robert Smith, Allen Rivkin. Prod: M-G-M.
  Cast: Mickey Rooney, Mamie Van Doren.
  Re-make of Joe Smith, American. Story of a sadistic gang-leader.

Under the Clock
  The Clock
  90 min.   b&w   1945
  Dir: Vincente Minnelli. Sp: Robert Nathan. Prod: M-G-M. Dist: Films Inc.
  Cast: Judy Garland, Robert Walker.
  A New York girl meets and marries a soldier on a 48-hour leave in New York.

The Man Who Hated People in *Saturday Evening Post*
  Lili
  81 min.   color   1953
  Dir: Charles Walters. Prod: M-G-M. Dist: Films Inc.
  Cast: Leslie Caron, Mel Ferrer, Zsa Zsa Gabor, Jean-Pierre Aumont.
  Joining a carnival puppet show, a shy 16-year-old French orphan girl becomes infatuated with a magician (who keeps his marriage a secret for "business reasons"), making the crippled puppeteer who loves her jealous.

GALLICO, PAUL (cont'd)

The Enchanted Hour
Next to No Time (Br.)
89 min.   b&w   1960
Dir: Henry Cornelius. Prod: Show-Corp. Dist: United Films.
Cast: Kenneth More, Betsy Drake, Roland Culver.
Comedy. A shy factory worker tries to put his automation plan into action.

Little Miracle (Br.)
Never Take No for an Answer
90 min.   b&w   1952
Prod: Souvaine Selective Pictures. Dist: Roa's.
Cast: Vittorio Manunta, Dennis O'Dea.
Peppino, the little seven-year-old businessman takes Violette, his sick donkey, to the crypt of St. Francis, where he is sure the donkey will recover.

The Night Before Christmas
No Time to Marry
7 reels   b&w   1937
Dir: Harry Lachman. Sp: Paul Gallico. Prod: Columbia Pictures Corp.
Cast: Richard Arlen, Mary Astor.
Assignments keep an ace reporter and journalist from getting to the altar.

Tight Wad
Wild Money
7 reels   b&w   1937
Dir: Louis King. Sp: Edward T. Lowe. Prod: Paramount.
Cast: Marguerite Roberts, Eddie Welch.
A skinflint auditor spends freely when he hits the trail of a good story.

GALSWORTHY, JOHN

The First and the Last (Br.)
21 Days Together
8 reels   b&w   1940
Dir: Basil Dean. Prod: Columbia Pictures Corp.
Cast: Laurence Olivier, Vivien Leigh.
A young lawyer and a girl decide to live a lifetime in 21 days.

GARDNER, EARL STANLEY

Granny Get Your Gun
Granny Get Your Gun
56 min.   b&w   1939

GARDNER, EARL STANLEY (cont'd)

Granny Get Your Gun (cont'd)
Dir: George Amy. Prod: First National Pictures. Dist: United Artists.
Cast: May Robson, Harry Davenport, Margot Stevenson, Hardie Albright.
Western comedy.

GARTH, DAVID

Don't Forget to Remember
   There Goes the Groom
   70 min.   b&w   1937
Dir: Joseph Santley. Sp: S. K. Lauren, Dorothy Yost, Harold Kusell. Prod: RKO.
Cast: Burgess Meredith, Ann Sothern.
Comedy. A man, blessed with sudden riches, has in-law troubles.

GARVEY, STANLEY

Three on a Mike
   Every Night at Eight
   80 min.   b&w   1935
Dir: Raoul Walsh. Prod: Paramount. Dist: Universal.
Cast: George Raft, Alice Faye, Frances Langford, Patsy Kelly.
Three office girls go on the radio and win fame and fortune.

GELZER, JAY

The House of the Flock in *Cosmopolitan* (September 1921)
   Driven
   6 reels   b&w   sil.   1923
Dir: Charles J. Brabin. Prod: Charles J. Brabin.
Cast: Emily Fitzroy, Burr McIntosh.
Rural melodrama. Two brothers, both bootleggers, want the same girl.

GIBBS, PHILIP HAMILTON

Darkened Rooms in *Cosmopolitan* (March-June 1928)
   Darkened Rooms
   7 reels   b&w   1929
Dir: Louis Gasnier. Prod: Paramount Famous Players—Lasky.
Cast: Evelyn Brent, Neil Hamilton.
Mystery melodrama. A young girl is saved from a false seeress.

Fellow Prisoners
   Captured
   72 min.   b&w   1933
Dir: Roy Del Ruth. Prod: Warner Bros. Dist: United Artists.
Cast: Leslie Howard, Douglas Fairbanks, Jr., Paul Lukas.

GIBBS, PHILIP HAMILTON (cont'd)

Captured (cont'd)
A dramatic story in a German prison camp where a husband learns that his best friend, also in prison, was his wife's lover.

GIDE, ANDRE

La Symphonie Pastorale
  Symphonie Pastorale (Fr., subtitles)
  105 min.   b&w   1948
  Dir: Jean Delanney. Prod: William Marshall Inc.
  Cast: Michele Morgan, Pierre Blanchar.

GILFORD, C. B.

Unidentified story in *Ellery Queen's Magazine*
  Joy Ride
  60 min.   b&w   1958
  Dir: Edward Bernds. Prod: Allied Artists. Dist: Hurlock Cine World.
  Cast: Regis Toomey, Ann Doran.
  Suspense drama. An "average man" terrorized by young punks turns the tables on them.

GILL, THOMAS

In the Mexican Quarter
  Border Cafe
  7 reels   b&w   1937
  Dir: Lew Landers. Sp: Lionel Houser. Prod: RKO
  Cast: John Beal, Harry Carey.
  Staid son settles in the West and fights a gang to protect his parents.

GILLESE, JOHN PATRICK

Kirby's Gander in *Kirby's Gander* (Toronto, 1957)
  Wings of Chance
  76 min.   color   1961
  Dir: Edward Dew. Prod: Universal.
  Cast: James Brown, Frances Rafferty.
  Drama. A pilot is stranded when his plane crashes in an uncharted wilderness.

GILROY, FRANK D.

The Last Notch
  The Fastest Gun Alive
  s.m. a TV play
  91 min.   b&w   1956
  Dir: Russell Rouse. Sp: Frank D. Gilroy, Russell Rouse. Prod: M-G-M. Dist: Films
    Inc.
  Cast: Glenn Ford, Jeanne Crain.
  Western. A peaceloving shopkeeper tries to keep his marksmanship a secret but
his town is threatened by a desparado.

GLASMAN, KUBEC

Nothing Down
  Saleslady
  8 reels   b&w   1938
  Dir: Arthur Greville Collins. Sp: Marion Orth. Prod: Monogram Pictures.
  Cast: Anne Nagel, Harry Davenport.
  An heiress gets a job as a saleslady working for the man who is ruining her
father's business.

GLIDDEN, FRED DILLEY see SHORT, LUKE (pseud.)

GOGOL, NIKOLAI

Diary of a Madman
  Diary of a Madman
  s.m. the play Diary of a Madman is in turn based on the story
  87 min.   1967
  Dir: Robert Carlisle. Sp: Dan Ertner, Tom Troupe. Prod: Robert Carlisle.
  Cast: Tom Troupe.
  A study of the mental disintegration of a man living in 19th century Europe.

Il Coppotto (It.)
  Il Coppoto
  93 min.   b&w   1953
  Dir: Alberto Lattvada. Prod: Farro.
  Cast: Renato Fascel, Yvonn Sanson.

Der Mantel (German)
  Der Mantel
  35 min.   color   1955
  Dir: Wolfgang Schieff.
  Cast: Marcel Marceau.

GOGOL, NIKOLAI (cont'd)

Shinel
  The Overcoat (Soviet)
  70 min.   b&w   1926
  Dir: Grigori Kozintsev, Leonid Trauberg. Dist: Audio Brandon, Museum of
      Modern Art.
  Cast: Andrei Dostrichkin, Sergei Gerasimov, Anna Zheimo.
A poor clerk's coat is stolen, he dies, and his ghost steals other coats.
Exaggerated gestures, distorted angles, and imaginative sets produce a bizarre effect.
The prologue tells of a frustrating youthful adventure of the same clerk.

  The Overcoat (English subtitles)
  73 min.   b&w
  Dir: Alexei Batalov. Prod: Lenfilm Studios. Dist: McGraw-Hill.
A screen version of the famous Gogol story in which a pathetic little clerk in a
grotesque and cruel world gets a new overcoat that changes his destiny.

  Shinel (Soviet)
  93 min.   b&w   1958
  Dir: Alexei Batalov. Sp: A. Solovyov. Dist: Contemporary/McGraw-Hill Films.
  Cast: Rolan Bykov, Y. Tolubayer.
A poor man's coat is stolen and he dies; his ghost takes the coats from the living.

GOLDMAN, RAYMOND LESLIE

Battling Bunyon Ceases to Be Funny in *Saturday Evening Post* (March 15, 1924)
  Battling Bunyon
  5 reels   sil.   b&w   1925
  Dir: Paul Hurst. Prod: Crown Prod.
  Cast: Wesley Barry, Molly Malone, Frank Campeau.
  If Arken Bunyon can raise $1,000 he can buy a partnership in a garage. When
a fighter makes passes at his girl, he fights him and a promoter gets the idea of
matching the two. Bunyon is badly beaten.

GOLDSMITH, L. S.

Man Who Stole a Dream
  Manhandled
  97 min.   b&w   1949
  Dir: Lewis R. Foster. Prod: Paramount. Dist: Select, United Films,
      Willoughby-Peerless.
  Cast: Dorothy Lamour, Dan Duryea.
  Turgid murder drama.

GOMBERG, SY

When Leo Came Marching Home
  When Willie Comes Marching Home
  82 min.   b&w   1950
  Dir: John Ford. Prod: 20th Century Fox. Dist: Films Inc.
  Cast: Dan Dailey, Corinne Calvet.
  The story of a West Virginian lad who goes into the Army during WWII and has
a series of adventures, including an interlude with a beautiful French leader of the
underground.

GOODEN, ARTHUR HENRY

Below the Deadline
  Below the Deadline
  5 reels   b&w   1920
  Dir: J. P. McGowan. Prod: Ascher Prod.

GOODLOE, ABBIE C.

Claustrophobia in *Book of Modern Short Stories*, ed. by D. Brewster (N.Y.,
  Macmillan, 1928)
  I Live My Life
  10 reels   b&w   1935
  Dir: W. S. Van Dyke. Sp: Joseph Mankiewicz. Prod: M-G-M.
  Cast: Joan Crawford, Brian Aherne.
  A hate-at-first-sight romance of a debutante and an archeologist.

GOODMAN, JACK

Magazine Story (jt. author Albert Rice)
  Gay Blades
  7 reels   b&w   1946
  Dir: George Blair. Sp: Albert Beich. Prod: Republic. Dist: Ivy.

GORKY, MAXIM

Her One True Love
  Her One True Love
  24 min.   color   1977
  Dir: Henry Comor. Prod: Bruce Raymond. Dist: Learning.
  Cast: Kate Reid, John Horton.
  Two agonizingly lonely people make fleeting contact: aging, illiterate Mae tries
gamely to fill the loveless void in her life by entertaining gentlemen callers; next
door, her rooming-house neighbor John passes his days in solitude.

GORKY, MAXIM (cont'd)

Twenty-Six and a Girl
   Nine and a Girl
   24 min.   b&w
   Dir and Prod: Michael Weiskopf. Dist: Viewfinders.
The story of nine pretzel bakers and a young girl who comes each day to pick up an order. In their fantasies she is the purest, kindest, most ideal of women. A new baker enters their lives and constantly brags of his conquests with women. They challenge him to arrange a tryst with the girl and he does.

GOULDING, EDMOND

Put and Take
   Applause
   Prod: Tiffany—Stahl Prod.

GRAND, GORDON

Major Denning's Trust Estate
   Sport of Kings
   68 min.   b&w   1947
   Dir: Robert Gordon. Sp: Edward Huebsch. Prod: Columbia.
   Cast: Paul Campbell, Gloria Henry.

GRANT, JAMES EDWARD

Big Brown Eyes
   Big Brown Eyes
   s.m. "Hahsit Babe"
   78 min.   b&w   1936
   Dir: Raoul Walsh. Prod: Paramount. Dist: Universal 16.
   Cast: Cary Grant, Joan Bennett, Walter Pidgeon, Lloyd Nolan.

Full Measure see Great Guy under Johnny Cave stories

Johnny Cave Stories in *Saturday Evening Post*
   Great Guy
   s.m. "Johnny Cave Goes Subtle," "Larceny on the Right," "Full Measure"
   73 min.   b&w   1937
   Dir: John G. Blystone. Prod: Grand National Films Inc. Dist: Budget, Em Gee
      Film Library, Cinema Eight/Cinema Concepts, Cinema Service/Vintage Films.
   Cast: James Cagney, Mae Clark.
As a live-wire operative in the City Department of Weights and Measures, Jimmy sets out to find the perpetrators of a savage beating which had placed his boss in the hospital. Along the way, he uncovers sources of graft and corruption in the city.

GRANT, JAMES EDWARD (cont'd)

Journal of Linnett Moore
  Proud Rebel
  90 min.   color   1958
  Prod: Formosa Prod. Dist: Roa's Films.
  Cast: Alan Ladd, Olivia De Havilland, David Ladd.
  The story tells of a "proud rebel" who travels North seeking medical aid for his
son, mute since seeing his mother die in the Battle of Atlanta. The stubborn efforts
of the man to find a cure for his son, the love of the boy for his dog, and the under-
standing of a strong farm woman are portrayed in a vivid, heart-warming film.

A Lady Came to Burkburnett
  Boom Town
  120 min.   b&w   1940
  Dir: Jack Conway. Sp: John Lee Mahin. Prod: M-G-M. Dist: Films Inc.
  Cast: Clark Gable, Spencer Tracy, Claudette Colbert, Hedy Lamarr.
  Brawling-sprawling action story about two rough 'n tough wildcatters on the
prowl for oil and women.

Larceny on the Right see Great Guy under Johnny Cave stories

Unidentified short stories
  She Had to Eat (jt. author Morris Musselman)
  6,698'   b&w   1937
  Dir: Jalcolm St. Clair. Sp: Samuel G. Engel. Prod: 20th Century Fox.

Whipsaw in *Liberty Magazine*
  Whipsaw
  9 reels   sd.   b&w   1935
  Dir: Sam Wood. Prod: Sam Wood Prod., M-G-M.
  Cast: Spencer Tracy, Myrna Loy.
  Loy plays a member of a jewel-robbing gang, Tracy is a detective.

GRANT, MAXWELL (pseud.)

The Fox Hound in *Shadow Magazine*
  International Crime
  87 min.   b&w   1938
  Dir: Charles Lamont. Prod: Grand National Films. Dist: United Films.
  Cast: Rod La Rocque, Valerie Hobson.
  A dashing reporter outwits the Police Commission, which doesn't recognize that
blowing up a safe was really a cover for murder.

GRANT, MAXWELL (cont'd)

The Ghost of the Manor*
  The Shadow Strikes
  63 min.   b&w   1937
  Dir: Lynn Shores. Sp: Al Martin. Prod: Grand National.
  *Note: Some sources credit this story to George H. Coxe.

The Shadow
  Invisible Avenger
  s.m. based on this character from radio series and *Street and Smith Magazine
  Stories.* Origin of the character is unknown.
  60 min.   b&w   1958
  Dir: James Won Howe, John Sledge. Sp: George Bellak, Betty Jeffries. Prod:
  Republic.

The Shadow (serial in 15 pts.)
  2 reels each   b&w   1940
  Dir: James W. Horne. Sp: Joseph Poland, Ned Dandy, Joseph O'Donnell. Prod:
  Columbia Pictures Corp.

The Shadow Returns
  61 min.   b&w   1946
  Dir: Phil Rosen. Sp: George Callahan. Prod: Monogram.

GRASHIN, MAURI

Chautauqua
  The Trouble with Girls
  s.m. novel by Day Keene and Dwight Babcock based on story by Mauri Grashin
  104 min.   b&w   1969
  Dir: Peter Tewksbury. Prod: M-G-M. Dist: Films Inc.
  Cast: Marilyn Mason, Nicole Jaffe, Sheree North.
  During the twenties, the manager of The Tolling Canvas College has the usual
irritations of placating small town politicians who think they have relatives with
talent.

GRAY, HUGH (jt. author) see River Gang under DAVID, CHARLES

GREEN, ALAN

Beauty on the Beat (jt. author Julian Brodie)
  Love on the Run
  80 min.   1936
  Dir: W. S. Van Dyke. Prod: M-G-M.

GREEN, ALAN (cont'd)

Love on the Run (cont'd)
Cast: Clark Gable, Joan Crawford, Franchot Tone.
Romantic comedy. Foreign correspondents in love travel around the world, fleeing from spies.

GREENE, GRAHAM

Across the Bridge in *Nineteen Stories* (N.Y., Viking, 1949)
Across the Bridge
103 min.   b&w   1958
Dir: Ken Annakin. Prod: Rank.
Cast: Rod Steiger, David Knight.
Drama. A crooked tycoon on the lam from Scotland Yard is cornered in Mexico.

The Basement Room
The Fallen Idol
94 min.   b&w   1948
Dir: Sir Carol Reed. Dist: Images.
Cast: Ralph Richardson, Michele Margan, Sonia Dresdel, Bobby Henrey.
The story of a lonely young boy who is left in the care of the family butler, whom he idolizes, while his parents are on a trip. He witnesses both the butler's clandestine love affair and the accidental death of the butler's wife. The boy believes the butler has murdered his wife and tries to save him, only to involve him more deeply with the police.

GREENE, HAROLD

Hide and Seek
Hide and Seek
90 min.   b&w   1964
Dir: Cy Endfield. Sp: David Stone. Prod: Albion Film Corp.
Drama comedy. A chemist tries to find his missing friend.

GREENE, WALTER

He Was One of the Boston Bullertons
Private Affairs
80 min.   b&w   1940
Dir: Albert S. Rogell. Sp: Charles Grayson, Leonard Spigelgass, Peter Milne.
    Prod: Universal Studios. Dist: Mogull's, "The" Film Center.
Cast: Robert Cummings, Hugh Herbert, Nancy Kelly.
Romantic drama. A young woman with problems goes to her father for advice. He hasn't seen her since her birth.

GREY, ZANE

Canyon Walls in *The Ranger and Other Stories* (N.Y., Harper, 1960)
Smoke Lightning
5,450'   b&w   1933
Dir: David Howard. Sp: Gordon Rigby, Sidney Mitchell. Prod: Fox.

The Last of the Duanes in *Argosy All-Story Weekly* (September 1914)
The Last of the Duanes
7 reels   sil.   b&w   1924
Dir: Lynn Reynolds. Prod: Fox.
Cast: Tom Mix, Marion Nixon.
The insults of Cal Bain force Buck Duane to fight and shoot him. Duane escapes
from the law, aids a rancher, and rescues his girlfriend Jenny from an outlaw band.

Last of the Duanes
5,120'   b&w   1941
Dir: James Tinling. Sp: Irving Cummings, Jr., William Conselman, Jr.
    Prod: 20th Century Fox.

The Last of the Duanes
6 reels   b&w   1930
Dir: Alfred L. Werker. Prod: Fox.
Cast: George O'Brien, Lucille Brown, Myrna Loy.
Songs were added to this version.

Lightning in Wright, Grey, ed.; *Hosses* (New York, 1927)
Lightning
7 reels   sil.   b&w   1927
Dir: James C. McKay. Adap: John Francis Natteford. Prod: Tiffany Prod.
Cast: Jobyna Ralston, Margaret Livingston, Robert Frazier.
Western drama. Famed horse-breakers Lee and Coon Stewart fail to capture the
wild stallion Lightning; later in Chicago they fail to tame two girls. By the end of
the film both the horse and the women are won.

The Water Hole in *Collier's* (October 8-December 24, 1927)
The Water Hole
7 reels   sil.   b&w   1928
Dir: F. Richard Jones. Prod: Paramount Famous Players—Lasky
Cast: Jack Holt, Nancy Carroll, John Boles.
Western melodrama. Judith vamps Philip Randolph when he comes East to
discuss business with her father. When he learns she is only kidding he angrily returns
to Arizona. Judith and her father follow and her fiancé follows them.

GRIFFIN, ELEANORE

Be It Ever So Humble* (jt. author William Rankin)
   Hi, Beautiful
   66 min.   b&w   1944
   Dir: Leslie Goodwins. Sp: Dick Irving Hyland. Prod: Universal.
   Cast: Martha O'Driscoll, Noah Beery, Jr., Hattie McDaniel.
   Comedy drama. Two young people win the "Happiest GI Couple" award, but
they are not married. *Note: Re-make of Love in a Bungalow (1937).

Class Prophecy
   When Love Is Young
   76 min.   b&w   1937
   Dir: Hal Mohr. Sp: Joseph Fields, Eve Greene. Prod: Universal.
   Cast: Virginia Bruce, Kent Taylor, Walter Brennan.
   Ambitious press agent takes a plain girl and turns her into a gorgeous singer.

GROSS, CORDELIA BAIRD

It's Hard to Find Mecca in Flushing see Protection for a Tough Racket

Protection for a Tough Racket
   This Could Be the Night
   s.m. It's Hard to Find Mecca in Flushing
   104 min.   b&w   1957
   Dir: Robert Wise. Sp: Isobel Lennart. Prod: M-G-M.
   Cast: Jean Simmons, Paul Douglas.
   Musical comedy. An innocent among the wolves of Broadway night life.

GRUBER, FRANK

Dog Show Murder
   Death of a Champion
   7 reels   b&w   1939
   Dir: Robert Florey. Sp: Stuart Palmer, Cortland Fitzsimmons.
      Prod: Paramount. Dist: Universal.
   Cast: Lynne Overman, Virginia Dale.
   Comedy mystery of the death of a champion dog.

GUITRY, SACHA

Bonne Chance
   Lucky Partners
   102 min.   b&w   1940
   Dir: Lewis Milestone. Prod: RKO. Dist: Films Inc.
   Cast: Ronald Colman, Ginger Rogers.
   Comedy. An artist shares a sweepstakes ticket with a girl and they win.

GULICK, BILL

Man from Texas in *Saturday Evening Post* (April 15, 1950)
  The Road to Denver
  90 min.　　　color　　　1955
  Dir: Joseph Kane. Prod: Republic. Dist: Ivy.
  Cast: John Payne, Lee J. Cobb.
  Western. Set in Colorado at the turn of the century, one brother owns a stage-
coach line and the other joins a gang of stagecoach hijackers.

HALE, EDWARD EVERETT

Man without a Country
  As No Man Has Loved (AKA The Man without a Country)
  10 reels　　　sil.　　　b&w　　　1925
  Dir: Rowland V. Lee. Prod: Fox.
  Cast: Edward Hearn.
  The hero, Philip Nolan, is sentenced to never see his country again.

Man without a Country
  21 min.　　　color　　　1938
  Prod: Warner Brothers. Dist: Syracuse University.

Man without a Country
  25 min.　　　b&w　　　1953
  Prod: Bing Crosby Prod. Dist: McGraw-Hill.
  Hale's classic story of Phillip Nolan, the man who denounced his country.

HALL, BLAIR

Easy Street in *Snappy Stories*
  The Easy Road
  5 reels　　　sil.　　　b&w　　　1921
  Dir: Tom Forman. Prod: Famous Players—Lasky.
  Cast: Thomas Meighan, Gladys George, Grace Goodall.
  Melodrama. Leonard Fayne, a novelist, marries wealthy Isabel, but her silliness
interferes with his creativity.

HALL, WILBUR (pseud. of Rudolph Edgar Block)

Johnny Cucabod in *Saturday Evening Post* (June 12, 1920)
    Broken Doll
    5 reels   sil.   b&w   1921
    Dir: Allan Dwan. Adap: Lillian Ducey. Prod: Allan Dawn Prod.
    Cast: Monte Blue, Mary Thurman.
    Rural melodrama. A cowhand is mistaken for a thief.

On the Threshold in *Saturday Evening Post*
    On the Threshold
    6 reels   sil.   b&w   1925
    Dir: Renaud Hoffman. Prod: Hoffman Prod.
    Cast: Gladys Hulette, Henry B. Walthall.
    Melodrama. When his wife dies in childbirth, Andrew Masters swears he will
prevent his daughter from marrying.

HALLIDAY, BRETT see also Blue, White and Perfect under CHASE, BORDEN

HALLIDAY, BRETT

Three on a Ticket
    Three on a Ticket
    s.m. character, Michael Shayne
    64 min.   b&w   1947
    Dir: Sam Newfield. Prod: Releasing Corp. Dist: Ivy, Mogull's.
    Cast: Hugh Beaumont.
    The plans for a secret weapon are on their way to a foreign power.

HAMLIN, JOHN HAROLD

Painted Ponies in *Western Story Magazine*
    Painted Ponies
    6 reels   sil.   b&w   1926
    Dir: Reeves Eason. Adap: Frank Beresford.
    Cast: Hoot Gibson, William Dunn.
    Western melodrama. Buck Sims drops into town and tries to win Mary from her
suitor, who is the town bully.

HADLEY, DOROTHY CURNOR

Room for Two
    Rosie the Riveter
    75 min.   b&w   1944
    Dir: Joseph Santley. Prod: Republic. Dist: Ivy.
    Cast: Jane Frazee, Frank Albertson.
    Musical comedy. A wacky rooming house boards wacky defense plant workers.

HANLON, BROOKE

Delicatessen in *Saturday Evening Post* (August 24, 1925)
  It Must Be Love
  7 reels   sil.   b&w   1926
  Dir: Alfred E. Green. Adap: Julian Josephson. Prod: John McCormick Prod.
  Cast: Colleen Moore, Jean Hersholt, Malcolm McGregor.
  Comedy drama. Fernie Schmidt hates the smells of her father's delicatessen/home.
She doesn't want to marry the sausage salesman Pop likes. Instead, she meets Jack
Dugan, who tells her he is in stocks. But Fernie is later resigned to her fate when
Jack buys a delicatessen.

HARMON, DAVID

The Man Who Owned the Town
  Johnny Concho
  84 min.   b&w   1956
  Dir: Don McGuire. Prod: United Artists.
  Cast: Frank Sinatra, Keenan Wynn.
  Western. A cowboy must face a fast gun.

HARRIS, KENNETH

Junk in *Saturday Evening Post* (December 25, 1920)
  The Idle Rich
  5 reels   sil.   b&w   1921
  Dir: Maxwell Karger. Adap: June Mathis. Prod: Metro Pictures.
  Cast: Bert Lytell, Virginia Valli.
  Comedy. Young, rich Sam Weatherbee is suddenly broke due to the business
speculations of his executor. He inherits an old house and sells the junk inside for
food, but for this his friends reject him.

HARRISON, WILLIAM C.

Petticoat Brigade
  The Guns of Fort Petticoat
  82 min.   color   1957
  Dir: George Marshall. Prod: Brown-Murphy Pictures. Dist: Modern, Roa's Films.
  Cast: Audie Murphy, Kathryn Grant, Hope Emerson.
  The story of the Texas territory during the Civil War when women and children
were left defenseless to withstand savage Indian attacks in a battle for survival,
while their menfolk marched off to battle.

Rollerball Murders
  Rollerball
  123 min.   color   1975
  Dir: Norman Jewison. Prod: United Artists.

HARRISON, WILLIAM C. (cont'd)

Rollerball (cont'd)
Cast: James Caan, Ralph Richardson, John Houseman.
A futuristic combination of rugby, roller-skating, and gladiator fight-to-the-death spectacles.

HART, WILLIAM S.

O'Malley of the Mounted
  O'Malley of the Mounted
  6 reels   sil.   b&w   1921
  Dir: Lambert Hillyer. Prod: Paramount.
  Cast: William S. Hart, Eva Novak.
  Sgt. O'Malley of the Royal Northwest Mounted Police tracks down a killer and then falls in love with the killer's sister.

  O'Malley of the Mounted
  70 min.   b&w   1936
  Dir: David Howard. Prod: 20th Century Fox. Dist: Lewis Film Service.
  Cast: George O'Brien, Irene Ware.

HARTE, BRET

The Idyll of Red Gulch
  The Man from Red Gulch
  6 reels   sil.   b&w   1925
  Dir: Edmund Mortimer. Prod: Hunt Stromberg Prod.
  Cast: Harry Carey, Harriet Hammond.
  At the time of the California Gold Rush, a woman runs off with the man who killed her husband, only to be pursued by her husband's partner.

M'liss, an Idyl of Red Mountain* in *The Luck of Roaring Camp and Other Stories*
  The Girl Who Ran Wild
  5 reels   sil.   b&w   1922
  Dir: Rupert Julian. Prod: Universal Film Manufacturing Co.
  Cast: Gladys Walton, Marc Robbins.
  Western melodrama. M'liss, a tomboy, is persuaded to tidy herself up and to get an education by the schoolmaster, with whom she falls in love.

  M'Liss
  7 reels   b&w   1936
  Dir: George Nicholls, Jr. Sp: Dorothy Yost. Prod: RKO.
  *Note: In 1915 and 1918 two versions were produced by World Film Corp. and Famous Players—Lasky.

HARTE, BRET (cont'd)

The Outcasts of Poker Flats*
Man Hunt
61 min.   b&w   1931
Dir: William Clemens. Prod: Pictures Co., rel. Warner Brothers, 1936. Dist:
    United Artists.
Cast: Ricardo Cortaz, Marguerite Churchill.
*Note: A 1910 Edison version and a 1919 Universal version were also
produced.

Outcasts of Poker Flats
68 min.   b&w   1937
Dir: Christy Cabanne. Prod: RKO.
Cast: Preston Foster.

Outcasts of Poker Flats
81 min.   b&w   1952
Dir: Joseph Newman. Prod: 20th Century Fox. Dist: Budget, Macmillan, Select,
    Willoughby-Peerless
Cast: Dale Robertson, Anne Baxter, Miriam Hopkins.
In Poker Flats, one of the roaring camps of the California Gold Rush days, the
townspeople, enraged by a robbery and murder, drive four "undesirables" (two
dance-hall ladies, a gambler, and the town drunk) from its precincts. The outcasts
pick up a young man and his girl and all are forced to seek shelter in a cabin, high
in the Sierras, due to an approaching blizzard.

Saint of Calamity Gulch in *Hutchinson's Magazine* (July 1925)
Taking a Chance
5 reels   sil.   b&w   1929
Dir: Norman Z. McLeod. Prod: Fox.
Cast: Rex Bell, Lola Todd.
Western melodrama.

Salomy Jane's Kiss*
Salomy Jane
s.m. "Salomy Jane," a play by Paul Armstrong
7 reels   sil.   b&w   1923
Dir: George Melford. Prod: Famous Players—Lasky.
Cast: Jacqueline Logan, George Fawcett.
Western melodrama. Salomy saves a stranger from hanging, who is later cleared
of his crime. *Note: A silent version was also made in 1914 by Alco.

HARTE, BRET (cont'd)

Salomy Jane's Kiss (cont'd)
    Wild Girl
    6,950'   b&w   1932
    Dir: Raoul Walsh. Prod: Fox.

Tennessee's Partner in *Booklover's Magazine* (July 1903)
    The Flaming Forties
    6 reels   sil.   b&w   1924
    Dir: Tom Forman. Prod: Stellar Prod.
    Cast: Harry Carey, William Norton.
    Western melodrama. Bill Jones saves Jack Desparde from drowning after
Desparde jumps off a steamboat that is taking him to be hanged.

    Tennessee's Partner
    87 min.   color   1955
    Prod: RKO. Dist: Cinema 8 (super 8 sound)
    Cast: Ronald Reagan, John Payne, Rhonda Fleming.
    A gambling queen, a gambler, and a cowpoke are all involved in a shooting and
double-crossing.

HARTLEY, L. P.

The Island
    The Island
    30 min.   color   1977
    Dir: Robert Fuest. Adap: Robert Fuest. Dist: Learning.
    Cast: John Hurt, Charles Gray.
    A sophisticated young WWI army officer, on overnight leave, motorcycles
buoyantly along, bound for the lavishly appointed Santander mansion on an otherwise deserted island. Captain Simmons' affair with the beautiful, wealthy Mrs.
Santander had been interrupted by his army service. There is something odd in the
reluctant attitude of the boatman who ferries him to the island, and at the house
the butler is peculiarly evasive. A pattern of small incidents grows to a crisis.

HARVEY, WILLIAM FRYER

The Beast
    The Beast with Five Fingers
    88 min.   b&w   1946
    Dir: Robert Florey. Sp: Curt Siodmak. Dist: United Artists.
    Cast: Robert Alda, Peter Lorre, Andrea King, Victor Francen, J. Carrol Naish.
    A horror thriller about a hand with an invisible body which commits murder
and terrorizes the entire household of a dead pianist.

HATTON, FANNY (jt. author) see HATTON, FREDERIC

HATTON, FREDERIC

The Azure Shore in *Harper's Bazaar* (March 1923)
    The Rush Hour (jt. author Fanny Hatton)
    7 reels   sil.   b&w   1927
    Dir: E. Mason Hopper. Adap: Zelda Sears.
    Cast: Marie Prevost, Harrison Ford.
    Comedy drama. Margie, a ticket agent, dreams of adventure and travel; her
fiancé dreams only of his business and marriage.

With the Tide in *Young's Magazine* (March 1923)
    South Sea Love
    7 reels   sil.   b&w   1927
    Dir: Ralph Ince. Prod: R-C Pictures.
    Cast: Patsy Ruth Miller, Lee Shumway.
    Romantic melodrama. While Fred slaves on an island to send money to Charlotte,
she is seeing another man.

HAVILAND-TAYLOR, KATHERINE

The Failure
    A Man to Remember
    79 min.   b&w   1938
    Dir: Garson Kanin. Sp: Dalton Trumbo. Prod: RKO.
    Cast: Edward Ellis, Anne Shirley.
    The son of the richest man in town wounds the doctor's daughter. The doctor
is compensated with the gift of a hospital.

    One Man's Journey
    8 reels   b&w   1933
    Dir: John Robertson. Sp: Lester Cohen, Sam Ornitz. Prod: RKO.

HAWKINS, DAVID (jt. author) see Shadow on the Window under HAWKINS,
    JOHN

HAWKINS, JOHN

Criminals Mark in *Saturday Evening Post*
    Crime Wave (jt. author Ward Hawkins)
    73 min.   b&w   1953
    Dir: Andre de Toth. Sp: Crane Wilbur. Prod: Warner Brothers.
    Cast: Sterling Hayden, Gene Nelson, Phyllis Kirk.
    Parolee Steve Lacey wants to go straight but three crooks pressure him into
robbing a bank.

HAWKINS, JOHN (cont'd)

The Missing Witness
  Shadow on the Window (jt. author David Hawkins)
  105 min.   b&w   1957
  Dir: William Asher. Prod: Columbia Pictures Corp. Dist: Institutional Cinema
    Service.
  Cast: John Barrymore, Jr., Betty Garrett, Peter Carey.
  A young boy wanders about in a daze, after having witnessed a brutal murder.
The police question the boy, and bit by bit put together the clues from his
incoherent story to solve the crime.

HAWKINS, WARD see Crime Wave under HAWKINS, JOHN

HAWTHORNE, NATHANIEL

Dr. Heidegger's Experiment
  Dr. Heidegger's Experiment
  15 min.   b&w   1954
  Prod: Dynamic Films. Dist: Audio Brandon
  Cast: Monty Woolley.
  The search for an elixir of youth.

  Dr. Heidegger's Experiment
  22 min.   color   1970
  Dist: Audio Brandon
  Two of the author's favorite themes are combined here: the consequences of
tampering with nature and rejecting conventional morality.

  Twice Told Tales
  s.m. "Rappaccini's Daughter," *The House of the Seven Gables*
  119 min.   color   1963
  Dir: Sidney Salkow. Sp: Robert E. Kent. Prod: United Artists. Dist: Audio
    Brandon.
  Cast: Vincent Price, Sebastian Cabot, Brett Halsey.
  Three adaptations of Hawthorne's stories. No. 1—Dr. Heidegger's Experiment, in
which two old men discover a way to return to their youth. No. 2—Rappaccini's
Daughter, in which a jealous father turns his daughter's blood to poison, killing
any man who touches her. No. 3—The House of the Seven Gables, which is cursed
by an innocent man who was burned for witchcraft three hundred years ago.

Rappaccini's Daughter see Twice Told Tales under Dr. Heidegger's Experiment

HAWTHORNE, NATHANIEL (cont'd)

Young Goodman Brown
  Young Goodman Brown
  30 min.   color   1973
  Dir: Donald Fox. Dist: Pyramid.
  Creatively visual adaptation of an enigmatic story of man's propensity for evil
and the Puritan method of handling it. Cine Golden Eagle. Special jury award,
Atlanta International Film Festival.

HAY, JACOB

Fractured Jaw (Br.)
  The Sheriff of Fractured Jaw
  102 min.   b&w   1959
  Dir: Raoul Walsh. Prod: 20th Century Fox. Dist: Films Inc.
  Cast: Kenneth Moore, Jayne Mansfield.
  Comedy western. A British gentleman tries to establish a gun business in the
wild and woolly West.

HAYCOX, ERNEST

Canyon Passage in *Saturday Evening Post*
  Canyon Passage
  92 min.   color   1946
  Dir: Jacques Tourneur. Sp: Ernest Pascal. Prod: Universal. Dist: The Movie
    Center.
  Cast: Dana Andrews, Brian Donlevy, Susan Hayword.
  Western, set in Oregon during frontier times. The owner of a general store
clashes with an outlaw.

Stage Coach to Lordsburg in *Collier's* (April 10, 1937)
  Stagecoach
  114 min.   b&w   1939
  Dir: John Ford. Prod: John Ford Prod. Dist: Films Inc., Images, Kit Parker
    Films.
  Cast: John Wayne, Claire Trevor, Thomas Mitchell, George Bancroft, Andy
    Devine.
  A group of passengers and stagecoach hands are on their way from Tonto to
Lordsburg. They include a medicine man, a gambler, a prostitute, a crooked banker,
a drunkard, the sheriff and his prisoner, and two members of Southern aristocracy.
Ford shows us each character's behavior under stress. A classic.

  Stagecoach
  115 min.   color   1966
  Dir: Gordon Douglas. Prod: 20th Century Fox.

HAYCOX, ERNEST (cont'd)

Stagecoach (cont'd)
Cast: Ann-Margret, Alex Cord, Bing Crosby, Red Buttons.
A re-make of Ford's "Stagecoach," about a handful of passengers who go
through a great deal before the final shootout.

Stage Station
　Apache Trail
　7 reels　　　　b&w　　　　1942
　Dir: Richard Thrope. Sp: Maurice Geraghty. Prod: M-G-M.
　Cast: Lloyd Nolan, Grant Withers, Gloria Holden.

　Apache War Smoke
　67 min.　　　b&w　　　　1952
　Dir: Harold Kress. Sp: Jerry Davis. Prod: M-G-M. Dist: Films Inc.
　Cast: Gilbert Roland, Glenda Farrell.
　A western spectacle. Re-make of Apache Trail.

HAYNES, MANNING

Man at the Gate
　Men of the Sea
　5 reels　　　　b&w　　　　1944
　Dir: Norman Walker. Prod: Releasing Corp. Dist: Mogull's.
　Cast: Sir Carol Reed.

HECHT, BEN

Actor's Blood see Actors and Sin under Concerning a Woman of Sin

Concerning a Woman of Sin in *Collected Stories* (N.Y., Crown, 1945)
　Actors and Sin
　s.m. "Actor's Blood," same collection
　90 min.　　　b&w　　　　1952
　Dir: Ben Hecht. Prod: United Artists. Dist: Budget.
　Cast: Edward G. Robinson, Marsha Hunt, Eddie Albert.
　Two 45-minute stories. Actor's Blood tells the story of a has-been performer
trying to save his daughter's career—with bizarre results. Woman of Sin is a
delicious satire on the film industry. Film executives are excited over a movie
scenario entitled Woman of Sin which they see as a great, torrid romance. Then
they meet the author—a precocious little girl.

HECHT, BEN (cont'd)

Crime without Passion in *Collected Stories* (N.Y., Crown, 1945)
    Crime without Passion
    72 min.   b&w   1934
    Dir: Ben Hecht, Charles MacArthur. Prod: Paramount. Dist: Universal 16.
    Cast: Claude Rains, Margo, Whitney Bourne.
    A Neitzchean defense lawyer whose flashy courtroom technique and shady
manipulation of evidence have earned him the title "Champion of the Damned"
murders his mistress. He attempts to concoct the perfect alibi, but the analytic
mind that served him so well in the courtroom brings him disaster in private life.
In a powerful, surprising conclusion, he ends up a haunted murderer rather than
the cynical manipulator of society he would like to be.

Specter of the Rose in *Collected Stories* (N.Y.; Crown, 1945)
    Specter of the Rose
    90 min.   b&w   1946
    Dir and Sp: Ben Hecht. Prod: Republic. Dist: Ivy.
    Cast: Judith Anderson, Ivan Kirov.
    Drama. A story about a young ballet dancer who is slowly losing his mind, and
the girl who loves him.

HECKELMANN, CHARLES N.

The Last Outpost to Hell
    Frontier Feud
    6 reels   b&w   1945
    Dir: Lambert Hillyer. Sp: Jess Bowers. Prod: Monogram.
    Cast: Johnny Mack Brown.
    A story about claim jumping.

HELLINGER, MARK

On the Nose
    Broadway Bill
    9,407'   b&w   1934
    Dir: Frank Capra. Sp: Robert Riskin. Prod: Columbia Pictures Corp.
    Cast: Myrna Loy, Warner Baxter, Lucille Ball.
    Story of a man, a maid, and a Cinderella racehorse named Broadway Bill.

Riding High
112 min.   b&w   1950
Dir: Frank Capra. Prod: Paramount.
Cast: Bing Crosby, Colleen Gray.
A re-make of Broadway Bill.

HEMINGWAY, ERNEST

The Killers
  The Killers
  105 min.   b&w   1946
  Dir: Robert Siodmak. Sp: Anthony Veiller. Prod: Universal.
  Cast: Edmond O'Brien, Ava Gardner, Burt Lancaster.
Former fighter Swede is double-crossed by hoodlums and his girl; he lies in bed
thinking about what happened while two hired killers wait for him.

  The Killers
  95 min.   color   1964
  Dir: Don Siegel. Prod: Universal. Dist: Twyman Films, Universal 16.
  Cast: Lee Marvin, Angie Dickinson.
An up-date of the 1946 version. The new plot also involves auto racing and a
$100,000,000 post-office robbery.

My Old Man
  My Old Man
  27 min.   color   1969
  Prod and Dist: Encyclopaedia Britannica.
Joe Butler must settle a conflict between reality and the preservation of his
illusions. The film was produced in Paris, using racetrack scenes and backgrounds.

  Under My Skin
  86 min.   b&w   1950
  Dir: Jean Negulesco. Prod: 20th Century Fox. Dist: Films Inc.
  Cast: John Garfield, Micheline Presle.
  A jockey tries to go straight.

Nick Adams Stories
  Hemingway's Adventures of a Young Man
  96 min.   color   1962
  Dir: Martin Ritt. Prod: Jerry Wald Prod.; rel. 20th Century Fox.
  Cast: Richard Beymer, Diane Baker, Paul Newman, Jessica Tandy, Eli Wallach,
     Dan Dailey.
To escape small town life, Nick joins an ambulance unit in the Italian Army
during WWI. Wounded and discouraged, he falls in love with a nurse who revives
his will to live.

The Short Happy Life of Francis Macomber in *Hemingway*, ed. by Malcolm Cowley
  (Viking, 1944)
  The Macomber Affair
  89 min.   b&w   1947

HEMINGWAY, ERNEST (cont'd)

The Macomber Affair (cont'd)
Dir: Zoltan Korda. Prod: Award Prod.
Cast: Gregory Peck, Joan Bennett, Robert Preston.
A love triangle involving a man, his wife, and a guide on an African hunting expedition.

The Snows of Kilimanjaro in *Great Modern Short Stories*, ed. by B. Cerf (N.Y.,
Modern Library, 1942)
The Snows of Kilimanjaro
117 min.   b&w   1952
Dir: Henry King. Prod: 20th Century Fox.
Cast: Gregory Peck, Susan Hayward, Ava Gardner, Hildegarde Neff.
A war melodrama.

Soldiers Home
Soldiers Home
41½ min.   color   1977
Dir: Robert Young. Sp: Robert Geller. Dist: Perspective.
Harold Krebs returns home after WWI unheralded by the local townsfolk. Krebs needs peace and time to work things out for himself, and he feels alienated from the crowded community.

HENDERSON, JESSIE

The Mouth of the Dragon in *Ainslee's* (March-April 1923)
The Perfect Flapper
7 reels   sil.   b&w   1924
Dir: John Francis Dillon. Prod: Associated First National.
Cast: Colleen Moore, Sydney Chaplin.
Romantic comedy. Wallflower Tommie Lou becomes unconventional to achieve more popularity.

HENRY, O. (pseud.)

During the early years of film (1900-1920), scores of films by Broadway Star Film Co., Biograph, Vitaphone, and other companies were based on O. Henry's stories, often uncredited. Space does not allow inclusion of films produced before 1920.

HENRY, O. (cont'd)

The Badge of Policeman O'Roon
    Doctor Rhythm
    81 min.   b&w   1938
    Dir: Frank Tuttle. Prod: Paramount. Dist: Universal 16.
    Cast: Bing Crosby, Beatrice Lillie, Mary Carlisle, Andy Devine.
    A Park Avenue doctor serves as the bodyguard of the daughter of a screwy
socialite to prevent her from marrying a smooth-talking heel.

Caballero's Way
    In Old Arizona
    7 reels   b&w   1929
    Dir: Raoul Walsh, Irving Cummings. Prod: Fox.
    Cast: Edmund Lowe, Dorothy Burgess.
    The caballero Cisco Kid, infatuated by a woman, is almost double-crossed by
her but she is shot instead of him. This is the most important Cisco Kid movie;
the others were made for the Saturday kiddie shows. *Note: The Cisco Kid was
a character created by O. Henry which appeared in a number of films including
the following: The Gay Amigo, The Gay Cavalier, Beauty and the Bandit, The
Cisco Kid and the Lady, The Gay Caballero, The Cisco Kid in Old Mexico, The
Cisco Kid Returns, The Daring Caballero, Girl from San Lorenzo, King of the
Bandits, South of Monterey, South of the Rio Grande, The Valiant Hobre, Viva
Cisco Kid, The Return óf the Cisco Kid, Lucky Cisco Kid, Ride on Vaquero, Riding
the California Trail, Satan's Cradle.

The Clarion Call see O. Henry Full House under The Cop and the Anthem

The Cop and the Anthem
    O. Henry's Full House
    s.m. "The Clarion Call," "The Ransom of Red Chief," "The Last Leaf," "The
        Gift of the Magi"
    117 min.   b&w   1952
    Dir: Jean Negulesco. Prod: 20th Century Fox. Dist: Films Inc.
    Cast: Charles Laughton, Marilyn Monroe, David Wayne, Dale Robertson, Richard
Widmark, Anne Baxter, Jean Peters, Fred Allen, Oscar Levant, Jeanne Crain,
Farley Granger.

Double Dyed Deceiver in *Everybody's Magazine* (December 1905)
    The Llano Kid
    8 reels   b&w   1939
    Dir: Edward D. Venturini. Sp: Wanda Tuchock. Prod: Paramount.
    Cast: Tito Guizar, Gale Sondergaard.
    The heroine refuses to turn in the Llano Kid even though she thinks he is a
bandit.

HENRY, O. (cont'd)

Dougle Dyed Deceiver (cont'd)
The Texas
79 min.   b&w   1930
Dir: John Cromwell. Prod: Paramount.
Cast: Gary Cooper, Fay Wray.

Fortune's Mask in *Cabbages and Kings*
Fortune's Mask
5 reels   sil.   b&w   1922
Dir: Robert Ensminger. Prod: Vitagraph.
Cast: Earle Williams, Patsy Ruth Miller.
Romantic drama. A newcomer to a Central American town successfully leads a revolution.

The Gift of the Magi see O. Henry's Full House under The Cop and the Anthem

The Last Leaf see O. Henry's Full House under The Cop and the Anthem

The Passing of Black Eagle
Black Eagle
8 reels   b&w   1948
Dir: Robert Gordon. Sp: Edward Huebsch, Hal Smith. Prod: Columbia.
Cast: William Bishop, Virginia Patton, Gordon Jones.
A hobo becomes involved in a quarrel between a female rancher and a group of swindlers.

The Ransom of Red Chief see also O. Henry's Full House under The Cop and the Anthem

The Ransom of Red Chief
The Big Chief
98 min.   b&w   1960
Dir: M. Verneuil. Prod: Continental Dist. Corp.
Cast: Fernandel, Gino Cervi, Papouf.
A French version of the story in which the kid devastates his kidnappers. In French.

The Ransom of Red Chief
color   1977
Dir: Tony Bill. Sp: Michael Kane. Prod and Dist: Learning Corp.
Cast: Harry Dean Stanton, Joe Spinell, Robbie Rist.

HENRY, O. (cont'd)

The Romantic Rogue
   The Cisco Kid
   65 min.   b&w   1931
   Prod: Fox. Dist: Budget.

Whistling Dick's Christmas Stocking in *Roads of Destiny* (New York, 1909)
   An Unwilling Hero
   5 reels   sil.   b&w   1921
   Dir: Clarence Badger. Prod: Goldwyn.
   Cast: Will Rogers, Molly Malone.
   Comedy drama. A hobo discovers other tramps are planning to rob a
plantation.

HERBERT, F. HUGH see also People Will Talk under KERR, SOPHIE

HERBERT, F. HUGH

A Guy Could Change in *Saturday Evening Post* (January 9, 1943)
   A Guy Could Change
   65 min.   b&w   1946
   Dir: William K. Howard. Prod: Republic. Dist: Ivy.
   Cast: Bobby Blake, Gerald Mohr.

HERGESHEIMER, JOSEPH

Tol'able David in *The Happy Life* (N.Y., 1919)
   Tol'able David
   8 reels   sil.   b&w   1921
   Dir: Henry King. Prod: Inspiration—First National. Dist: Cinema 8.
   Cast: Richard Barthelmess.
   A young man takes care of his mother after his father and older brother were
killed by a ruthless gang of murderers; eventually, he meets the gang.

   Tol'able David
   8 reels   b&w   1930
   Dir: John Blystone. Prod: Columbia Pictures Corp.
   Cast: Richard Cromwell, Henry B. Walthall.

HERRICK, KIMBALL

Night Patrol
   Trouble at Midnight
   s.m. screen story "Midnight Raider"
   69 min.   b&w   1938

HERRICK, KIMBALL (cont'd)

Trouble at Midnight (cont'd)
Dir: Ford Beebe. Sp: Ford Beebe, Maurice Geraghty. Prod: Universal.
Cast: Noah Beery, Jr., Catherine Hughes (Kay Huges), Larry Blake.
Drama. Mystery of a theft of dairy cows.

HERVEY, HARRY

Burnt Offering
A Passport to Hell
6,820'   b&w   1932
Dir: Frank Lloyd. Prod: Fox.

Shanghai Express
Peking Express
s.m. Shanghai Express (movie) which was based on the story "Shanghai Express"
95 min.   b&w   1951
Dir: William Dieterle. Prod: Paramount.
Cast: Joseph Cotten, Corinne Calvet, Edmund Gwenn.
Melodrama. Adventure aboard a speeding train with a doctor and a wandering
lady. A re-make of Shanghai Express.

Shanghai Express
84 min.   b&w   1932
Dir: Joseph Von Sternberg. Prod: Paramount Publix Corp. Dist: Twyman Films,
     Universal 16.
Cast: Marlene Dietrich, Clive Brook, Anna May Wong, Warner Oland, Eugene
     Palette.
Re-made in 1951 and re-titled Peking Express. "It took more than one man
to change my name to Shanghai Lily," drawls Dietrich as she embarks on a train
journey from Peking to Shanghai during a Chinese civil war. The film is dedicated
to the proposition of unconditional love, with all its most fatalistic implications
of capitulating to the mask while seeing only the face.

HICHENS, ROBERT SMYTHE

Snake-bite in *Snake-bite and Other Stories* (London, 1919)
The Lady Who Lied
8 reels   sil.   b&w   1925
Sp: Edwin Carewe. Adap: Lois Leeson. Prod: First National Pictures.
Cast: Lewis Stone, Virginia Valli, Louis Rayne.
Melodrama. Fay Kennion breaks her engagement to Horace Pierpont when she
finds him in a seemingly compromising situation with another woman. She marries
an alcoholic doctor, who is later in a position to save Pierpont from a snake-bite,
but the doctor refuses to help until Fay feigns love for the doctor.

HICKS, EDWIN P.

Capital Offense
  Hot Summer Night
  86 min.   b&w   1957
  Dir: David Friedkin. Sp: Morton Fine. Prod: M-G-M.
  Cast: Leslie Nielson, Colleen Miller.
  Crime melodrama. An unemployed newspaperman is kidnapped in the Ozarks
after he interviews a gangster.

HILLMAN, GORDON MALHERBE

The Great Man Votes
  The Great Man Votes
  70 min.   b&w   1939
  Dir: Garson Kanin. Prod: RKO. Dist: Contemporary/McGraw-Hill Films,
      Films Inc.
  Cast: John Barrymore, Virginia Weidler.
  Drama. A scholar who drinks too much reforms when the Children's Society
threatens to take his children away from him.

Here I Am a Stranger
  Here I Am a Stranger
  7,674'   b&w   1939
  Dir: Roy Del Ruth. Sp: Milton Sperling. Prod: Fox.
  Cast: Richard Greene, Brenda Joyce

HITTLEMAN, CARL K. see 36 Hours under DAHL, ROALD

HOFFMAN, CHARLES

Untitled
  It Could Happen To You
  6,360'   b&w   1939
  Dir: Alfred Werker. Prod: 20th Century Fox.

HOLDING, ELIZABETH SANXAY

The Bride Comes Home
  The Bride Comes Home
  85 min.   b&w   1935
  Dir: Wesley Ruggles. Prod: Paramount. Dist: Universal 16.
  Cast: Claudette Colbert, Fred MacMurray, Robert Young.
  Comedy about a love triangle.

HOLMES, MILTON

Bundles for Freedom
    Mr. Lucky
    100 min.   b&w   1943
    Dir: H. C. Potter. Prod: RKO. Dist: Films Inc.
    Cast: Cary Grant, Laraine Day.
    Comedy. A professional gambler seeks to raise money by operating a war-drive bazaar.

HOPPER, JAMES MARIE

Father and Son in *Saturday Evening Post* (October 25, 1924)
    Win That Girl
    6 reels   sd. effects and mus.   b&w   1928
    Dir: David Butler. Prod: Fox
    Cast: David Rollins, Sue Carol, Tom Elliot.
    Comedy of a football rivalry between two families.

HORTON, ROBERT J.

A Man of Action in *Western Story Annual*
    Rip Roarin' Roberts
    5 reels   sil.   b&w   1924
    Dir: Richard Thorpe. Prod: Approved Pictures.
    Cast: Buddy Roosevelt, Brenda Lane.
    Western melodrama. To collect a reward a man has himself appointed sheriff.

HOUGH, DONALD

Calaboose
    Calaboose
    5 reels   b&w   1943
    Dir: Hal Roach, Jr. Sp: Arnold Belgard. Prod: Hal Roach Studios.
    Cast: Noah Beery, Jr.
    A situation comedy about screwballs in the calaboose.

HOUSTON, NORMAN

Private Property
    A Royal Romance
    62 min.   b&w   1930
    Dir: Erle C. Kenton. Prod: Columbia Pictures Corp.

HOWARD, GEORGE BRONSON

Black Room
  Man from Headquarters
  65 min.   b&w   1928
  Dir: Duke Warne. Prod: Rayart Pictures. Dist: Select (8mm silent)
  Cast: Cornelius Keefe, Edith Roberts.

HOWELL, DOROTHY

Black Sheep
  Guilty*
  71 min.   sil. or sd.   b&w   1930
  Dir: George B. Seitz. Prod: Columbia Pictures Corp.
  Cast: Virginia Valli, John Holland.
  Society melodrama. The daughter of a senator sentenced to prison for
bribery is ostracized by her friends. *Note: According to the AFI, publication
was not verified.

HUGGINS, ROY

Now You See It
  The Fuller Brush Man
  93 min.   b&w   1948
  Dir: S. Sylvan Simon. Prod: Columbia. Dist: Macmillan, Modern.
  Cast: Red Skelton, Janet Blair.
  Street sweeper Skelton proposes to his girl Blair, but she refuses and tells him
that he must amount to something before she will accept. Red decides to sell
Fuller brushes and his comical adventures take him to a deserted warehouse where
a band of crooks come out second best.

HUGHES, LANGSTON

Thank You, M'am
  Thank You, M'am
  12 min.   color   1976
  Dir: Andrew Sugerman. Dist: Phoenix Films.
  A night nurse at a large city hospital is on her way home early in the morning. A
10-year-old boy begins following her and soon attempts to grab her pocketbook. She
grabs him instead and brings him to her apartment.

HUGHES, LLEWLLYN

Chap Called Bardell in *Liberty Magazine* (February 23, 1929)
  Sky Hawk
  7 reels   b&w   1929
  Dir: John G. Blystone. Prod: Fox.

HUGHES, LLEWLLYN (cont'd)

Sky Hawk (cont'd)
Cast: Helen Chandler, John Garrick.
War melodrama. Pilot Jack Bardell, accused of crashing his plane to avoid serving on the French front, proves his bravery.

HUGHES, RUPERT

Bitterness of Sweets in *Long Ever Ago* (N.Y., Harper, 1918)
Look Your Best
6 reels   sil.   b&w   1923
Prod: Samuel Goldwyn
Cast: Colleen Moore, Antonio Moreno.
Comedy drama. A poor girl is given a chance to replace a chorus girl who has grown too fat.

Canavan, the Man Who Had His Way in *Long Ever Ago* (N.Y., Harper, 1918)
Hold Your Horses
5 reels   sil.   b&w   1921
Dir: E. Mason Hopper. Prod: Goldwyn.
Cast: Tom Moore, Sylvia Ashton.
Comedy. Dan Canavan, an immigrant from Ireland, goes from street cleaner to husband of society belle Beatrice Newness.

It Had to Happen
7,184'   b&w   1936
Dir: Roy Del Ruth. Sp: Howard Ellis Smith, Kathryn Soola. Prod: 20th Century
    Fox.
Cast: George Raft, Rosalind Russell.
An Italian immigrant becomes a big political boss and falls for the banker's wife.

Don't You Care in *Saturday Evening Post* (July 4, 1914)
Don't
6 reels   sil.   b&w   1925
Dir: Alf Goulding. Prod: M-G-M.
Cast: Sally O'Neil, John Patrick.
A story about a parent-defying flapper.

From the Ground Up in *Cosmopolitan* (October 1921)
From the Ground Up
5 reels   sil.   b&w   1921
Dir: E. Mason Hopper. Adap: Rupert Hughes. Prod: Goldwyn Pictures.
Cast: Tom Moore, Helene Chadwick.

HUGHES, RUPERT (cont'd)

From the Ground Up (cont'd)
Comedy. Philena Mortimer refuses to marry the man her father has chosen because he needs a loan from the man's bank.

The Girl on the Barge in *Hearst's International Cosmopolitan* (October 1927)
The Girl on the Barge
8 reels   sil.   b&w   1929
Dir: Edward Sloman. Adap: Charles Kenyon, Nan Cochrane. Prod: Universal.
Cast: Jean Hersholt, Sally O'Neill.
Melodrama. Erie McCadden, the daughter of a mean barge captain, falls in love with a tugboat pilot.

Money Talks
Money Talks
6 reels   sil.   b&w   1926
Dir: Archie Mayo. Adap: Jessie Burns. Sp: Jessie Burns, Bernard Vorhaus. Prod: M-G-M.
Cast: Ned Sparks, Owen Moore, Claire Windsor.
A gun-running villain is thwarted by a gun-toting hero.

Obscurity
Breach of Promise
7 reels   b&w   1932
Dir: Paul L. Stein. Sp: Ben Verschleiser. Prod: E. W. Mannons.

The Old Nest in *Saturday Evening Post* (June 3, 1911)
The Old Nest
8 reels   sil.   b&w   1921
Dir: Reginald Barker. Prod: Goldwyn.
Cast: Dwight Crittenden, Mary Alden.
Domestic drama. The saga of a large family.

The Patent Leather Kid in *Patent Leather Kid and Several Others* (New York, 1927)
The Patent Leather Kid
127 min.   b&w   1927
Dir: Alfred Santell. Adap: Adela Rogers St. Johns.
Cast: Richard Barthelmess, Molly O'Day, Arthur Stone.
He was a fighter, in peace and in war. She was full of fire and fight. Their love was savage, primitive. Then came war—and the glorification of love through sacrifice, danger, and death!

HUGHES, RUPERT (cont'd)

She Goes to War in *She Goes to War and Other Stories* (New York, 1929)
    She Goes to War
    b&w   1929
    Dist: Em Gee Film Library.

True as Steel in *Cosmopolitan* (December 1923)
    True as Steel
    7 reels   sil.   b&w   1924
    Dir: Rupert Hughes. Prod: Goldwyn.
    Cast: Aileen Pringle, Huntley Gordon, Cleo Madison.
    Drama. Frank Parry becomes infatuated with another woman on a business trip
to New York.

Unidentified story
    FBI Girl
    74 min.   b&w   1951
    Dir: William Berke. Prod: Lippert. Dist: Mogull's
    Cast: Audrey Totter, George Brent.
    A clerk is the bait to obtain evidence on a mob trying to uncover the governor's
former criminal record.

HUNYADY, SANDER

The Girl Downstairs
    The Girl Downstairs
    8 reels   b&w   1938
    Dir: Norman Taurog. Sp: Harold Goldman, Felix Jackson, Karl Noti. Prod:
      M-G-M.
    Cast: Franciska Gaal, Franchot Tone.
    The heroine is a naive domestic who wins a man-about-town from the affections
of her rich employer.

HURST, FANNIE

Back Pay in Wick, J., compiler; *Stories Editors Buy & Why* (N.Y., Small, 1921)
    Back Pay
    7 reels   sil.   b&w   1922
    Dir: Frank Borzage. Prod: Cosmopolitan Prod.
    Cast: Seena Owen, Matt Moore, J. Barney Sherry, Ethel Duray.
    Country girl Hester Bevins, in love with delivery boy Jerry Newcombe, doesn't
want to settle down to a dull poor life. In New York she falls in with a wealthy
businessman, but leaves him when she learns that Jerry, wounded in the war in
France, is blind and will soon die. She marries Jerry.

HURST, FANNIE (cont'd)

Back Pay (cont'd)
Back Pay
77 min.   b&w   1930
Dir: William A. Seiter. Prod: Warner Brothers. Dist: United Artists.
Cast: Montagu Love, Corinne Griffith.
A girl rebels against her small town background.

Four Daughters
Young at Heart
117 min.   color   1954
Dir: Gordon Douglas. Prod: Warner Brothers.
Cast: Frank Sinatra, Doris Day, Gig Young, Ethel Barrymore, Dorothy Malone.
A cynical, hard-luck musician gets a new outlook on life when he meets and
falls for a small-town girl.

Give This Little Girl a Hand in *Procession* (New York, 1929)
The Painted Angel
7 reels   b&w   1929
Dir: Millard Webb. Prod: First National Corp. and Vitaphone.
Cast: Billie Dove, Edmund Lowe.
Melodrama. A violinist stops the bullet that is intended for an entertainer.

The Good Provider in *Saturday Evening Post* (August 15, 1914)
The Good Provider
8 reels   sil.   b&w   1922
Dir: Frank Borzage. Prod: Cosmopolitan Prod.
Cast: Vera Gordon, Dore Davidson.
Society melodrama. Jewish immigrants struggle with changing business practices
and city life before returning to the country.

Humoresque in *Humoresque*
Humoresque
6 reels   b&w   sil.   1920
Dir: Frank Borzage. Prod: Cosmopolitan Prod.
Cast: Alma Rubens.

Humoresque
125 min.   b&w   1947
Dir: Jean Negulesco. Sp: Clifford Odets, Zachary Gold.
Cast: Joan Crawford, John Garfield, Oscar Levant.
A poor but gifted musician is sponsored by a wealthy society woman who loves
him, but he decides that his career is more important than she is.

HURST, FANNIE (cont'd)

Just Around the Corner in *Just Around the Corner* (New York, 1914)
Just Around the Corner
7 reels   sil.   b&w   1921
Dir and Adap: Frances Marion. Prod: Cosmopolitan Prod.
Cast: Margaret Seddon, Lewis Sargent, Sigrid Holmquist.
Melodrama. Ma Birdsong repeatedly asks her daughter, Essie, to bring home her
fiancé, Joe Ullman, a crooked ticket speculator. He refuses to come even when Ma
is on her deathbed. Essie gets a stranger to impersonate Joe and later marries Joe's
impersonator.

The Nth Commandment in *Every Soul Hath Its Song* (New York, 1916)
The Nth Commandment
8 reels   sil.   b&w   1923
Dir: Frank Borzage. Prod: Cosmopolitan
Cast: Colleen Moore, James Morrison.
Drama. Flattered by the attentions of a sophisticated man, Sarah breaks her
previous engagement.

Roulette in *The Vertical City* (New York, 1922)
Wheel of Chance
7 reels   sil.   b&w   1929
Dir: Alfred Santell. Adap: Gerald C. Duffy. Prod: First National Pictures.
Cast: Richard Barthelmess, Warner Oland.
Melodrama. During the Czarist regime a Russian family, saddened by the death
of a son, comes to America. Later the son is found to be alive.

HUTCHINSON, BRUCE

Park Avenue Logger in *Saturday Evening Post* (November 29, 1935)
Tall Timber
67 min.   b&w   1937
Dir: David Howard. Prod: George A. Hirliman. Dist: Film Classics Exchange,
    Mogull's
Cast: George O'Brien, Marjorie Reynolds.
A young man in society exposes the foreman of a lumber camp to be a crook.
Prior movie title was Park Avenue Logger.

HUXLEY, ALDOUS

The Giaconda Smile
A Woman's Vengeance
96 min.   b&w   1948
Dir: Zoltan Korda. Sp: Aldous Huxley. Prod: Universal. Dist: Universal 16.

HUXLEY, ALDOUS (cont'd)

A Woman's Vengeance (cont'd)
Cast: Jessica Tandy, Charles Boyer, Ann Blyth.
Mystery drama. A man who falls in love with a shop girl is put on trial for poisoning his wife.

Young Archimedes
Prelude to Fame
78 min.   b&w   1950
Prod: Two Cities Films; rel. Universal.
Drama. A professor saves a young Italian conductor from exploitation.

HYDE, ROBERT

Just Another Dame
Not a Ladies Man
6 reels   b&w   1942
Dir: Lew Landers. Sp: Rian James. Prod: Columbia Pictures Corp.

HYMER, JAMES

The Lost Game
Law of the Underworld (jt. author Samuel Shipman)
s.m. stage production by John B. Hymer
60 min.   b&w   1938
Dir: Lew Landers. Prod: RKO. Dist: Films Inc.
Cast: Chester Morris, Anne Shirley, Walter Abel.
A ruthless gang leader has a change of heart and saves a young couple from harm.

INGHAM, TRAVIS

Biddy
Most Precious Thing in Life
7 reels   b&w   1934
Dir: Lambert Hillyer. Sp: Ethel Hill, Dore Schary. Prod: Columbia Pictures Corp.

INGHAM, TRAVIS (cont'd)

Most Precious Thing in Life (cont'd)
Cast: Jean Arthur, Donald Cook.
A charwoman is really the mother of a spoiled young aristocrat.

IRVING, WASHINGTON

The Bold Dragoon
   The Bold Dragoon
   15 min.   b&w   1954
   Prod: Dynamic Films. Dist: Audio Brandon.
   Cast: Monty Woolley.
   An innkeeper rids himself of a bothersome guest by giving him a haunted room.

The Legend of Sleepy Hollow
   Biograph, Selig, and Thanhouser are among the companies which produced early
silent versions of The Legend of Sleepy Hollow.

   The Headless Horseman
   8 reels   sil.   b&w   1922
   Dir: Edward Venturini. Dist: Killiam.
   Cast: Will Rogers, Lois Meredith.
   Ichabod Crane rides again in this 1922 Hollywood version of Washington Irving's
The Legend of Sleepy Hollow. Brought to the screen amid the vintage early Ameri-
can charm of the Hudson River locale.

   Ichabod and Mr. Toad
   s.m. for Mr. Toad is Wind in the Willows by Kenneth Grahame
   68 min.   color   1949
   Prod: Walt Disney.
   Voices: Basil Rathbone, Bing Crosby.
   Animated.

   The Legend of Sleepy Hollow
   13 min.   color   1972
   Prod: Pyramid/Bosustow. Dist: Pyramid and Bosustow.
   Animated.

   Tales of Washington Irving
   45 min.   color
   Dist: Audio-Brandon
   Ichabod Crane and Rip Van Winkle are among the many wonderful residents of
the Dutch settlement in the Hudson River valley.

IRVING, WASHINGTON (cont'd)

Rip Van Winkle
  Rip Van Winkle
  1 reel   sil.   1924
  Prod: Universal.
  Cast: Charles Dudley, Fay Holderness.

IRWIN, WALLACE

American Beauty in *Saturday Evening Post* (January 8, 1927)
  American Beauty
  7 reels   sil.   b&w   1927
  Dir: Richard Wallace. Prod: First National Pictures.
  Cast: Billie Dove, Lloyd Hughes, Walter McGrail.
  Romantic drama. A young, beautiful, but poor girl attempts to win a wealthy
man for her husband, but her poverty is discovered after she "borrows" a gown
from the laundry run by her mother.

Sophie Semenoff in *Saturday Evening Post* (November 27, 1920)
  Making the Grade
  5 reels   sil.   b&w   1921
  Dir: Fred J. Butler.
  Cast: David Butler, Helen Ferguson.
  A wealthy, freewheeling American lad marries a Russian school teacher and takes
her back to the U.S., only to find that she is really a princess escaping the Bolsheviks.

ISHERWOOD, CHRISTOPHER

Berlin Stories
  Cabaret
  s.m. musical play by Jose Masteroff; play I Am a Camera by John Van Druten;
      both based on "Goodbye to Berlin" in *Berlin Stories.*
  123 min.   color
  Dir: Bob Fosse. Prod: Allied Artists and ABC Pictures Corp. Dist: Cine World.
  Cast: Liza Minnelli, Michael York, Helmut Griem, Joel Grey.

  I Am a Camera
  98 min.   b&w   1955
  Dir: Henry Cornelius. Dist: Audio-Brandon.
  Cast: Julie Harris, Laurence Harvey, Shelley Winters.
  Sally Bowles is a zany nightclub singer in pre-Hitler Germany.

JACCARD, JACQUES

Hard Rock
  The Galloping Ace
  5 reels   sil.   b&w   1924
  Dir: Robert North Bradbury. Prod: Universal.
  Cast: Jack Hoxie, Margaret Morris.
  Western melodrama. War hero Jim Jordon takes a job on a ranch, and falls in love
with the woman who owns it.

JACKSON, FRED

High Speed in *Argosy Magazine* (June 1, 1918)
  High Speed
  5 reels   b&w   1924
  Dir: Herbert Blanche. Prod: Universal.
  Cast: Herbert Rawlinson, Carmelita Geraghy.
  Comedy melodrama. Athlete Hi Moreland tries to win the hand of the daughter
of a bank president, but he is framed by a competitor.

Morocco Box in *Argosy Magazine* (January 6, 1923)
  Love Letters
  5 reels   sil.   b&w   1924
  Dir: David Soloman. Prod: Fox.
  Cast: Shirley Mason, Gordon Edwards.
  Melodrama. Two sisters try to retrieve passionate love letters they wrote as young
girls, and had sent to a notorious rake.

JACKSON, JOSEPH

The Champ
  Be Yourself
  67 min.   b&w   1930
  Dir: Thorton Freeland. Prod: United Artists. Dist: Mogull's, Blackhawk (sale).
  Cast: Fannie Brice, Robert Armstrong.
  The hero challenges a champion.

JACKSON, SHIRLEY

The Lottery
    The Lottery
    18 min.   color   1969
    Prod and Dist: Encyclopaedia Britannica.
    The inhabitants of a small town in America chose a person to be stoned to death
each year.

JACOBS, WILLIAM WYMARK

The Interruption (novelette) in *World's Greatest Mystery Stories*, ed. by W. J.
    Cuppy (N.Y., World, 1943)
    Footsteps in the Fog
    90 min.   b&w   1955
    Dir: Arthur Lubin. Prod: Film's Locations Ltd. Dist: Macmillan, Modern, Roa's
        Films.
    Cast: Stewart Granger, Jean Simmons.
    A gaslight suspense thriller set in London at the turn of the century. A patrician
householder (Granger) poisons his wife, and a servant girl (Simmons) blackmails him.
In an atmosphere of chilly Victorian elegance, the two match wits in a lethal game
of cat and mouse.

The Monkey Box
    Our Relations
    70 min.   b&w   1936
    Dir: Harry Lachman. Prod: M-G-M. Dist: Budget, Em Gee Film Library, Kit
        Parker, Macmillan, Select, Swank.
    Cast: Laurel and Hardy, Alan Hale.
    Life is ever-so-peaceful for our friends until long-lost twin brothers turn up
unexpectedly, then a riot of mistaken identities and incredible frustrations take
place.

The Monkey's Paw
    Monkey's Paw
    s.m. play by Louis Napoleon Parker
    56 min.   b&w   1932
    Dir: Wesley Ruggles. Sp: Graham John. Prod: RKO.
    Cast: C. Aubrey Smith, Ivan Simpson, Louis Carter.
    Everything turns out to be a dream.

Monkey's Paw
    64 min.   b&w   1948
    Dir: Norman Dee. Sp: N. Lee, Barbara Toy. Prod: Butchers Film. Dist: Kay Film.
    Cast: Milton Rosmer, Megs Jenkins, Joan Seton, Norman Shelley.

JACOBS, WILLIAM WYMARK (cont'd)

Monkey's Paw (cont'd)
A couple obtains a monkey's paw, which grants wishes but always at great cost.

Tales from the Crypt
   s.m. comic book series "All Thru the House," "Reflection of Death," "Poetic
     Justice," "Blind Alleys," and "Wish You Were Here," (in turn based on "The
     Monkey's Paw") by William M. Gaines, Albert B. Feldstein, and Johnny Craig
   92 min.   color   1972
   Dir: Freddie Francis. Prod: Cinerama. Dist: Swank.
   Cast: Sir Ralph Richardson, Joan Collins, Martin Boddey.
Horror. On a tour through a subterranean burial ground five unrelated sightseers find themselves locked in a crypt where various horrific experiences from their future (or past?) lives are exposed to them by cryptkeeper Sir Ralph Richardson.

JAMES, HENRY

The Jolly Corner
   The Jolly Corner
   43 min.   color   1977
   Dir: Arthur Barron. Sp: Arthur Barron. Dist: Perspective.
Brydon, an expatriate American who fled from the Civil War, returns to New York 35 years later. He is at once repelled and lured on by the lust for profit and power, and wonders what would have happened had he remained. To find out he makes frequent visits to the house where he spent his youth.

JAMES, MONTAQUE R.

Casting the Runes in *Ghosts and Marvels*, comp. by V. H. Collins
   Curse of the Demon (Br.)
   95 min.   b&w   1958
   Dir: Jacques Tourneur. Prod: Columbia Pictures Corp.
   Cast: Dana Andrews, Peggy Cummins.
Fearsome monster from the past returns to wreck havoc in London. Former title was Night of the Demon.

JANIS, ELSIE (jt. author) see Close Harmony under MARKEY, GENE

JARRICO, PAUL

Private Miss Jones
   Thousands Cheer (jt. author Richard Collins)
   126 min.   color   1944
   Sp: George Sidney. Prod: M-G-M. Dist: Films Inc.

JARRICO, PAUL (cont'd)

Thousands Cheer (cont'd)
Cast: Kathryn Grayson, Gene Kelly, Mary Astor.
Musical. An all-star extravaganza about a soldier and the colonel's daughter.

JENKINS, WILL F.

The Purple Hieroglyph in *Snappy Stories* (March 1, 1920)
Murder Will Out
7 reels   b&w   1930
Dir: Clarence Badger. Prod: First National Pictures.
Cast: Jack Mulhall, Lila Lee, Noah Beery, Jr.
Mystery ensues when blackmail, poisoning, attempted murder, and a kidnapping plague a young couple in upper crust Washington, D.C., society.

JOHNSON, DOROTHY

Man Called Horse in *Collier's* (January 7, 1950)
A Man Called Horse
114 min.   color   1970
Dir: Elliot Silverstein. Prod: Cinema Center. Dist: Swank.
Cast: Richard Harris, Dame Judith Anderson.
Richard Harris plays a man called "Horse" in this extraordinary story of an English aristocrat in the 1700s, who is captured by Sioux Indians. His only chance for escape is to prove his manhood in their savage culture, an effort which culminates in the ritual "Vow to the Sun," one of the most brutal events ever filmed.

The Man Who Shot Liberty Valance in *Indian Country* (New York, 1953)
The Man Who Shot Liberty Valance
122 min.   b&w   1962
Dir: John Ford. Prod: Paramount. Dist: Films Inc.
Cast: James Stewart, John Wayne, Lee Marvin, Edmond O'Brien.
Eastern lawyer (Stewart) is determined to rid a Western town of its resident terror, Liberty Valance, through organization of the citizens, elections, etc. Wayne, the other leading strong gun, watches Stewart's ineffectual, idealistic efforts with amusement, then does the job himself by simply shooting Liberty. The townsfolk consider Stewart the hero and launch him on a successful political career. Meanwhile, Wayne dies in obscurity.

JOHNSON, NUNNALLY

Rough House Rosie in *Saturday Evening Post* (June 12, 1926)
Rough House Rosie
5,952'   sil.   b&w   1927
Dir: Frank Strayer. Sp: Louise Long, Ethel Doherty. Prod: Famous Players–Lasky.

JOHNSON, NUNNALLY (cont'd)

Rough House Rosie (cont'd)
Cast: Clara Bow, Reed Howes.
Society comedy. Story of a girl who wants to be a dancer and a boxer.

JOHNSON, OWEN

The Lawrenceville Stories
The Happy Years
110 min.   color   1950
Dir: William Wellman. Prod: M-G-M. Dist: Films Inc.
Cast: Dean Stockwell, Darryl Hickman, Leo G. Carroll, Scotty Beckett, Leon
    Ames.

The exasperating experiences of a pint-sized terror to teachers and parents who
is sent to the Lawrenceville, New Jersey, prep school, where, despite himself, he
becomes civilized—and almost loveable. Set in the 1890s.

JOHNSTON, CALVIN

Temple Dusk in *Saturday Evening Post* (October 16, 1920)
Without Limit
7 reels   sil.   b&w   1921
Dir: George D. Baker. Prod: S-L Pictures.
Cast: Anna Qu. Nilsson, Robert Frazer.
Society melodrama. The son of a clergyman gambles away his money.

JONES, HERBERT A.

The Mystery Ship
Suicide Fleet
9 reels   b&w   1931
Dir: Albert Rogell. Sp: Lew Lipton. Prod: RKO.
Cast: William Boyd, Ginger Rogers, Robert Armstrong.
Two brawling sailors fight over the same girl.

JORDAN, ANNE

Kitchen Privileges
Luckiest Girl in the World
68 min.   b&w   1936
Dir: Edward Buzzell. Sp: Herbert Fields, Henry Myers. Prod: Universal.
Cast: Jane Wyatt, Louis Hayward, Nat Pendleton.
Comedy drama. A wealthy society girl must live on $150 a month to prove to her
father that she can stand being married to a poor man.

JORGENSON, IVAR (pseud.)

Deadly City in *If: Worlds of Science Fiction* (March 1953)
    Target Earth
    75 min.   b&w   1954
    Dir: Sherman A. Rose. Sp: William Raynor. Prod: Allied Artists.
    Cast: Richard Denning, Virginia Grey, Kathleen Crowley.
    A girl awakens alone in the city; everyone else has fled because giant robots
with death rays have arrived from Venus.

JOSSELYN, TALBERT

Navy Bound in *Collier's* (December 14, 1935)
    Navy Bound
    61 min.   b&w   1951
    Dir: Paul Landres. Prod: Monogram. Dist: Institutional Cinema Service.
    Cast: Tom Neal, Regis Toomey, Wendy Waldon.
    Action packed drama of a Navy boxing champion and the touching gratitude
he feels for his foster father.

KAFKA, FRANZ

The Hunger Artist
    The Hunger Artist
    10 min.   color   1976
    Dir: Fred Smith, Maura Smith. Prod: Paramount Oxford.
    The hero is engaged in the crowd-gathering spectacle of starving, attracting the
curious and the scornful.

KAFKA, JOHN

The Woman Who Came Back
s.m. story suggested by Philip Yordan
    The Woman Who Came Back
    69 min.   b&w   1945
    Dir: Walter Colmer. Prod: Republic Pictures Corp. Dist: Ivy.
    Cast: John Loder, Nancy Kelly.

KAHLER, HUGH MACNAIR

Fool's First in *Saturday Evening Post* (November 20, 1920)
Fools First
6 reels   sil.   b&w   1922
Dir: Marshall Neilan. Prod: Marshall Neilan Prod.
Cast: Richard Dix, Claire Windsor.
Crime melodrama. Once released from prison, Tommy robs a bank with his girl-friend, but at the last minute changes his mind and tries to return the money.

Once a Peddler in *Saturday Evening Post* (September 3, 1921)
The Little Giant
7 reels   sil.   b&w   1926
Dir and Adap: William Nigh. Prod: Universal.
Cast: Glenn Hunter, Edna Murphy.
Elmer, the sales manager of a large manufacturing company, launches a successful sales campaign, which is sabotaged by the son of the company's president.

KALEY, J.

Deuces Wild
Saddle Aces
57 min.   b&w   1935
Prod: Republic Pictures Corp. Dist: Thunderbird.
Cast: Rex Bell.

KANTOR, MacKINLEY

Gun Crazy in *Saturday Evening Post* (February 3, 1940)
Gun Crazy
87 min.   b&w   1948
Dir: Joseph Lewis. Prod: United Artists. Dist: Hurlock-Cine World.
Cast: Peggy Cummins, John Dall.
An early variation of the Bonnie and Clyde theme; a tribute to reckless love and non-stop action. Former title was Deadly Is the Female.

Mountain Music
Mountain Music
8 reels   b&w   1937
Dir: Robert Florey. Sp: John C. Moffett, Duke Atteberry, Russell Crouse,
     Charles Lederer. Prod: Paramount.
Cast: Bob Burns, Martha Raye.
Slapstick comedy of an amnesiac.

KAUFFMAN, REGINALD WRIGHT

Our Undisciplined Daughters
  School for Girls
  8 reels   b&w   1934
  Dir: William Nigh. Prod: Liberty Pictures.

KEEFE, FREDERICK L.

The Interpreter
  Before Winter Comes
  108 min.   color   1969
  Dir: J. Lee Thompson. Prod: Columbia Pictures Corp. Dist: Budget, Charard
    Motion Pictures, Macmillan, Modern, Welling Motion Pictures.
  Cast: David Niven, Anna Karina, Topol.
A refugee camp in occupied Austria after WWII is run by British Major Giles
Burnside (Niven), a stickler for regulations. He must assign displaced persons of
the border camp to either the American or Russian zones. With all its human
misery, the camp is in shambles until one of the refugees, Janovic (Topol), steps
forward to help out. Janovic serves as a multi-lingual interpreter, a mediator
between British and Russian military brass, and an efficient camp orderly. Ulti-
mately, in a friendly rivalry, he challenges Burnside's authority.

KEELER, HARRY STEPHEN

Twelve Coins of Confucius
  Mysterious Mr. Wong
  56 min.   b&w   1935
  Dir: William Nigh. Prod: Monogram. Dist: Budget, Classic Film Museum, Em
    Gee Film Library, United Artists, Wholesome Film Center.
  Cast: Bela Lugosi, Wallace Ford.
Twelve coins, given by Confucius on his death bed to his trusted friends in the
province of Keelat, were circulated and lost over the years. Legend says that if one
man could amass all twelve gold pieces he would gain extraordinary powers, and
Wong (Lugosi) believes he is that man. He will stop at nothing to locate the missing
twelfth coin.

KELLAND, CLARENCE BUDINGTON

Backbone in *Saturday Evening Post*
  Backbone
  7 reels   sil.   b&w   1923
  Dir: Edward Sloman. Prod: Distinctive Pictures.
  Cast: Edith Roberts, Alfred Lunt, William B. Mack.
Romantic drama. André de Mersay, a lumber tycoon separated from his sweet-
heart Yvonne de Chausson, reminisces about his ancestor, Louis XV of France.

KELLAND, CLARENCE BUDINGTON (cont'd)

Knots and Windshakers in *Everybody's Magazine* (April 1920)
French Heels
7 reels   sil.   b&w   1922
Dir: Edwin L. Hollywood. Adap: Eve Unsell. Prod: Holtre Prod.
Cast: Irene Castle, Ward Crane.
Melodrama. A soldier returning home from the war must tell a young girl that her brother was killed. She goes to work in a cabaret to support herself. Later when she marries the soldier, his parents object.

Scattergood Baines Stories (suggestion for)
Scattergood Baines
68 min.   b&w   1941
Dir: Guy Kibbee. Prod: Pyramid Pictures Corp., rel. RKO. Dist: Roa's Films.
Cast: Christy Cabanne.
The sage of Coldriver selects a new teacher, keeps control of his community railroad, defeats the syndicate, and stills gossipy tongues. Other films: Scattergood Meets Broadway (1941), Scattergood Pulls the String (1941), Scattergood Rides High (1942).

Stand-In in *Saturday Evening Post* (February 13, 1937)
Stand-In
90 min.   b&w   1937
Dir: Tay Garnett. Prod: United Artists. Dist: Macmillan, Mogull's Films Inc.
Cast: Leslie Howard, Joan Blondell, Humphrey Bogart.
An alcoholic producer (Bogart) and a ravishing former child star (Blondell) come to the aid of a befuddled financial expert (Howard), who is trying to save a movie studio from bankruptcy.

Thirty-Day Princess in *Ladies Home Journal* (July 1933)
Thirty-Day Princess
76 min.   b&w   1934
Dir: Marion Gering. Prod: Paramount.
Cast: Sylvia Sidney, Cary Grant.
A princess on a good-will tour gets the mumps and a replacement must be found.

KELLY, T. HOWARD

His Buddy's Wife in *Smart Set*
His Buddy's Wife
6 reels   sil.   b&w   1925
Dir: Tom Teriss. Prod: Associated Exhibitors.
Cast: Glenn Hunter, Edna Murphy.

KELLY, T. HOWARD (cont'd)

His Buddy's Wife (cont'd)

Melodrama. A war buddy asks Jim to look after his family if anything happens to him. When Bill does not return from a patrol, Jim goes to Bill's farm to care for his family. When the neighbors begin to gossip, Jim decides to marry Bill's wife Mary, but Bill returns on the eve of the wedding.

Lover's Island in *Smart Set*
    Lover's Island
    5 reels   sil.   b&w   1925
    Dir: Henri Diamont-Berger. Prod: Encore Pictures
    Cast: Hope Hampton, James Kirkwood.
    Clemmy, who has been attacked, names Avery as her attacker. Her father vows he will make the responsible party marry her, but Avery already has a financeé.

KENEDI, ALEXANDER G. (jt. author) see Marry the Boss' Daughter under FARAGO, SANDOR

KENT, ROBERT E.

Assigned to Danger
    Assigned to Danger
    66 min.   b&w   1948
    Dir: Oscar Boetticher. Sp: Eugene Ling.
    Cast: Gene Raymond, Noreen Nash.
    The adventure of an insurance investigator who brings about the capture of a gang of payroll bandits.

KEOUN, ERIC

Sir Tristram Goes West
    The Ghost Goes West (Br.)
    85 min.   b&w   1936
    Dir: Reme Clair. Sp: Robert E. Sherwood, Geoffrey Kerr. Prod: London Film
        Prod. Dist: Macmillan, Mogull's, Audio Brandon.
    Cast: Robert Donat, Jean Parker.
    Comedy fantasy. When the castle of Lord Tristram is moved stone-by-stone to America its resident spirit follows. The castle, having been reconstructed in America, is inhabited by a young and pretty lady who quickly becomes aware of her houseguest.

KERR, SOPHIE

Beauty's Worth in *Saturday Evening Post* (February 14, 1920)
    Beauty's Worth
    7 reels   sil.   b&w   1922
    Dir: Robert G. Vignola. Prod: Cosmopolitan.
    Cast: Marion Davies, Forest Stanley.
    Society melodrama. A sophisticated neighbor flirts with a Quaker girl though
he is really not interested in her.

KAYO, OKE

People Will Talk
    People Will Talk
    s.m. "Such a Lovely Couple," by F. Hugh Herbert
    7 reels   b&w   1935
    Dir: Alfred Santell. Sp: Herbert Fields. Prod: Paramount.
    Cast: Cary Grant, Jeanne Crain.
    A physician falls in love with a girl that is pregnant, and is accused of malpractice by a jealous colleague.

Relative Values in *Saturday Evening Post* (January 27, 1923)
    Young Ideas
    5 reels   sil.   b&w   1924
    Dir: Robert Hill. Prod: Universal.
    Cast: Laura La Plante, T. Roy Barnes.
    Comedy. Octavia supports a large family, all of whom pretend ailments to avoid
work.

Sweetie Peach in *Confetti, a Book of Short Stories* (New York, 1927)
    The House That Jazz Built
    6 reels   sil.   b&w   1921
    Dir: Penrhyn Stanlaws. Prod: Realart Pictures.
    Cast: Wanda Hawley, Forrest Stanley.
    Domestic drama. Frank and Cora Rodham begin married life as a modest suburban couple. When Frank acquires a good position with a company in New York,
she becomes fat and slovenly. Frank becomes infatuated with another woman until
Cora regains her figure.

KETCHUM, PHILLIP

The Town in Hell's Backyard
    The Devil's Trail
    b&w   1941
    Dir: Lambert Hillyer. Sp: Robert Lee Johnson. Prod: Columbia Pictures Corp.

KETCHUM, PHILLIP (cont'd)

The Devil's Trail (cont'd)
Cast: Bill Elliott, Tex Ritter.
Western.

KEYES, DANIEL

Flowers for Algernon in *Magazine of Fantasy and Science Fiction* (short story and
later a novel)
Charly
103 min.   color   1968
Dir: Ralph Nelson. Prod: Cinerama. Dist: Films Inc.
Cast: Cliff Robertson, Claire Bloom.
Charly, a 30-year-old with the mental capabilities of a 6-year-old, undergoes
experimental treatment in a mental retardation clinic. He achieves normalcy, only
to learn he will soon revert to his former state.

KILBOURNE, FANNIE

The Girl Who Was the Life of the Party in *American Magazine* (December 1923)
Girls Men Forget
6 reels   sil.   b&w   1924
Dir: Maurice Campbell. Prod: Principal Pictures.
Cast: Johnnie Walker, Patsy Ruth Miller.
Comedy melodrama. Kitty Shayne, life of the party, learns that the men in her
life marry the quiet girls.

Sunny Goes Home in *Saturday Evening Post*
The Major and the Minor
s.m. Connie Goes Home, play by Edward Childs Carpenter
100 min.   b&w   1942
Prod: Paramount. Dist: Universal.
Cast: Ginger Rogers, Ray Milland, Rita Johnson, Robert Benchley, Diana Lynn.
A career woman impersonates a 12-year-old girl in order to save on train fare
and then must continue the masquerade while biding time in a boys' military
academy.

You're Never Too Young
102 min.   b&w   1955
Dir: Norman Taurog. Prod: Paramount.
Cast: Dean Martin, Jerry Lewis.
Jerry is a wacky barber forced to pose as a child because a murderer is on his
trail. A re-make of The Major and the Minor.

KING, BASIL

The Ghost's Story in *Spreading Dawn*
Earthbound
6,035'   b&w   1940
Dir: Irving Pichel. Sp: Samuel G. Engel, John Howard Lawson. Prod: Fox.
Cast: Warner Baxter, Andrea Leeds.
The spirit of a man returns to earth.

KING, RUFUS

The Case of the Constant God
Love Letters of a Star
66 min.   b&w   1936
Dir: Lewis R. Foster, Milton Carruth. Sp: Lewis R. Foster, Milton Carruth,
    James Mulhauser. Prod: Universal.
Cast: Henry Hunter, Polly Rowles, C. Henry Gordon.
Murder mystery. A girl commits suicide because she was blackmailed over letters
she wrote to a stage star.

Murder by the Clock
Murder by the Clock
s.m. Murder by the Clock, a play by Charles Beahan.
74 min.   b&w   1931
Dir: Edward Sloman. Sp: Henry Myers. Prod: Paramount.
Cast: William Boyd, Lilyan Tashman, Irving Pichel, Regis Toomey.

Secret Beyond the Door
Museum Piece Number 13 in *Redbook*
99 min.   b&w   1948
Dir: Fritz Lang. Sp: Silvia Richards. Prod: Diana Prod. Dist: Ivy.
Cast: Joan Bennett, Michael Redgrave.
Mystery. A beautiful woman married after a whirlwind romance suspects that
her husband wants to kill her.

KIPLING, RUDYARD

The King's Ankus
Jungle Book
s.m. other Mowgli stories
115 min.   color   1942
Dir: Zoltan Korda. Sp: Laurence Stallings. Dist: Images.
Cast: Sabu, Joseph Calleia, John Qualen.
A boy strays from his village as an infant and is raised by a she-wolf. As he grows
up, Mowgli discovers a vast treasure in the jungle and must protect it from the
villagers.

KIPLING, RUDYARD (cont'd)

The Man Who Would Be King
   The Man Who Would Be King
   127 min.   color   1976
   Dir: John Huston. Sp: Gladys Hill, Huston. Prod: Columbia/Allied Artists.
      Dist: Hurlock Cine World.
   Cast: Sean Connery, Michael Caine, Christopher Plummer.
   Tongue-in-cheek Danny Dravot and acolyte Peachy are fearless boyhood heroes
who teach the tribesmen to slaughter enemies like civilized men. Allah smiles until
Danny, installed as divine king of Kafiristan, succombs to the oldest temptation on
earth and brings disaster to Peachy and himself.

Mowgli stories
   The Jungle Book
   78 min.   color   1967
   Dir: Wolfgang Reitherman. Sp: Larry Clemmons, Ralph Wright, Ken Anderson,
      Vance Gerry. Prod: Buena Vista.
   Voices: George Sanders, Phil Harris, Sebastian Cabot, Louis Prima.
   Animated.

   Mowgli's Brothers
   26 min.   color   1977
   Prod: Chuck Jones. Dist: Xerox
   Voices: Roddy McDowall, June Foray.
   Animated. Wolves adopt and raise a human baby called Mowgli. From them, he
learns about love, justice, and the jungle code of loyalty.

Rikki-Tikki-Tavi
   Rikki-Tikki-Tavi
   26 min.   color   1977
   Prod: Chuck Jones. Dist: Xerox
   Animated. Orson Welles narrates the adventures of a mongoose who is saved from
drowning by an Indian family. The loveable pet becomes a loyal member of the
family and protects them from two dreaded cobras that live nearby.

Soldiers Three in *Soldiers Three and Other Stories*
   Soldiers Three
   95 min.   b&w   1951
   Dir: Tay Garnett. Sp: Marguerite Roberts, Tom Reed, Malcolm Stuart Boylan.
      Prod: M-G-M. Dist: Films Inc.
   Cast: Stewart Granger, Walter Pidgeon.
   Soldiers in India.

KIPLING, RUDYARD (cont'd)

Toomai of the Elephants
    Elephant Boy
    80 min.   b&w   1937
    Dir: Robert Flaherty, Zoltan Korda. Prod: London Film Prod. Dist: Budget,
       Roa's Films.
    Cast: Sabu.
Because of his friendship with Kala Nag, a tremendously large elephant, Tomai
saves his village from stampeding wild elephants.

The White Seal
    The White Seal
    26 min.   color   1977
    Prod: Chuck Jones. Dist: Xerox.
    Animated. Narrated by Roddy McDowall. Kotick, the white seal, learns to
survive in the Bering Sea and puts his knowledge to work to protect his friends too.
When seal hunters invade his island, he guides fellow seals to a safe haven.

Without Benefit of Clergy
    Without Benefit of Clergy
    6 reels   sil.   b&w   1921
    Dir: James Young. Prod: Pathe.
    Cast: Percy Marmont.
    Drama. English engineer John Holden rescues a woman from an
unwelcome suitor in Lahore.

KIRK, LAWRENCE

A Cargo of Innocents
    Stand by for Action
    109 min.   b&w   1942
    Dir: Robert Z. Leonard. Sp: George Bruce, John Balderston, Herman Mankiewicz.
      Prod: Loew's.
    Cast: Robert Taylor
    A boat full of mothers and their children are rescued.

KIRK, RALPH G.

Malloy Campeador in *Saturday Evening Post* (September 17, 1921)
    The Scrapper
    5 reels   sil.   b&w   1922
    Dir: Hobart Henley. Prod: Universal.
    Cast: Herbert Rawlinson, Gertrude Olmstead.
    Romantic drama. A construction engineer falls in love with the contractor's
daughter.

KIRK, RALPH G. (cont'd)

United States Flavor in *Saturday Evening Post* (June 14, 1924)
    Men of Steel
    10 reels   sil.   b&w   1926
    Dir: George Archainbaud. Prod: First National.
    Cast: Milton Sills, Doris Kenyon.
A fugitive mine laborer rises to leadership among the workers at a steel mill
and becomes engaged to the mill owner's daughter, only to have his past catch up
with him.

KIRKLAND, JACK

Honor Bright
    Now and Forever (jt. author Melville Baker)
    82 min.   b&w   1934
    Dir: Henry Hathaway. Prod: Paramount. Dist: Universal.
    Cast: Carole Lombard, Gary Cooper.
A jewel theif tries to go straight for the sake of his little girl. When circumstances
lead him back into crime, he violates the "honor bright" compact he made with his
daughter.

KOMROFF, MANUEL

The Thousand Dollar Bill
    The Small Town Boy
    6 reels   1937
    Dir and Sp: Glenn Tryon. Prod: Grand National Films.
    Cast: Stuart Erwin, Joyce Compton.
A small, timid boy is an easy mark for everyone.

KUTTNER, HENRY see PADGETT, LEWIS (pseud.)

KYNE, PETER B.

All for Love
    Valley of Wanted Men
    b&w   1935
    Prod: Maurice Conn Prod.

Back to Yellow Jacket
    Back to Yellow Jacket
    6 reels   sil.   b&w   1922
    Dir and Prod: Ben Wilson.
    Cast: Roy Stewart, Kathleen Kirkham, Earl Metcalf.

KYNE, PETER B. (cont'd)

Back to Yellow Jacket (cont'd)

Western melodrama. Carmen, wife of Sunny Jim Ballantyne, a prospector, is dissatisfied with her life and attends a public dance with Flush Kirby, a gambler. Eventually she is reconciled with her husband.

Blue Blood and the Pirates in *Saturday Evening Post* (March 30, 1912)

Breed of the Sea

6 reels   sil.   b&w   1926

Dir: Ralph Ince. Adap: J. G. Hawks. Prod: R-C Pictures.

Cast: Ralph Ince, Margaret Livingstone.

Melodrama. Two brothers are in love with the same girl, who is the dean's daughter.

Bread upon the Waters in *Hearst's International Magazine*

A Hero on Horseback

6 reels   sil.   b&w   1927

Dir: Del Andres. Adap: Mary Alice Scully, Arthur Statter. Prod: Universal.

Cast: Hoot Gibson, Ethlyne Clair.

Western melodrama. Billy Gardor, a happy-go-lucky cowboy, loses almost $500 gambling, but he invests $50 in a grubstake with an old prospector, who finds a mine.

Brothers under Their Skins in *Cosmopolitan* (December 1921)

Brothers under the Skin

6 reels   sil.   b&w   1922

Dir: E. Mason Hopper. Prod: Goldwyn Pictures.

Cast: Pat O'Malley, Helene Chadwick.

Comedy drama. Newton Craddock, a shipping clerk, and the vice president of the company have similar marital problems—suspicious, spendthrift wives.

Cappy Ricks stories (a character that appeared in some of Kyne's novels and short stories)

The Affairs of Cappy Ricks

61 min.   b&w   1937

Dir: Ralph Staub. Prod: Republic. Dist: Ivy.

Cast: Walter Brennan, Lyle Talbot.

Cappy, an old codger, sends his family to a desert island to teach them a lesson.

KYNE, PETER B. (cont'd)

Cappy Ricks
6 reels   sil.   b&w   1921
Dir: Tom Forman. Prod: Paramount.
Cast: Thomas Meighan, Agnes Ayres.
Sea melodrama. Cappy objects to the man his daughter loves.

Cornflower Cassie's Concert in *Cosmopolitan* (February 1924)
Beauty and the Bad Man
6 reels   sil.   b&w   1925
Dir: William Worthington. Adap: Frank E. Woods. Prod: Penisual Studios.
Cast: Mabel Ballin, Forrest Stanley, Russell Simpson.
Western melodrama. An orphan marries the organist of the church, but she leaves him when she discovers his low character.

Dog Meat
Blue Blood
72 min.   b&w   1951
Dir: Lew Landers. Prod: Monogram. Dist: Newman.
Cast: Bill Williams, Jane Nigh.
A veteran trainer convinces a wealthy girl to let him train a horse headed for oblivion.

Flaming Guns
Flaming Guns
57 min.   b&w   1932
Dir: Arthur Rosson. Sp: Jack Cunningham. Prod: Universal.
Cast: Tom Mix.
Western.

The Great Mono Miracle (suggestion for)
A Face in the Fog
60 min.   b&w   1936
Dir: Robert Hill. Prod: Victory Picture Corp. Dist: Mogull's.
Cast: June Clude, Lloyd Hughes.
A girl reporter joins the search for a murderer.

The Harbor Bar in *Redbook* (April 1914)
Loving Lies
7 reels   sil.   b&w   1924
Dir: W. S. Van Dyke.
Cast: Evelyn Brent, Monte Blue, Joan Lowell.
Melodrama. Hazards in the line of duty cause marriage problems for the captain of a harbor tugboat.

KYNE, PETER B. (cont'd)

Humanizing Mr. Winsby in *Redbook* (April-May 1915)
  Making a Man
  6 reels   sil.   b&w   1922
  Dir: Joseph Henabery. Prod: Famous Players—Lasky.
  Cast: Jack Holt, J. P. Lockney, Eva Novak.
  Drama. A rich man from California falls upon hard times in New York, only to
be redeemed by the love of the girl who had spurned him in California.

The Light to Leeward
  Homeward Bound
  7 reels   sil.   b&w   1923
  Dir: Ralph Ince. Prod: Paramount.
  Cast: Thomas Meighan.
  Melodrama. First mate Jim Bedford wins his girl and her father's blessing when
he proves his bravery.

Lionized
  Racing Blood
  61 min.   b&w   1936
  Dir and Prod: Maurice Conn.
  Cast: Frankie Darro.
  A boy rescues a crippled horse about to be slaughtered and turns it into a
race horse.

The Man in Hobbles in *Saturday Evening Post* (March 29, 1913)
  The Man in Hobbles
  6 reels   sil.   b&w   1928
  Dir: George Archainbaud. Prod: Tiffany-Stahl.
  Cast: John Harron, Lila Lee.
  A young photographer has to contend with his wife's shiftless family until he
makes good.

A Motion to Adjourn in *Saturday Evening Post* (September 1914)
  A Motion to Adjourn
  6 reels   sil.   b&w   1921
  Dir: Roy Clements. Prod: Ben Wilson Prod.
  Cast: Harry Rattenberry, Roy Stewart.
  Comedy about the disinherited playboy son of a wealthy New York broker and
his induction into the "Ornery and Worthless Men of the World" in a western mining
community.

KYNE, PETER B. (cont'd)

The New Pardner
Hot Off the Press
6 reels   b&w   1935
Dir: Al Herman. Sp: Victor Potel, Gordon S. Griffith. Prod: Victory Pictures.
Cast: Jack LaRue, Monte Blue.
A story about rival newspapers, one backed by crooks.

On Irish Hill
Kelly of the Secret Service
73 min.   b&w   1936
Prod: Principal Prod.
Cast: Lloyd Hughes, Sheila Manners.
A bomb is perfected to keep the enemy fleet from U.S. shores.

One Day's Work
Rio Grande Romance
7 reels   b&w   1936
Dir: Bob Hill. Sp: Al Martin. Prod: Victory Picture Corp.

One Eighth Apache in *Redbook*
Danger Ahead
6 reels   b&w   1935
Dir: Al Herman. Sp: Al Martin. Prod: Victory Picture Corp.
Cast: Lawrence Gray, Sheila Manners.
A gang tries to swindle a sea captain out of $40,000.

One Eighth Apache
6 reels   sil.   b&w   1922
Dir: Ben Wilson. Prod: Berwilla Film Corp.
Cast: Roy Stewart, Kathleen Kirkham.
A man uses murder and scandal to prevent the marriage of his former sweetheart to the son of a cattle and oil baron.

The Parson of Panamint in *The Parson of Panamint and Other Stories* (New
    York, 1929)
The Parson of Panamint
84 min.   b&w   1941
Dir: William McGann. Prod: Paramount.
Western. In a wild town that grew up with a gold strike, a gentle parson is
almost executed as a murderer.

KYNE, PETER B. (cont'd)

The Parson of Panamint (cont'd)
    While Satan Sleeps
    6,069'   sil.   b&w   1922
    Dir: Joseph Henabery. Prod: Famous Players—Lasky.
    Cast: Jack Holt, Wade Boteler, Mabel Van Buren.
    Western melodrama. Phil Webster, alias Slick Phil, son of a minister, escapes
from prison and disguises himself as a minister.

Rustling for Cupid in *Hearst's International Cosmopolitan* (February 1926)
    Rustling for Cupid
    5 reels   sil.   b&w   1926
    Dir: Irving Cummings. Prod: Fox.
    Cast: George O'Brien, Anita Stewart.
    A young man returns from college to his father's ranch and discovers his father
engaging in cattle rustling.

Shipmates
    Taming the Wild
    6 reels   b&w   1936
    Dir: Bob Hill. Sp: Al Martin. Prod: Victory Picture Corp.
    Cast: Brian Washburn, Rod La Rocque.
    A family lawyer protects a headstrong heiress from gangsters.

Ten Dollar Raise in *Saturday Evening Post* (December 4, 1909)
    He Hired the Boss
    6,533'   1942
    Dir: Thomas Z. Loring. Sp: Ben Markson, Irving Cummings, Jr. Prod: Fox.
      Dist: Films Inc.
    Cast: Stuart Erwin, Evelyn Venable.
    A bookkeeper wants a raise and is sold options on lots instead.

    Ten Dollar Raise
    6 reels   sil.   b&w   1921
    Dir: Edward Sloman. Prod: J. L. Frothingham.
    Cast: William V. Mong, Marguerite De La Motte.
    Society melodrama. Wilkins, a bookkeeper for 20 years, does not receive an
expected raise and can't marry Emily. He strikes oil on his property.

    $10 Raise
    6,482'   b&w   1935
    Dir: George Marshall. Sp: Henry Johnson, Louis Breslow. Prod: Fox.
    Cast: Edward Everett Horton, Karen Morley.
    A timid bookkeeper invests in property sold to him by a con man.

KYNE, PETER B. (cont'd)

Thoroughbreds in *Hearst's International Cosmopolitan* (September 1925)
    The Golden Strain
    6 reels   sil.   b&w   1925
    Dir: Victor Schertzinger. Prod: Fox.
    Cast: Hobart Bosworth, Kenneth Harlan.
    Western melodrama. A newly commissioned lieutenant assigned to a cavalry post
fails to lead his men in the first attack by the Indians, but later redeems himself.

The Three Godfathers*
    Bronco Billy and the Baby
    1 reel   sil.   b&w   1908
    Cast: G. M. Anderson.
    Bronco Billy, an outlaw, gives up his freedom to help a lost child and is reformed
by love. Re-issued by Essanay in 1915 as The Three Outlaws. *Note: In 1974
ABC made a TV movie entitled The Godchild, also based on this story.

Hell's Heroes
    7 reels   b&w   1930
    Dir: William Wyler. Adap: Tom Reed. Prod: Universal.
    Cast: Charles Bickford, Raymond Hatton.
    Western melodrama. Three bandits, escaping from the sheriff, come upon a woman
dying during childbirth. She asks them to be the godfathers of her child and to take
the baby to New Jerusalem to its father. Two bandits die on the way; the third dies
after placing the baby on the steps to the church.

The Three Godfathers
    8 reels   b&w   1936
    Dir: Richard Boleslawski. Sp: Edward E. Paramore, Jr., Manuel Seff. Prod:
      M-G-M.
    Cast: Chester Morris, Lewis Stone, Walter Brennan.
    A trio of fugitive gunmen rescue a newborn baby found in a covered wagon with
its dying mother.

Three Godfathers
    105 min.   color   1948
    Dir: John Ford. Sp: Laurence Stallings, Frank S. Nugent. Prod: Argosy Pictures.
    Cast: John Wayne, Pedro Armendariz.
    Set in 19th century Arizona, three robbers become godfathers.

Tidy Toreador in *Cosmopolitan* (April 1927)
    Galloping Fury
    6 reels   sil.   b&w   1927
    Dir: Reaves Eason. Prod: Universal.
    Cast: Hoot Gibson, Otis Harlan.

KYNE, PETER B. (cont'd)

Galloping Fury (cont'd)
Western comedy drama. Infected with poison ivy, a ranch foreman treats it with mud from a marsh, which also improves his looks. The whole town wants to buy some mud.

The Tie That Binds (suggestion for)
Flaming Frontiers (serial)
2 reels each   b&w   1938
Dir: Ray Taylor, Alan James. Sp: Wyndham Gittens, George Plympton, Basil Dickey, Paul Perez. Dist: Thunderbird.
Cast: John Mack Brown, Eleanor Hansen.
A young Indian scout aids a beautiful girl whose brother, the owner of a gold mine, has been framed for murder.

Vengeance of the Lord
Bars of Hate
6 reels   b&w   1936
Dir: Al Herman. Sp: Al Martin. Prod: Victory Pictures.

Without Orders
Without Orders
64 min.   b&w   1936
Dir: Lew Landers. Sp: J. Robert Bren, Edmund L. Hartmann. Prod: RKO.
Cast: Robert Armstrong, Sally Eilers.
A story about the responsibility of airline pilots for their crews.

LACROSSITT, HENRY

The Mob
Homicide Squad
70 min.   b&w   1931
Dir: George Melford. Prod: Universal.
Cast: Leo Carrillo, Noah Beery.
Drama. The police hunt a big-time gangster, whose own son is forced to frame him.

LAMBERT, RIETA

Clipped Wings
  Hello Sister
  62 min.   b&w   1930
  Dir: Alan Crosland, Erich von Stronheim. Prod: Sono Art World Wide Pictures.
    Dist: Films Inc.
  Cast: ZaSu Pitts, James Dunn.

L'AMOUR, LOUISE

The Gift of Cochise in *Collier's*
  Hondo
  93 min.   color   1955
  Dir: John Farrow. Prod: Wayne-Fellows Prod.
  Cast: John Wayne, Geraldine Page.
  Hondo Lane (1874) works as a dispatch rider for the U.S. Cavalry. He comes
upon a woman and her son who have been deserted by her husband after an Apache
attack.

  Hondo and the Apaches
  1967
  Dir: Lee Katzin. Sp: Andrew Fenady. Prod: M-G-M.
  Cast: Robert Taylor, Ralph Taeger, Noah Beery, Jr.
  A re-make of Hondo for TV and overseas markets.

Plunder
  The Tall Stranger
  81 min.   color   1957
  Dir: Thomas Carr. Prod: Allied Artists. Dist: Ivy.
  Cast: Joel McCrea, Virginia Mayo.
  Western. A wagon train of settlers fight off desperados.

Unidentified story
  Four Guns to the Border
  83 min.   color   1954
  Dir: Richard Carlson. Sp: George Van Marter, Franklin Coen. Prod: Universal.
  Cast: Rory Calhoun, Colleen Miller, George Nader.
  Western. After a bank robbery, an outlaw gang helps an ex-gunslinger and his
beautiful daughter fight off Apaches.

LANGELAAN, GEORGE

The Fly in *Science Fiction: Greatest Science Fiction and Fantasy*
  The Fly
  95 min.   color   1958

LANGELAAN, GEORGE (cont'd)

The Fly (cont'd)
Dir: Kurt Neumann. Prod: 20th Century Fox. Dist: Budget, Macmillan, Roa's,
Select
Cast: Vincent Price, Patricia Owens.

A scientist discovers a method of disintegrating objects and then materializing them at a distance. When he experiments on himself, a housefly intrudes in the experiment, and their atoms become confused. The man's head ends up on the fly's, and vice versa. The Return of the Fly, based on the characters in the original, was produced in 1959 as was The Curse of the Fly in 1965, both by 20th Century Fox.

LANHAM, EDWIN

The Senator Was Indiscreet
The Senator Was Indiscreet
81 min.   b&w   1947
Dir: George S. Kaufman. Sp: Charles MacArthur. Prod: Universal.
Cast: William Powell, Ella Raines.

Comedy drama. A boisterous senator who wants to be the next President, decides that the way to win the nomination is to repeatedly state that he is not a candidate for the office.

Unidentified story
It Shouldn't Happen to a Dog
6,279'   b&w   1946
Dir: Herbert I. Leeds. Sp: Eugene Ling, Frank Gabrielson. Prod: 20th Century
Fox. Dist: Films Inc.
Cast: Carol Landis, Allyn Joslyn.

A reporter flirts with a lady cop to get an exclusive story.

LARDNER, JOHN (jt. author) see Finger Man under LIPSIUS, MORRIS

LARDNER, RING

Alibi Ike
Alibi Ike
72 min.   b&w   1935
Dir: Ray Enright. Prod: Warner Bros. Dist: United Artists.
Cast: Joe E. Brown, Olivia De Havilland.

Romantic comedy. A modest baseball player nearly forfeits his team's chances by modestly denying his real love.

LARDNER, RING (cont'd)

Champion in *American Omnibus*, ed. by Carl Van Doren (Doubleday, 1933)
 Champion
 99 min.   b&w   1948
 Dir: Mark Robson. Prod: Screen Players Corp. Dist: Budget, Ivy, Kit Parker,
  Macmillan.
 Cast: Kirk Douglas, Arthur Kennedy.
 A young man's ruthlessness takes him to the top of the prizefighting profession.
This film received an Academy Award for best editing and won four other
nominations.

LARKIN, JOHN FRANCIS

Customer's Girl
 She Had to Say Yes
 64 min.   b&w   1933
 Dir: Busby Berkeley. Prod: First National Pictures and Vitaphone. Dist: United
  Artists.
 Cast: Loretta Young, Lyle Talbot.
 A girl entertains an out-of-town buyer and gets in trouble.

LAWRENCE, DAVID HERBERT

The Rocking Horse Winner
 The Rocking Horse Winner
 91 min.   b&w   1950
 Dir: Anthony Pelessier. Prod: Two Cities Films. Dist: Janus.
 Cast: John Mills, Valerie Hobson.
 Paul Grahame, a sensitive 10-year-old boy, hears his parents fighting about money.
He is given a toy rockinghorse and soon begins discussing the art of racing and
handicapping with the handyman. He chooses many winners, but first he must race
his own rockinghorse and soon the strain is too much for him.

 The Rocking-Horse Winner
 30 min.   color   1977
 Dir: Peter Medak. Adap: Julian Bond. Dist: Learning Corp.
 Cast: Kenneth More.
 A young boy is disturbed by the arguments between his father and mother over
money. Convinced by his mother that lack of luck is to blame, Paul becomes
obsessed by the need to be lucky. On his rocking-horse he suddenly learns how to
predict the outcome of the races with disastrous results.

LEA, FANNY HEASLIP

The Peacock Screen
  Cheaters
  68 min.   b&w   1934
  Dir: Phil Rosen. Prod: Liberty Pictures Corp.

LEE, CONNIE

Unidentified story
  Swing It Professor
  6 reels   b&w   1937
  Dir: Marshall Neilan. Sp: Nicholas H. Barrows, Robert St. Clair. Prod:
    Ambassador Pictures.

LE FANU, SHERIDAN

Carmilla in *In a Glass Darkly*
  Blood and Roses
  74 min.   color   1961
  Dir: Roger Vadim. Prod: Paramount. Dist: Films Inc.
  Cast: Mel Ferrer, Elsa Martinelli, Annette Stroyberg.
  Vampire-spirit Carmilla, who has been dormant for several hundred years, takes
over the body and soul of a look-alike relative when an Army mine frees her spirit.

  Terror in the Crypt (Br. title Crypt of Horror)
  84 min.   b&w   1960
  Dir: Thomas Miller. Dist: Audio Brandon.
  A father must deal with the spirit of a vampire which has been reincarnated into
the body of his daughter. Horrified by her bloodlust, the Count employs an exorcist
to vanquish the demon.

  The Vampire Lovers (Br.)
  88 min.   color   1970
  Dir: Roy Ward Baker. Sp: Tudor Gates. Dist: United Films.
  Cast: Ingrid Pitt, Pippa Steel.
  Horror. Carmilla befriends and kills young women. Two sequels were made: Lust
for a Vampire (1970) and Twins of Evil (1971).

  Vampyr
  66 min.   b&w   1931
  Dir: Carl Dreyer. Sp: Christen Jul, Carl Dreyer.
  Cast: Julian West, Sybille Schmitz, Maurice Schutz.
  The story of David Gray and his misadventures in vampire-laden Eastern Europe.
The director is known for use of his settings to convey dark moods and heavy texture.

LEIGHTON, FLORENCE (pseud. of Florence Leighton Pfalzgraf)

Heaven's Gate
  Our Little Girl
  63 min.   b&w   1935
  Prod: Fox
  Cast: Shirley Temple, Joel McCrea.
  A troubled only child tries to patch up her parents' differences.

LEIGHTON, WILL R.

The Able-Minded Lady in *Saturday Evening Post*
  The Ableminded Lady
  5 reels   sil.   b&w   1922
  Dir: Ollie Sellers. Prod: Pacific Film Co.
  Cast: Henry B. Walthall, Elinor Fair, Helen Raymond.
  A cowboy bachelor works for a three-time widow who eventually wins him, too.

LEINSTER, MURRAY (pseud. of WILL F. JENKINS)

The Purple Hieroglyph in *Snappy Stories* (March 1, 1920)
  Murder Will Out
  6 reels   b&w   1930
  Dir: Clarence Badger. Prod: First National Pictures.
  Cast: Lila Lee, Jack Mulhall, Noah Beery.
  A Chinese gang blackmails a businessman.

LE NOIR, PHILIP

The Man Who Wouldn't Take Off His Hat in *Argosy All-Story Weekly*
  (August 19, 1922)
  The Devil's Bowl
  5 reels   sil.   b&w   1923
  Dir: Neal Hart. Prod: William Steiner Prod.
  Cast: Catherine Bennett, W. J. Allen, Neal Hart.
  Western melodrama. Sam rescues his sister from marriage to a horse thief.
Re-issued or re-made in 1924 under the title Branded a Thief.

LEONARD, ELMORE

The Captives
  The Tall T
  78 min.   1957
  Dir: Budd Boetticher. Prod: Columbia.
  Cast: Randolph Scott, Richard Boone.
  Western. Scott battles Boone and his band of outlaws.

LEONARD, ELMORE (cont'd)

3:10 to Yuma
   3:10 to Yuma
   92 min.   b&w   1957
   Dir: Delmer Daves. Prod: Columbia. Dist: Audio Brandon.
   Cast: Glenn Ford, Van Heflin, Felicia Farr.
   A rancher is faced with the responsibility of putting a notorious killer on the
gallows-bound train to Yuma. As other volunteers quit or are killed by the outlaw's
gunmen, he alone is left with the prisoner.

LEWIS, HERBERT CLYDE

D-Day in Las Vegas
   Lady Luck
   97 min.   b&w   1946
   Dir: Edwin L. Marin. Prod: RKO. Dist: Films Inc.
   Cast: Robert Young, Barbara Hale.
   Comedy drama. A nice girl tries to tame a high-rolling gambler by marrying him.

LEWIS, SINCLAIR

Bongo
   Fun and Fancy Free
   s.m. "Jack and the Beanstalk" (fairy tale)
   73 min.   color   1947
   Prod: Walt Disney Prod. Dist: Films Inc., Roa's Films.
   Animated. Narration and songs by Dinah Shore and Jiminey Cricket. A story
of Bongo the circus bear, and other Disney characters.

The Ghost Patrol in *Selected Short Stories* (Garden City, N.Y., 1935)
   The Ghost Patrol
   5 reels   sil.   b&w   1923
   Dir: Ralph Graves. Prod: Universal.
   Cast: Ralph Graves, Bessie Love, George Nichols.
   Drama. Kind policeman Donald Dorgan helps Terry go straight and wins approval
from his girls' father.

Let's Play King in *Selected Short Stories*
   Forbidden Adventure
   6,950'   b&w   1931
   Dir: Norman Taurog. Sp: Edward E. Paramore, Jr., Joseph L. Mankiewicz.
     Prod: Paramount.
   Cast: Mitzi Green, Jackie Searl.
   A story of the enmity between two jealous women.

LIEBE, HAPSBURG

Trimmed and Burned in *Collier's* (September 1921)
    Trimmed
    5 reels   sil.   b&w   1922
    Dir: Harry Pollard. Prod: Universal.
    Cast: Hoot Gibson, Patsy Ruth Miller.
    Western comedy drama. A man, expected by the political boss to be easy to manipulate, remains an honest sheriff.

LINDNER, ROBERT M.

Destiny's Tot in *The Fifty Minute Hour*
    Pressure Point
    89 min.   b&w   1962
    Dir: Hubert Cornfield. Prod: Larcus. Dist: United Artists.
    Cast: Sidney Poitier, Bobby Darin, Peter Falk.
    A tense drama of a Nazi Bundist in America in the 1930s and the black prison psychiatrist who tries to straighten out his mind.

LINDSEY, JUDGE BEN

Little Colored White Cloud
    One Mile from Heaven
    7 reels   b&w   1937
    Dir: Allan Dwan. Prod: Fox.
    Cast: Clair Trevor, Sally Blane.
    A young Negro woman brings up a white child and battles in court to keep her.

LIPSIUS, MORRIS

Finger Man
    Finger Man (jt. author John Lardner)
    82 min.   b&w   1955
    Dir: Harold Schuster. Sp: Warren Douglas. Prod: Allied Artists. Dist: Ivy.
    Cast: Frank Lovejoy, Forrest Tucker.
    Crime melodrama. To avoid prison, an ex-convict turns informer and assists the FBI in breaking up a syndicate.

LITTLETON, SCOTT

Inside Story
    Night Editor
    s.m. radio show Night Editor
    68 min.   b&w   1946
    Dir: Henry Levin. Prod: Columbia.
    Cast: William Gargan, Janis Carter.
    Melodrama. A B-picture about a crooked cop and a luscious, but mean, woman.

LOCKRIDGE, FRANCIS see LOCKRIDGE, RICHARD

LOCKRIDGE, RICHARD

Several stories about Mr. and Mrs. North (jt. author Frances Lockridge)
Mr. and Mrs. North
s.m. a play by Owen Davis about these characters
7 reels b&w   1942
Dir: Robert B. Sinclair. Prod: M-G-M.
Cast: Gracie Allen, William Post, Jr.
A mystery farce.

LOFTS, NORA

Chinese Finale in *I Met a Gypsy* (London, 1935)
Seven Women
93 min. color   1966
Dir: John Ford. Sp: Janet Green, John McCormick. Prod: M-G-M. Dist: Films Inc.
Cast: Anne Bancroft, Sue Lyon, Margaret Leighton.
In China during the turbulent 1930s, an isolated missionary post is headed by a
strait-laced spinster. She eagerly awaits the new resident doctor, who turns out to
be breezy, profane, drinking, chain-smoking Bancroft dressed in riding breeches.

LONDON, JACK

The Abysmal Brute
Conflict
63 min. b&w   1936
Dir: David Howard. Sp: Charles A. Logue, Walter Weems. Prod: Universal.
Cast: John Wayne, Jean Rogers.
Drama. A beautiful girl reporter tries to discover if a lumberjack is actually in
cahoots with a fake fight racket.

All Gold Canyon
All Gold Canyon
21 min. color   1973
Prod: Kratky Film, Prague. Dist: Indiana University.
A prospector discovers gold, works his claim, and is ambushed. The prospector's
struggle to overcome his enemy is shown, with an open-ended conclusion.

Brown Wolf
Brown Wolf
30 min. color   1972
Dir: George Kaczender. Dist: Learning Corp., Syracuse University.
Two people attempt to possess a wild and beautiful dog after it is separated from
its master. When the master returns after two years, the couple let the dog chose its
future master.

LONDON, JACK (cont'd)

Demetrios Cantos in *Tales of the Fish Patrol* (New York, 1905)
  Devil's Skipper
  6 reels   sil.   b&w   1928
  Dir: John G. Adolfi. Prod: Tiffany Prod.
  Cast: Belle Bennett, Montagu Love.
  Drama. The female commander of a slave ship lures aboard a man who has caused
her suffering, and has him tortured. She then turns over the young girl with him to
her crew, but learns later that the girl is her own daughter.

Flush of Gold in *Lost Face and Children of the Frost* (N.Y., Macmillan)
  Alaska
  8 reels   b&w   1944
  Dir: George Archainbaud. Sp: George Wallace Sayre, Harrison Orkow. Prod:
    Monogram.

Gold Hunter of the North
  North to the Klondike
  s.m. story by William Castle adapted from Jack London's story
  70 min.   b&w   1941
  Dir: Erle C. Kenton. Sp: Clarence Upson Young, Lew Sarecky, George Bricker.
    Prod: Universal. Dist: Mogull's.
  Cast: Broderick Crawford, Lon Chaney, Jr.
  Adventure. Gold is discovered on the land owned by a beautiful girl.

The Mexican
  The Fighter
  78 min.   b&w   1952
  Dir: Herbert Kline. Prod: G. H. Prod. Dist: Budget.
  Cast: Richard Conte, Lee J. Cobb.
  A poor Mexican patriot comes to America at the turn of the century. To obtain
money for guns so that his people can free themselves from ruthless dictators, he
becomes a fighter.

A Raid on the Oyster Pirates in *Tales of the Fish Patrol*
  Tropical Nights
  6 reels   b&w   sil.   1928
  Dir: Elmer Clifton. Prod: Tiffany-Stahl.
  Cast: Patsy Ruth Miller, Malcolm McGregor.
  Melodrama. A young woman thinks she is responsible for the death of a
businessman dealing in pearls.

LONDON, JACK (cont'd)

The Siege of the Lancashire Queen in *Tales of the Fish Patrol*
　　Prowlers of the Sea
　　6 reels　　　　sil.　　　　　b&w　　　　　1928
　　Dir: John G. Adolfi. Prod: Tiffany-Stahl.
　　Cast: Carmel Myers, Ricardo Cortez.
　　Drama. An honest man is put in charge of the Coast Guard, but he succumbs to
the charms of a beautiful, dishonest woman.

Son of the Wolf in *Tales of the Far North*
　　Son of the Wolf
　　5 reels　　　　sil.　　　　　b&w　　　　　1928
　　Dir: Norman Dawn. Prod: Tiffany-Stahl.
　　Cast: Wheeler Oakman, Edith Roberts.
　　Melodrama. Scruff Mackenzie falls in love with his Indian ward, Chook-Ra, but
he must prove he loves her to her Indian people.

The Story of Jees Uck in *Faith of Men and Other Stories* (N.Y., 1904)
　　The Mohican's Daughter
　　5 reels　　　　sil.　　　　　b&w　　　　　1922
　　Dir: S. E. V. Taylor. Prod: PTB Inc.
　　Romantic drama. A half-breed girl defies Indian law by getting medicine for a
sick child, and flees to the trading post manager for help.

That Spot
　　Sign of the Wolf
　　80 min.　　　　b&w　　　　　1941
　　Dir: Howard Bretherton. Prod: Monogram. Dist: Mogull's.
　　Cast: Michael Whelan, Grace Bradley.
　　Two dogs battle in the Canadian wilds.

A Thousand Deaths
　　Torture Ship
　　57 min.　　　　b&w　　　　　1939
　　Prod: Producers Releasing Corp. Dist: United Films.
　　Cast: Lyle Talbot, Sheila Bromley.

To Build a Fire
　　To Build a Fire
　　56 min.　　　　color　　　　　1969
　　Dir: David Cobham. Dist: Audio Brandon, Kit Parker.
　　Cast: Ian Hogg.
　　Narrated by Orson Welles. A lone man travels through the -75° weather of the
Alaskan wilderness.

LONDON, JACK (cont'd)

To Build a Fire (cont'd)
> To Build a Fire
> 14½ min.   color   1975
> Dir: Robert Stitzel. Dist: BFA.
> The encounter between man and nature in freezing cold weather.

The Unexpected
> By the Law (USSR)
> 61 min.   sil.   b&w   1926
> Dir: Lev Kuleshov. Dist: Kit Parker.
> Cast: Sergei Komarov, Alexandra Khokhlova.
> A psychological drama. A member of a party goes on a killing rage in a log cabin in Alaska.

White and Yellow in *Tales of the Fish Patrol*
> The Haunted Ship
> 5 reels   sil.   b&w   1927
> Dir: Forrest K. Sheldon. Adap: E. Morton Hough. Prod: Tiffany-Stahl.
> Cast: Dorothy Sebastian, Montagu Love.
> Thinking his wife was unfaithful, Captain Simon Grant sets her and their son afloat in a small boat.

The White Silence in *Best Short Stories* (N.Y., Sun Dial, 1945)
> Romance of the Redwoods
> 63 min.   b&w   1939
> Dir: Charles Vidor. Prod: Columbia. Dist: Institutional Cinema Service.
> Cast: Jean Parker, Charles Bickford.
> Adventure, photographed in the Redwood country. The story concerns men and women in a logging camp.

Wife of the King
> Wife of the King
> 1928
> Prod: Tiffany-Stahl Prod.

Yellow Handkerchief in *Brown Wolf and Other Jack London Stories*, ed. by Franklin K. Mathiews (New York, 1920)
> Stormy Waters
> 6 reels   sil.   b&w   1928
> Dir: Edgar Lewis. Adap: Harry Dittmar. Prod: Tiffany-Stahl.
> Cast: Eve Southern, Malcolm McGregor, Roy Stewart.
> Melodrama. Though David is engaged to be married, he succumbs to the temptation of Lola, a barfly, while on a seafaring trip to Buenos Aires.

LONG, AMELIA REYNOLDS

The Thought-Monster
    Fiend Without a Face
    75 min.   b&w   1958
    Dir: Arthur Crabtree. Dist: Modern.
    Cast: Marshall Thompson, Kim Parker, Terence Kilburn.
    In a small Canadian town, the U.S. Air Force has set up a secret radar station.
Agaonizing deaths occur when the radar is at full power. Autopsies reveal that the
brains and spinal cords of the victims are missing.

LORD, MINDRET

Unidentified story
    Alias Nick Beal
    93 min.   1949
    Dir: John Farrow. Prod: Paramount.
    Cast: Ray Milland, Thomas Mitchell.
    An honest District Attorney is sidetracked by a mysterious satanic stranger.

LOVECRAFT, H. P.

Case of Charles Dexter Ward
    The Haunted Palace
    85 min.   color   1963
    Dir: Roger Corman. Prod: Roger Corman. Dist: Audio Brandon.
    Cast: Vincent Price, Debra Paget, Lon Chaney, Jr.
    Though the title is taken from Poe's story, the film is based almost entirely on
Lovecraft's story. A warlock, burned at the stake, returns to possess the body of
his sole descendant.

The Colour Out of Space in *Amazing Stories* (September 1927)
    Die, Monster, Die!
    80 min.   color   1965
    Dir: Daniel Haller. Prod: American International. Dist: Budget, Roa's,
        Macmillan.
    Cast: Boris Karloff, Nick Adams, Patrick Magee.
    Because of a radioactive meteor, the ancient lord of a mouldering estate is slowly
transformed into a monster, gradually losing his sanity and his human qualities.

The Dreams in the Witch-House (uncredited)
    The Crimson Cult
    87 min.   color   1970
    Dir: Vernon Sewall. Dist: Budget, Macmillan, Modern.
    Cast: Boris Karloff, Christopher Lee, Mark Eden, Barbara Steele.

LOVECRAFT, H. P. (cont'd)

The Crimson Cult (cont'd)
A young man seeking his brother goes to Grey Marsh Lodge. At the family grave-yard he finds a witches' shrine with a crimson sacrificial altar; more horrors await him.

The Dunwich Horror
   The Dunwich Horror
   90 min.   color   1970
   Dir: Daniel Haller. Sp: Curtis Lee Hanson. Dist: Audio Brandon, Wholesome Film
      Center.
   Cast: Sandra Dee, Dean Stockwell, Sam Jaffe.
The town of Dunwich turns into a haven for the practice of the black mass and black magic. Stockwell plays a student of the Devil who lures Sandra Dee to his estate.

The Shuttered Room in *The Shuttered Room and Other Pieces* (Sauk City, Wis., 1959)
   The Shuttered Room (Br.)
   100 min.   color   1968
   Dir: David Greene. Prod: Warner Bros. Dist: Kerr, Modern, Roa's.
   Cast: Gig Young, Carol Lynley, Oliver Reed, Flora Robson.
An attractive couple assume their inheritance. They insist on seeing their house, and the mystery of the shuttered room is revealed.

LOWNDES, MRS. BELLOC

Shameful Behavior in *Studies in Wives* (New York, 1910)
   Shameful Behavior?
   6 reels   sil.   b&w   1926
   Dir: Albert Kelley. Prod: Preferred Pictures.
   Cast: Edith Roberts, Richard Tucker.
   Romantic comedy. A young flapper poses as Sally, an escapee from an insane asylum, but the joke wears thin.

LUNDQUIST, ARTHUR

A series of unidentified stories
   The Time of Desire
   1958
   Prod: Europa Films.

LUTHER, BARBARA

Moon Walk in *Ladies Home Journal* (February 1962)
   A Ticklish Affair
   89 min.   color   1963

LUTHER, BARBARA (cont'd)

A Ticklish Affair (cont'd)
Dir: George Sidney. Sp: Ruth Brooks Flippen. Prod: M-G-M. Dist: Films Inc.
Cast: Shirley Jones, Gig Young, Red Buttons.
Comedy. The escapades of a widow, her three sons, and a naval officer.

LYLE, EUGENE P., JR.

The Ringtailed Galliwampus in *Saturday Evening Post* (July 15, 1922)
Try and Get It
6 reels   sil.   b&w   1924
Dir: Cullen Tate. Adap: Jules Furthman.
Cast: Bryant Washburn, Billie Dove.
Comedy drama. Two young bill collectors must collect a debt.

LYNCH, JAMES CHARLES

Battle of Pilgrim Hill in *Saturday Evening Post*
Hurricane at Pilgrim Hill
65 min.   b&w   1953
Dir: Richard Bare. Prod: Howco. Dist: Budget, Macmillan.
Cast: Clem Bevans, Cecil Lellaway, David Bruce.
Pop Snedley, a cantankerous old screwball, visits his son in the quiet town of Pilgrim Hill and soon sets it on its ear.

LYNDON, BARRE

A *Saturday Evening Post* story
Sundown
90 min.   b&w   1941
Dir: Henry Hathaway. Prod: United Artists. Dist: Films Inc.
Cast: Gene Tierney, Bruce Cabot, George Sanders.
Melodrama. A British settlement in Africa is aided by a jungle girl in defeating the Nazis.

MaCAULEY, RICHARD
Ready, Willing and Able
  Ready, Willing and Able
  93 min.   b&w   1937
  Dir: Ray Enright. Prod: Warner Bros. Dist: United Artists.
  Cast: Jane Wyman, Ruby Keeler.
  Musical. A stage-struck girl pretends to be a London musical star.

Special Arrangement
  Melody for Two
  60 min.   b&w   1936
  Dir: Louis King. Prod: Warner Brothers and Vitaphone. Dist: United Artists.
  Cast: James Melton, Patricia Ellis.
  Musical. A clash between rival singers.

Unidentified story
  Riding on Air
  70 min.   b&w   1937
  Eir: Edward Sedgwick. Prod: RKO. Dist: Mogull's.
  Cast: Joe E. Brown, Guy Kibbee.
  Joe Brown takes up flying.

MacDONALD, JOHN D.
Taint of the Tiger in *Cosmopolitan* (March 1958)
  Man-Trap
  93 min.   b&w   1961
  Dir: Edmond O'Brien. Sp: Ed Waters. Prod: Tiger Prod.
  Cast: Jeffrey Hunter, David Janssen.
  Melodrama. Matt Jameson becomes involved in the recovery of $3,500,000 for a
Central American dictator.

MacGRATH, HAROLD
You Can't Always Tell in *Redbook Magazine* (December 1925)
  Womanpower
  7 reels   sil.   b&w   1926
  Dir: Harry Beaumont. Prod: Fox.

MacGRATH, HAROLD (cont'd)

Womanpower (cont'd)
Cast: Ralph Graves, Kathryn Perry.
Comedy drama. A rich, young idler becomes a fighter.

MACHARG, WILLIAM BRIGGS

The Price of a Party in *Cosmopolitan*
The Price of a Party
6 reels   sil.   b&w   1924
Dir: Charles Giblyn. Prod: Howard Estabrook Prod.
Cast: Hope Hampton, Harrison Ford.
A broker hires a poor, but beautiful cabaret dancer to prevent a hated business rival from exercising a valuable option.

Wine in *Hearst's International Magazine* (March 1922)
Wine
7 reels   sil.   b&w   1924
Dir: Louis J. Gasnier. Prod: Universal.
Cast: Clara Bow, Forrest Stanley.
Melodrama. Facing financial ruin, John joins up with the bootleggers.

MacISAACS, FRED

Unidentified story
Mysterious Crossing
56 min.   b&w   1936
Dir: Arthur Lubin. Sp: Jefferson Parker, John Grey. Prod: Universal.
Cast: James Dunn, Jean Rogers.
Mystery. A reporter tries to solve the murder of a man killed on a Mississippi boat.

MACK, WILLARD

The Public Be Damned
Night of Terror
65 min.   b&w   1933
Dir: Benjamin Stoloff. Sp: Beatrice Van, William Jacobs, Lester Nielson. Prod:
    Columbia.
Cast: Bela Lugosi, George Meeker, Tully Marshal.
A maniac killer is on the loose.

MAC ORLAN, PIERRE

Port of Shadows
   Port of Shadows
   90 min.   b&w   1939
   Dir: Marcel Carne. Prod: Film Alliance. Dist: Contemporary McGraw-Hill.
   Cast: Jean Gabin, Michele Morgan.

MAGRUDER, MARY

Courage in *Young's Magazine*
   Satan and the Woman
   7 reels   sil.   b&w   1928
   Dir: Burton King. Prod: Excellent Pictures.
   Cast: Claire Windsor, Cornelius Keefe.
   Drama. A ruthless old woman tries to crush the romance of her heir and a grand-
daughter whose blood relationship she had refused to acknowledge.

MALAMUD, BERNARD

Angel Levine in *Commentary* (December 1955)
   The Angel Levine
   107 min.   color   1970
   Dir: Jan Kadar, Chiz Schultz. Dist: Macmillan.
   Cast: Zero Mostel, Harry Belafonte, Ida Kaminska.
   Down on his luck, a tailor finds a black man sitting in his kitchen who claims that
he can work a miracle if the tailor has faith in him.

MALLOY, DORIS (jt. author) see Mad Parade under ORR, GERTRUDE

MANN, E. B.

Stampede
   Stormy Trails
   59 min.   b&w   1936
   Prod: Grand National
   Cast: Rex Bell.
   A fighting cowpoke.

MANN, THOMAS

Tonio Kröger (novella) in *Death in Venice*
   Tonio Kröger (Fr./W. Ger., English subtitles)
   90 min.   b&w   1968
   Dir: Rolf Thiele. Prod: Pathe Contemporary. Dist: Contemporary McGraw-Hill.
   Cast: Jean-Claude Brialy, Nadja Tiller, Gert Frobe.
   A story about growing up in Germany in the late 19th century.

MANNES, MARYA

The Woman Who Was Scared
   Forever Darling
   91 min.   color   1956
   Dir: Alexander Hall. Prod: M-G-M. Dist: Films Inc.
   Cast: Lucille Ball, Desi Arnaz.
   A guardian angel who looks like a movie star saves the marriage of a scatter-
brained wife and her long-suffering husband.

MANSFIELD, KATHERINE

The Garden Party
   The Garden Party
   24 min.   color   1974
   Prod: Gurian/Sholder Prod. Dist: Paramount Communications.
   After World War II, a young girl makes her first acquaintance with death when a
neighboring farmer is killed in an accident the day of her mother's party. She is upset
and wants her mother to call off the party.

MARCIN, NATALIE

You Can't Fool a Marine
   Anchors Aweigh
   140 min.   color & b&w   1945
   Dir: George Sidney. Prod: M-G-M. Dist: Films Inc.
   Cast: Gene Kelly, Frank Sinatra.
   Two prowling gobs on a damsel-hunting expedition in Hollywood: one is a sea-
going Don Juan, the other a slightly backward, gawky chump.

MARKEY, GENE

Blinky in *Blue Book* (January 1923)
   Blinky
   6 reels   sil.   b&w   1923
   Dir: Edward Sedgwick. Prod: Universal.
   Cast: Hoot Gibson.
   Romantic comedy. Blinky proves his worth to the cavalry.

Close Harmony (jt. author Elsie Janis)
   Close Harmony
   7 reels   b&w   1929
   Dir: John Cromwell, Edward Sutherland. Adap: Percy Heath. Prod: Paramount
      Famous Players—Lasky.
   Cast: Charles Rogers, Nancy Carroll.
   Musical comedy drama. A girl interferes with a band's big chance.

MARMUR, JACLAND

No Home of His Own in *Saturday Evening Post*
   Return from the Sea
   80 min.   b&w   1954
   Dir: Lesley Selander. Prod: Allied Artists. Dist: Hurlock Cine World.
   Cast: Neville Brand, Jan Sterling.
   A chief mate finds romance in San Diego before shipping out again.

MARQUAND, JOHN PHILLIPS

Only a Few of Us Left in *Saturday Evening Post* (January 1922)
   High Speed Lee
   5 reels   sil.   b&w   1923
   Dir and Adap: Dudley Murphy. Prod: Atlantic Features.
   Cast: Reed Howes.
   Society comedy drama. A wealthy, idle young man falls for a young girl, who is
unhappy because he does not take an interest in the family tire business. When he
does, the executives quit.

The Right That Failed in *Four of a Kind* (New York, 1923)
   The Right That Failed
   5 reels   sil.   b&w   1922
   Dir: Bayard Veiller. Prod: Metro Pictures.
   Cast: Bert Lytell, Virginia Valli.
   A boxing champ, resting at a summer resort, falls in love with a society girl with
the approval of her father and the opposition of her stuffy finané.

That Girl and Mr. Moto
   Think Fast, Mr. Moto
   5,961'   b&w   1937
   Dir: Norman Foster. Sp: Howard Ellis Smith, Norman Foster. Prod: Fox. Dist:
      Warner Brothers.
   Cast: Peter Lorre.
   A suave, sinister man solves baffling crimes.

MARTIN, THORNTON (jt. author) see The Band Plays On under STUHLDREHER,
HARRY

MASON, FRANK VAN WYCK

International Team
   The Spy Ring
   70 min.   b&w   1938
   Dir: Joseph H. Leiws. Sp: author. Prod: Trem Carr. Dist: Universal.

MASON, FRANK VAN WYCK (cont'd)

The Spy Ring (cont'd)
Cast: William Hall, Jane Wyman.
Drama. Spies are hot on the trail of a young inventor.

MASON, GRACE SARTWELL

Clarissa and the Post Road in *Saturday Evening Post* (July 14, 1923)
Man Crazy
6 reels   sil.   b&w   1927
Dir: John Francis Dillon. Adap: Perry Nathan. Prod: Charles R. Rogers Prod.
Cast: Dorothy Mackaill, Jack Mulhall.
Against her grandmother's wishes, a carefree daughter of an aristocratic New England family falls for a handsome truckdriver, and aids him in a fight against bootleggers.

Speed in *Saturday Evening Post* (October 18-25, 1924)
Speed
6 reels   sil.   b&w   1925
Dir: Edward J. Le Saint. Prod: Banner Prod.
Cast: Betty Blythe, Pauline Garon.
Melodrama. Jazz-mad young people pursue pleasure recklessly until the heroine is kidnapped.

MATSON, NORMAN

Larger Than Life
He Couldn't Say No*
s.m. Larger Than Life, a play by Joseph Shrank in turn based on the story
7 reels   b&w   1937
Dir: Lewis Seiler. Prod: Warner Brothers. Dist: United Artists.
Cast: Jane Wyman, Frank McHugh.
An office clerk is harrassed by his girlfriend's mother. *Note: Prior movie title was Larger Than Life.

MATTIESSON, PETER

Travelin Man in *Harper's* (February 1957)
The Young One (Mex.)
96 min.   b&w   1961
Dir: Luis Bunuel. Prod: Olmec Prod.
Cast: Zachary Scott, Bernie Hamilton, Kay Meersman.
A black man fleeing the law is drawn into a web of danger.

MAUGHAM, W. SOMERSET

The Alien Corn see Quartet under Facts of Life

The Ant and the Grasshopper
    Encore
    s.m. "Winter Cruise," "Gigolo and Gigolette"
    90 min.   1951
    Dir: Pat Jackson. Prod: Two Cities Films.
    Cast: Glynis Johns, Kay Walsh, Nigel Patrick.
    In one story a playboy tries to get money from his brother; in another, a spinster
makes things rough on a ship. A high-dive artist fears an accident in the third tale.

The Colonel's Lady see Quartet under Facts of Life

Facts of Life
    Quartet (Br.)
    s.m. "The Alien Corn," "The Kite," "The Colonel's Lady"
    108 min.   b&w   1949
    Dir: Ken Annakin, Arthur Crabtree, Harold French, Ralph Smart. Prod: J. Arthur
        Rank. Dist: Walter Reade 16.
    Cast: Mai Zetterling, Cecil Parker, George Cole.
    Four stories ranging from the comic to the dramatic.

Gigolo and Gigolette see Encore under The Ant and the Grasshopper

The Kite see Quartet under Facts of Life

The Letter (a short story and a play)
    The Letter
    97 min.   b&w   1940
    Dir: William Wyler. Prod: Warner Brothers. Dist: United Artists.
    Cast: Bette Davis, Herbert Marshall, Gale Sondergaard.
    A wife, on trial for murdering her lover, must retrieve an incriminating letter.

    The Letter
    1963
    Prod: M-G-M.

Theatre
    Adorable Julia (Fr./Aust., subtitles)
    s.m. unidentified short stories
    106 min.   b&w   1963

MAUGHAM, W. SOMERSET (cont'd)

Adorable Julia (cont'd)
Dir: Alfred Weidenmann. Dist: Kit Parker.
Cast: Lili Palmer, Charles Boyer, Jean Sorel, Jeanne Valerie.
Comedy. An actress fighting an apparently losing battle with middle age pretends that her 18-year-old son is 15, and then takes on a very young lover.

Lord Mountdrago
Three Cases of Murder
s.m. "In the Picture," by Roderick Wilkinson
99 min.   1955
Dir: George More O'Ferrall for Lord Mountdrago; Wendy Toye for In the Picture.
Cast: Orson Welles, Alan Badel, for Lord Mountdrago; Alan Badel, Hugh Pryse, for In the Picture.
A trio of tales, two of which are based on short stories. In Lord Mountdrago, a hex is put on a man who is placed in embarrassing situations in his dreams. In the Picture is about a mad artist who lives within a painting at a museum; he entices people to enter it and they never leave.

Mr. Know All see Trio under The Verger

Rain in *The Trembling of a Leaf* (New York, 1921)
Miss Sadie Thompson
91 min.   1953
Dir: Curtis Bernhardt. Sp: Harry Kleiner. Prod: Columbia.
Cast: Rita Hayworth, Jose Ferrer.

Rain
91 min.   b&w   1932
Dir: Lewis Milestone. Prod: Feature Prod. Dist: Thunderbird.
Cast: Joan Crawford, Walter Huston, Guy Kibbee.
The most celebrated version of the story, vividly capturing the lives of several very different people during a fierce monsoon. Joan Crawford plays a prostitute, whom the minister tries to reform.

Sadie Thompson
s.m. Rain, a play by John Colton and Clemence Randolph
9 reels   sil.   b&w   1929
Dir: Raoul Walsh. Prod: Gloria Swanson Prod.
Cast: Gloria Swanson, Lionel Barrymore, Raoul Walsh.
Melodrama. A minister saves a woman from her immorality, but later tries to seduce her.

MAUGHAM, W. SOMERSET (cont'd)

The Verger
   Trio (Br.)
   s.m. "Mr. Know All," "The Sanitorium"
   91 min.   b&w   1951
   Dir: Ken Annakin. Prod: Gainsborough Pictures. Dist: Walter Reade 16.
   Cast: Jean Simmons, Michael Rennie.
   Three separate stories about a church verger, an obnoxious passenger on a ship,
and a romance in a sanitorium.

The Vessel of Wrath in *Box Office*, comp. by Marjorie Barrows and George Eaton
   (New York, 1943)
   Beachcomber
   88 min.   b&w   1939
   Dir: Erich Pommer. Prod: Laughton Pommer-Mayflower Prod. Dist: Budget,
      Kit Parker.
   Cast: Charles Laughton, Elsa Lanchester.
   Comedy drama. A delightful non-conformist finds that his life takes a somersault
when a prim reformer invades his South Sea Island home.

The Beachcomber
   82 min.   color   1955
   Dir: Muriel Box. Prod: United Artists.
   Cast: Robert Newton.
   A bum meets a missionary's sister on a tropical island and his life is changed.

Winter Cruise see Encore under The Ant and the Grasshopper

MAUPASSANT, GUY DE

Angel and Sinner (Boule de Suif)
   Angel and Sinner (Fr.)
   90 min.   b&w   1946
   Dist: Film Classic Exchange.

The Woman Disputed (subtitles)
   s.m. The Woman Disputed, a play by Denison Clift
   9 reels   b&w   sil.   1928
   Dir: Henry King, Sam Taylor. Prod: United Artists.
   Cast: Norma Talmadge, Gilbert Roland.
   War drama. An Austrian and a Russian soldier reform a prostitute who helps
save the lives of 10,000 men.

MAUPASSANT, GUY DE (cont'd)

He

He (Fr., subtitles)
85 min.   b&w   1933
Prod: Astor Pictures. Dist: Trans-National Films.
Cast: Fernandel.

The House of Madame Tellier see Le Plaisir under The Mask

The Horla
Diary of a Madman
s.m. based on three stories, primarily "La Horla" in *Gil Blas* (October 26, 1886);
    the other two are unidentified
96 min.   color   1962
Dir: Reginald Le Borg. Sp: Robert E. Kent. Dist: United Artists.
Cast: Vincent Price, Nancy Kovack, Ian Wolfe.
A possessed man is forced to kill.

The Job in *Little Rogue and Other Stories* (N.Y., Knopf, 1924)
Boccaccio '70
s.m. the film consists of "acts" and the second act is based on this story
145 min.   color   1962
Dir: Frderico Fellini, Luchino Visconti, Vittorio de Sica. Prod: Concordia cia
    cinematographie—Cineraz. Dist: Macmillan.
Cast: Sophia Loren, Romy Schneider.
Three episodes. The first, The Raffle, is about a timid soul who wins a liaison
with a girl; The Bet is about an aristocrat's wife who takes a job as his mistress;
in The Temptation of Dr. Antonio a voluptuous poster comes alive for a puritani-
cal fanatic.

Mademoiselle Fifi
Mademoiselle Fifi
68 min.   b&w   1944
Dir: Robert Wise. Prod: RKO. Dist: Films Inc.
Cast: Simone Simon, Jason Robards, Sr.
A young laundress repulses a German officer and joins the French underground.

The Mask
Le Plaisir (Fr.)
s.m. "The Model," "The House of Madame Tellier"
95 min.   b&w   1953
Dir: Max Ophuls. Prod: Stera Films. Dist: Kit Parker.
Cast: Danielle Darrieux, Claude Dauphin.

MAUPASSANT, GUY DE (cont'd)

Le Plaisir (cont'd)
In The Mask a wife describes to a doctor how her aging husband visits a dance hall wearing a mask to hide his wrinkles. The House of Madame Tellier concerns a woman who closes her brothel so she and her girls can attend her niece's first communion. The Model is about a young painter who has an affair with a model. She throws herself from a window because of her love for him, and breaks her legs.

The Model see Le Plaisir under The Mask

Paul's Mistress (Le Femme de Paul)
Masculine-Feminine
s.m. "The Sign"
103 min.   b&w   1966
Dir: Jean Luc-Godard. Prod: Columbia. Dist: Swank.
Cast: Jean-Pierre Leaud.
An updated portrayal of youthful Paris, mingling sex with violence, in the story of a callow young man and a free-wheeling young woman.

The Sign see Masculine-Feminine

Unidentified stories
End of Desire (Fr.)
86 min.   1962
Dir: Alexander Astruc. Prod: Contintental.
Cast: Maria Schell, Christian Marquand.
A wealthy girl discovers that her husband married her so he could pay off his debts.

McCALL, MARCY C., JR.

Fraternity
On the Sunny Side
69 min.   b&w   1941
Dir: Harold Schuster. Prod: 20th Century Fox. Dist: Select.
Cast: Roddy McDowall, Jane Sarwell.
A London lad whose family was bombed out by the blitz comes to live with an American family. The American son becomes jealous of him.

Revolt
Scarlet Dawn
58 min.   b&w   1932
Dir: William Dieterle. Prod: Warner Brothers. Dist: United Artists.
Cast: Douglas Fairbanks, Jr., Nancy Carroll, Lilyan Tashman.

McCALL, MARCY C., JR. (cont'd)

Scarlet Dawn (cont'd)
During the height of the Russian Revolution, a prince, saved by a devoted female servant, marries her and together they flee to Paris.

Mc CULLEY, JOHNSTON

The Brute Breaker in *All-Story Weekly* (August 10, 1918)
The Ice Flood
6 reels   sil.   b&w   1926
Dir: George B. Seitz. Prod: Universal. Dist: Mogull's.
Cast: Kenneth Harlan, Viola Dana.
Melodrama. Jack cleans up the tough timber camps on his northwest property.

El Torbellino
The Black Pirates
73 min.   color   1954
Dir: Allen H. Miner. Sp: Fred Freiberger. Prod: Salvador Films. Dist; Newman.
Cast: Anthony Dexter.
Adventure melodrama. A band of pirates forces terrorized villagers to dig for buried treasure.

King of Cactusville
Outlaw Deputy
60 min.   b&w   1935
Dir: Otto Brower. Prod: Puritan Picture Corp. Dist: Trans-American.
Cast: Tim McCoy.
A reformed outlaw becomes a sheriff.

The Sign of Zorro
s.m. Zorro stories and *The Curse of Capistrano*, a magazine serial later published
    as a novel
90 min.   b&w   1960
Dir: Norman Foster, Lewis R. Foster. Prod: Walt Disney Prod. Dist: Roa's Films.
Cast: Guy Williams, Henry Calvin.
Re-edited from the TV shows. The daring escapades of the romantic rogue who righted the wrongs of evil-doers in early Spanish California.

Unidentified stories
Mark of the Renegade
81 min.   color   1951
Dir: Hugo Fregonese. Sp: Robert Hardy Andrews, Louis Solomon. Prod:
    Universal.

Mc CULLEY, JOHNSTON (cont'd)

Mark of the Renegade (cont'd)
Cast: Ricardo Montalban, Cyd Charisse, J. Carrol Naish.
Western, set in 1824. A renegade is forced to romance a beautiful girl.

McGIBNEY, DONALD

Two Arabian Nights in *McClure's Magazine*
Two Arabian Nights
9 reels   sil.   b&w   1927
Dir: Lewis Milestone. Prod: Caddo Co.
Cast: William Boyd, Mary Astor.
Romantic comedy. Two Army men are imprisoned by the Germans but escape
disguised as Arabs.

When the Desert Calls in *Ladies Home Journal* (May 1920)
When the Desert Calls
6 reels   sil.   b&w   1922
Dir: Ray C. Smallwood. Prod: Pyramid Pictures.
Cast: Violet Heming, Robert Frazer.
Melodrama. Discredited, a man feigns suicide. His wife finds shelter with a
sheik's widow.

McGIVERN, WILLIAM

The Big Heat, serialized in *Saturday Evening Post* (begun December 27, 1952)
The Big Heat
90 min.   b&w   1953
Dir: Fritz Lang. Prod: Columbia. Dist: Audio Brandon.
Cast: Glenn Ford, Lee Marvin, Gloria Grahame.
Dave Bannion (Ford), a police detective, is determined to expose the circum-
stances surrounding a fellow officer's suicide, although he is warned by his superior
to give up the investigation.

McGRATH, HAROLD

Beautiful Bullet in *Redbook* (November 1927)
Danger Street
6 reels   sil.   b&w   1928
Dir: Ralph Ince. Sp: Enid Hibbard. Prod: FBO Prod.
Cast: Warner Baxter, Martha Sleeper.
Underworld melodrama. A society clubman, weary of life, purposely gets
involved in a gun fight with local gangs.

McGUINESS, JAMES K.

Pearls and Emeralds
   Cocktail Hour
   8 reels   b&w   1933
   Dir: Victor Schertzinger. Sp: Gertrude Purcell. Prod: Columbia.

McHUGH, MARTIN J. (jt. author) see The Rising of the Moon under
O'CONNOR, FRANK

McKENNEY, RUTH

Several unidentified stories
   Margie (jt. author Richard Bransten)
   94 min.   b&w   1946
   Dir: Henry King. Prod: Fox. Dist: Macmillan, Select.
   Cast: Jeanne Crain, Glenn Langan.
   Comedy of high school life in the 1920s.

McNEILE, H. C. see SAPPER (pseud.)

McNUTT, WILLIAM SLAVENS

His Good Name in *Collier's* (July 22, 1922)
   Trifling with Honor
   8 reels   sil.   b&w   1923
   Dir: Harry A. Pollard. Prod: Universal.
   Cast: Rockliffe Fellowes, Fritzi Ridgeway.
   Drama. A former convict makes good as a baseball player.

Leander Clicks
   Hot Tip
   7 reels   b&w   1935
   Dir: Ray McCarey, James Gleason. Sp: Hugh Cummings, Olive Cooper, Louis
      Stevens. Prod: RKO.
   A man risks his family fortune at the racetrack.

McSHERRY, GARY

Good Boy
   Scandal at Scourie
   90 min.   color   1953
   Dir: Jean Negulesco. Sp: Leonard Spigelgass, Karl Tunberg. Prod: Loew's. Dist:
      Films Inc.
   Cast: Greer Garson, Walter Pidgeon.
   A story about the problems of a Canadian couple living in a small town who want
to adopt an orphan.

MELVILLE, BAKER see Now and Forever under KIRKLAND, JACK

MELVILLE, HERMAN

Bartleby, the Scrivener in *Selected Writings of Herman Melville* (Modern Library, 1952)
Bartleby
28 min.　　color　　1969
Prod and Dist: Encyclopaedia Britannica
Story of the man who "preferred not to."

Bartleby (Br.)
1972
Dir: Anthony Friedman. Sp: Rodney Carr-Smith, Anthony Friedman. Prod: Maron.
Cast: Paul Scofield, John McEvery.
An updated version of the story in which the boss, though he empathizes with Bartleby, must fire him. But Bartleby won't go.

The Happy Failure
　The Happy Failure
　15 min.　　b&w　　1955
　Prod: Dynamic Films. Dist: Macmillan.
　Cast: Monty Woolley.
　An old man is taught by his nephew that material success is less important than happiness.

The Lightning-Rod Man
　The Lightning-Rod Man
　16 min.　　color　　1975
　Dir: John DeChancie. Dist: Pyramid.
　A heated debate between an aggressive lightning-rod salesman and a home owner who relishes rather than fears the excitement of an electrical storm.

MÉRIMÉE, PROSPER

Carmen in *Golden Tales from Merimee* (N.Y., Dodd, 1929)
　Carmen was made as four silent films: Carmen (U.S., 1913); Carmen (U.S., 1915); Us (U.S., with Charlie Chaplin), and Carmen (Fr., 1926).
　Carmen (subtitles)
　85 min.　　b&w　　1947
　Prod: Scalera Films, Rome. Dist: Modern.
　Cast: Viviane Romance, Jean Marias, Eli Parvo.
　Carmen, a Spanish gypsy employed in a tobacco factory in Seville, is ruthless and without conscience; she lives solely for her own pleasure.

MÉRIMÉE, PROSPER (cont'd)

Carmen (cont'd)
Carmen, Baby (U.S., Yugoslavia, Ger.)
90 min.   color   1967
Dir: Rodley Metzger. Sp: Jesse Vogel.
Cast: Uta Leuka, Claude Ringer.
An updating of the story with rock 'n' roll music and a good deal of sex.

Carmen Jones
105 min.   1955
Dir: Otto Preminger. Prod: Caryle Productions.
Cast: Dorothy Dandridge, Harry Belafonte, Pearl Bailey.
An updating of the Oscar Hammerstein II play based on the story.

The Devil Made a Woman (Spain)
s.m. Carmen, a play by Georges Bizet, Henri Meilhac, Ludovic Halevy
90 min.   color   1962
Dir: Tulio Demicheli.
Cast: Sarita Montiel, George Mistral.
Antonio, a leader of the Spanish guerillas (1812), takes refuge with Carmen.

The Loves of Carmen
98 min.   color   1948
Dir: Charles Vidor. Prod: Beckworth Corp.
Cast: Rita Hayworth, Glenn Ford.
The story of a soldier's love for a gypsy.

MERRICK, LEONARD

Laurels and the Lady in *The Man Who Understood Women and Other Stories*
(London, 1908)
Fool's Paradise
9 reels   sil.   b&w   1921
Dir: Cecil B. DeMille. Prod: Famous Players—Lasky.
Cast: Dorothy Dalton.
Melodrama. An ex-service man falls in love with Rosa; he is tricked by a dancer
into marrying.

Magnificent Lie
8 reels   b&w   1931
Dir: Berthold Viertel. Sp: Vincent Laurence, Samson Raphaelson. Prod:
Paramount Publix.
Cast: Ralph Bellamy, Ruth Chatterton.
A cafe singer impersonates a French actress.

MICHENER, JAMES A.

Until They Sail in *Return to Paradise*
Until They Sail
95 min.   b&w   1957
Dir: Robert Wise. Sp: Charles Schnee. Prod: M-G-M. Dist: Films Inc.
Cast: Joan Fontaine, Sandra Dee, Piper Laurie, Jean Simmons.
A four-part soap opera about four sisters during wartime in New Zealand.

MILLER, ALICE DUER

The Adventuress
The Keyhole
69 min.   b&w   1933
Dir: Michael Curtiz. Prod: Warner Bros. Dist: United Artists.
Cast: Kay Francis, George Brent.
A jealous husband hires a detective, and lives to regret it.

Are Parents People? in *Are Parents People?* (New York, 1924)
Are Parents People?
5 reels   sil.   b&w   1925
Dir: Malcolm St. Clair. Prod: Famous Players—Lasky. Dist: Cinema 8 (8mm)
Cast: Betty Bronson, Adolphe Menjou, Florence Vidor, André Beranger.
Comedy. Lita reconciles her parents by getting expelled from school, after they
file for a divorce.

The Charm School in *Saturday Evening Post*
The Charm School
5 reels   sil.   b&w   1920
Dir: James Cruze. Prod: Famous Players—Lasky.

The Princess and the Plumber in *Bishop's Nephew* (originally published in *Saturday
Evening Post*, December 14-28, 1929)
The Princess and the Plumber
7 reels   b&w   1930
Dir: Alexander Korda. Sp: Howard J. Green. Prod: Fox.
Cast: Charles Farrell, Maureen O'Sullivan.
Romantic comedy. An unsophisticated princess goes vacationing in the moun-
tains with a rich American and a Baron; she falls in love with the American.

MILLER, ARTHUR

Esquire story
The Misfits
124 min.   b&w   1961
Dir: John Huston. Sp: Arthur Miller. Prod and Dist: United Artists.

MILLER, ARTHUR (cont'd)

The Misfits (cont'd)
Cast: Clark Gable, Marilyn Monroe, Montgomery Clift.
The story of three sometime-cowboys and a recent divorcee whom they meet in
Reno. Each sees the woman as an idealized image—of mother, wife, sweetheart,
mistress. The woman herself is confused but loving, and passionately desires freedom.

MILLER, MARY ASHE (jt. author) see The Man Who Married His Own Wife under
WILSON, JOHN FLEMING

MILLER, SETON I.

Public Enemy No. 1
"G" Men
85 min.   b&w   1935
Dir: William Keighley. Prod and Dist: United Artists.
Cast: James Cagney, Lloyd Nolan, Margaret Lindsay.
A young man, raised and educated by an unknown gang leader, joins the G-Men
to track down racketeers.

MILLHOLLAND, RAY

Island Doctor
Girl from God's Country
54 min.   b&w   1940
Dir: Sidney Salkow. Prod: Republic. Dist: Ivy.
Cast: Jane Wyatt, Charles Bickford.
A nurse in Alaska helps a doctor in trouble with the law for the mercy killing
of his father.

MITCHELL, RUTH COMFORT

Into Her Kingdom in Redbook Magazine
Into Her Kingdom
7 reels   sil.   b&w   1926
Dir: Svende Gade. Adap: Carey Wilson. Prod: Corinne Griffith Prod.
Cast: Corinne Griffith, Einar Hanson.
Romantic drama. A Russian peasant is sent to Siberia for allegedly insulting the
Grand Duchess of Tatiana; seven years later, upon her release, she joins the
Bolsheviks.

MOFFITT, JACK

Hawk's Mate
Central Airport
75 min.   b&w   1933

MOFFITT, JACK (cont'd)

Central Airport (cont'd)
Dir: William Dieterle. Prod: First National and Vitaphone. Dist: United Artists.
Cast: Richard Barthelmess, Sally Eilers.
A love triangle in the aviation game.

MONTAYNE, CHARLES EDWARD

Her Night of Nights in *Snappy Stories* (October 10-25, 1921)
Her Night of Nights
5 reels   sil.   b&w   1922
Dir: Hobart Henley. Prod: Universal.
Cast: Marie Prevost, Edward Hearn.
Romantic comedy drama. Molly, a model, spurns the advances of the boss's son
in favor of a shipping clerk.

Judith in *Action, and Other Stories* (Garden City, N.Y., 1929)
True Heaven
6 reels   sd. effects   b&w   1929
Dir: James Tinling. Prod: Fox.
Cast: George O'Brien, Lois Moran.
War melodrama. A British soldier falls in love with a German agent.

MOONEY, MARTIN

Special Agent
Special Agent
76 min.   b&w   1935
Dir: William Keighley. Prod: Warner Bros. Dist: United Artists.
Cast: Bette Davis, George Brent.
A mystery melodrama about a newspaperman who plays ball with an evil
racketeer, in order to obtain some incriminating evidence.

MOORE, OLGA

Quintuplets to You
You Can't Beat Love
7 reels   b&w   1937
Dir: Christy Cabanne. Sp: David Silverstein, Maxwell Shane. Prod: RKO.
Cast: Joan Fontaine, Preston Foster.
The daughter of a mayoralty candidate dares a playboy to become her father's
rival.

MORGAN, BYRON see also The Band Plays On under STUHLDREHER, HARRY

MORGAN, BYRON

The Hell Diggers in *Saturday Evening Post* (October 2, 1920)
    The Hell Diggers
    5 reels   sil.   b&w   1921
    Dir: Frank Urson. Prod: Famous Players–Lasky.
    Cast: Wallace Reid, Lois Wilson.
    Melodrama. A construction superintendent falls in love with a farmer's daughter.
Her father leads a group opposed to the destruction of the land.

Too Much Speed in *Saturday Evening Post* (May 28, 1921)
    Too Much Speed
    5 reels   sil.   b&w   1921
    Dir: Frank Urson. Prod: Famous Players–Lasky.
    Cast: Wallace Reid, Agnes Ayres.
    Action melodrama. Pat retires from racing to please his father-in-law-to-be, but
eventually goes back to it.

MORRIS, EDMUND

San Siandro Killings
    The Savage Guns
    73 min.   color   1962
    Dir: Michael Carreras. Sp: author. Prod: M-G-M. Dist: Films Inc.
    Cast: Richard Basehart, Don Taylor.
    Bandits oppose a ranger in Mexico.

MORRIS, GORDON

Auf Wiedersehen (jt. author Morton Barteau)
    Six Hours to Live
    78 min.   b&w   1932
    Dir: William Dieterle. Sp: Bradley King. Prod: Fox.
    Cast: Warner Baxter, Irene Ware, George Marion.
    A murdered diplomat returns to life and catches the murderer.

MORRIS, GOUVERNEUR

The Man Who Played God
    The Man Who Played God
    s.m. The Silent Voice, a play based on the story
    6 reels   sil.   b&w   1922
    Dir: Harmon White. Prod: Distinctive-United Artists.
    Cast: George Arliss.
    Drama. A musician loses his hearing; his depression sorely tests his wife.

MORRIS, GOUVERNEUR (cont'd)

The Man Who Played God (cont'd)
    The Man Who Played God
    83 min.   b&w   1932
    Dir: John Adolfi. Prod: Warner Bros. Dist: United Artists.
    Cast: George Arliss, Bette Davis.
    A great musician who becomes deaf goes into a depression. Eventually he learns
to read lips and finds meaning in life again.

You Can't Get Away With It in *Incandescent Lily, and Other Stories* (New York,
    1914)
    You Can't Get Away With It
    6 reels   sil.   b&w   1923
    Dir: Rowland V. Lec. Prod: Fox.
    Cast: Percy Marmont, Malcolm McGregor.
    Romantic drama. Jill enters into an illicit alliance with her employer when his wife
refuses to divorce him.

MORRIS, REBECCA

The Good Humor Man in *New Yorker*
    One Is a Lonely Number
    97 min.   color   1972
    Dir: Mel Stuart. Prod: M-G-M. Dist: Films Inc.
    Cast: Trish Van Devere, Monte Markham, Janet Leigh, Melvyn Douglas.
    Suddenly abandoned by her husband, a young woman faces the lonely task of find-
ing her own identity, earning a living, and seeking a new life.

MORROW, HONORE

Benefits Forgotten (novelette)
    Of Human Hearts
    110 min.   b&w   1938
    Dir: Clarence Brown. Prod: M-G-M. Dist: Films Inc.
    Cast: Walter Huston, James Stewart.
    A study of rural life where a young man rebels against his religion.

MOSS, GEOFFREY MAJOR

Unidentified story
    Isn't Life Wonderful
    99 min.   sil.   b&w   1924
    Dir: D. W. Griffith. Dist: Audio Brandon, Museum of Modern Art.
    Cast: Carol Dempster, Neil Hamilton, Helen Lowell.
    The painful struggle for food is offset by the powerful love between Inga (Carol)
and Hans (Neil).

MUIR, AUGUSTUS

Ocean Gold
  The Phantom Submarine
  7 reels   b&w   1940
  Dir: Charles Barton. Sp: Joseph Krumgold. Prod: Columbia.

MUMFORD, ETHEL WATTS

Everything Money Can Buy in *Hearst's International* (August 27, 1924)
  After Business Hours
  5,600'   sil.   b&w   1925
  Dir: Mal St. Clair. Prod: Columbia.
  Cast: Elaine Hammerstein, Lou Tellegen.
  Society melodrama. June marries a wealthy young man in order to have whatever
money can buy, but he refuses to give her money of her own.

MUNI, BELLE

Unwanted
  The Deceiver (jt. author Abem Finkel)
  7 reels   b&w   1931
  Dir: Louis King. Adap: Charles Logue. Prod: Columbia.

MUNSON, AUDREY

Studio Secrets in *Hearst's Sunday Magazine*
  Heedless Moths
  s.m. "Life Story" and others
  6 reels   sil.   b&w   1921
  Dir: Robert Z. Leonard. Prod: Perry Plays.
  Cast: Holmes E. Herbert, Hedda Hopper.
  Melodrama. A model is asked to pose for a Greenwich Village painter but his
intentions are not wholly artistic. She flees and is found by an old man who introduces her to a famed sculptor.

MURPHY, DUDLY see Jazz Heaven under FORNEY, PAULINE

MUSSELMAN, MORRIS see She Had to Eat under GRANT, JAMES EDWARD

MYGATE, GERALD

Two Can Play in *Saturday Evening Post* (February 25–March 4, 1922)
  Two Can Play
  6 reels   sil.   b&w   1926
  Dir: Nat Ross. Prod: Encore Pictures.

MYGATE, GERALD (cont'd)

Two Can Play (cont'd)
Cast: George Fawcett, Allan Forrest.
Society melodrama. A wealthy man who disapproves of his daughter's fiancé tries to discredit him.

NASON, LEONARD

Rodney in *Gallant Horses* (N.Y., Macmillan, 1938)
    Keep 'em Rolling
    b&w   1934
    Prod: RKO.

NAZARRO, RAY (jt. author) see Jimmy the Gent under DOYLE, LAIRD

NEBEL, FREDERICK

The Bribe
    The Bribe
    98 min.   b&w   1949
    Dir: Robert Z. Leonard. Sp: Marguerite Roberts. Prod: M-G-M. Dist: Films Inc.
    Cast: Robert Taylor, Ava Gardner.
    A war surplus racket in the tropics is broken up.

No Hard Feelings
    Smart Blonde
    59 min.   b&w   1936
    Dir: Frank McDonald. Prod: Warner Brothers and Vitaphone. Dist: United Artists.
    Cast: Glenda Farrell, Barton MacLane.
    A mettlesome reporter named Torchy Blane, aided by an irate police lieutenant, nabs the villian.

    A Shot in the Dark
    60 min.   b&w   1941
    Dir: William McCann. Prod: Warner Bros. Dist: United Artists.
    Cast: William Lundigan, Ricardo Cortez.
    A reporter tracks down a murderer.

NEIDIG, WILLIAM J.

The Snob in *Saturday Evening Post* (September 28, 1918)
    The Snob
    5 reels   sil.   b&w   1921
    Dir: Sam Wood. Prod: Realart.
    Cast: Wandy Hawley, Edwin Stevens.
    Drama. Kathryn snubs a poor boy working his way through college.

Tracked to Earth in *Saturday Evening Post*
    Tracked to Earth
    5 reels   sil.   b&w   1922
    Dir: William Worthington. Prod: Universal.
    Cast: Frank Mayo, Virginia Valli.
    A railroad agent, though innocent, is arrested as a horse thief.

NEWHOUSE, EDWARD

Come Again Another Day
    Shadow in the Sky
    78 min.   b&w   1951
    Dir: Fred M. Wilcox. Sp: Ben Maddow. Prod: M-G-M. Dist: Films Inc.
    Cast: Ralph Meeker, Nancy Davis.
    A war-shocked veteran disrupts the lives of his relatives who have given him a home.

Several unidentified stories
    I Want You
    102 min.   b&w   1952
    Dir: Mark Robson. Prod: Samuel Goldwyn. Dist: Macmillan.
    Cast: Dana Andrews, Dorothy McGuire.
    The effect of the Korean War on the typical American family is dramatized.

NEWSOM, J. D.

The Rest Cure
    We're in the Legion Now
    8 reels   color   1937
    Dir: Crane Wilbur. Sp: Roger Whately. Prod: Edward L. Alperson.
    Cast: Reginald Denny, Esther Ralston.
    Two confidence men join the Legion.

Sowing Glory
    Trouble in Morocco
    7 reels   b&w   1937
    Dir: Ernest B. Schoedsack. Sp: Paul Franklin. Prod: Columbia.

NORRIS, KATHLEEN

Manhattan Love Song
  Change of Heart
  87 min.   b&w   1943
  Dir: Albert Rogell. Prod: Fox. Dist: Ivy.
  Cast: Susan Hayward, John Carroll.
  A midwest song writer thinks a young song publisher has stolen her song.

Poor, Dear Margaret Kirby in *Poor, Dear Margaret Kirby and Other Stories* (New
  York, 1913)
  Poor, Dear Margaret Kirby
  5 reels   sil.   b&w   1921
  Dir: William P. S. Earle. Prod: Selznick Pictures.
  Cast: Elaine Hammerstein, William B. Donaldson.
  A society woman is forced to take in boarders when her husband, beset with
financial difficulties, attempts suicide and becomes seriously ill.

OATES, JOYCE CAROL

In the Region of Ice
  In the Region of Ice
  38 min.   b&w   1977
  Prod: A. Guttfreund, P. Werner. Dist: Phoenix Films.
  Cast: Fionnoulla Flanagan, Peter Lempert.
  A brilliant, but disturbed Jewish student seeks help from his college English pro-
fessor, a Catholic nun named Sister Irene. She is touched but unable to help.

O'CONNOR, FLANNERY

A Circle in the Fire
  A Circle in the Fire
  49½ min.   color   1976
  Dir: Victor Nunez. Dist: Perspective Films.
  The security of the Cope farm is shattered by a visit from three teen-aged boys.
Jealous of the farm's tranquility, the boys slowly destroy that which they cannot
possess—first with petty vandalism, finally with cruel malice.

O'CONNOR, FLANNERY (cont'd)

Comforts of Home
    Comforts of Home
    40 min.   color   1974
    Dir: Jerome Shore. Prod: Leonard Lipson. Dist: Phoenix Films.
    A seemingly happy mother-son relationship is disrupted by a young girl who
enters the family household. She has a tremendous effect on them both, tragically for
the mother.

The Displaced Person
    The Displaced Person
    57½ min.   color   1977
    Dir: Glenn Jordan. Sp: Horton Foote. Dist: Perspective.
    Cast: Irene Worth, John Houseman.
    The "displaced person" is a conscientious but driven Polish refugee who arrives
on a Georgia farm in the late 1940s. An elderly priest means well, but fails in his
efforts to integrate the Pole with the people on the farm.

Good Country People
    Good Country People
    32 min.   color   1975
    Dir, Prod, and Dist: Jeff Jackson.
    A traveling salesman seduces an unattractive woman with a wooden leg, who
has returned to her hometown with a Ph.D. in philosophy and finds she is out of
place.

O'CONNOR, FRANK

The Majesty of the Law
    The Rising of the Moon
    s.m. "The Minutes Wait," a story by Martin J. McHugh and The Rising of the
      Moon, a play by Lady Gregory
    81 min.   b&w   1957
    Dir: John Ford. Prod: Four Province Prod. Dist: Warner Bros.
    Cast: Noel Purcell, Denis O'Dea.

OLIVER, JENNIE HARRIS

Several unidentified stories
    Mokey
    9 reels   b&w   1942
    Dir: Wells Root. Sp: Root, Jan Fortune. Prod: M-G-M.
    Cast: Bobby Blake, Donna Reed.
    A child must get used to his stepmother.

OPPENHEIM, E. PHILIPS

Numbers of Death in *Spies and Intrigues* (Boston, Little, 1936)
 Monte Carlo Nights
 70 min.   b&w   1934
 Dir: William Nigh. Prod: Monogram. Dist: Mogull's.
 Cast: Mary Brain, John Darrow.
 A young man, convicted of murder, escapes and with one club he is able to find the real murderer.

OPPENHEIMER, GEORGE

Baby Face (jt. author George Bruce)
 Killer McCoy
 103 min.   b&w   1947
 Dir: Roy Rowland.Prod: M-G-M. Dist: Films Inc.
 Cast: Mickey Rooney, Brian Donlevy.

ORNITZ, SAMUEL

Tong War
 Chinatown Nights
 83 min.   b&w   1929
 Dir: William Wellman. Prod: Paramount. Dist: Universal.
 Cast: Wallace Beery, Florence Vidor.
 A society woman, caught in the midst of a tong war in Chinatown, is rescued.

ORR, GERTRUDE

Women Like Men (jt. author Doris Malloy)
 Mad Parade
 7 reels   b&w   1931
 Dir: William Beadine. Sp: Henry McCarthy, Frank R. Conklin. Prod: Paramount.

ORR, MARY

The Wisdom of Eve
 All about Eve
 s.m. a radio play
 139 min.   b&w   1950
 Dir: Joseph L. Mankiewicz. Prod: 20th Century Fox. Dist: Films Inc.
 Cast: Bette Davis, Anne Baxter, George Sanders.
 An older actress, near the end of her fabulous career, does battle with a calculating, treacherous newcomer.

OSBOURNE, LLOYD

The Man Who in *Saturday Evening Post* (January 1, 1921)
    The Man Who
    6 reels   sil.   b&w   1921
    Dir: Maxwell Karger. Adap: Arthur J. Zellner. Prod: Metro Pictures.
    Cast: Bert Lytell, Lucy Cotton.
    To protest the soaring price of shoes and to gain importance in the eyes of a rich girl, a poor bank clerk refuses to wear shoes on the street and causes a sensation in New York.

OXFORD, JOHN BARTON

The Man-Tamer in *Redbook* (April 1918)
    The Man Tamer
    5 reels   sil.   b&w   1921
    Dir: Harry B. Harris. Prod: Universal.
    Cast: Gladys Walton, Rex De Roselli.
    A female lion-tamer is called upon by a profligate millionaire to tame his hard-drinking son.

PACKARD, FRANK L.

The Iron Rider in *All-Story Magazine* (March 11-April 8, 1916)
    Smiles Are Trumps
    5 reels   sil.   b&w   1922
    Dir: George E. Marshall. Prod: Fox.
    Cast: Maurice B. Flynn, Ora Carew.
    Melodrama. A young man discovers that his boss is cheating the company.

The Wrecking Boss in *The Night Operator* (New York, 1919)
    The Crash
    8 reels   sil.   b&w   1928
    Dir: Eddie Cline. Prod: First National Pictures.
    Melodrama. A man's jealousy and drinking cause his wife to leave him.

PADGETT, LEWIS (pseud. of Henry Kuttner)

The Twonky
    The Twonky
    72 min.   b&w   1953
    Dir and Sp: Arch Oboler. Prod: United Artists.
    Cast: Hans Conreid, Billy Lynn, Gloria Blondell.
    Science fiction. A creature from the future invades a TV set and tries to protect
and serve the set's owner, but the owner kills it.

PAGANO, JO

Double Jeopardy
    Murder Without Tears
    64 min.   b&w   1953
    Dir: William Beaudine. Prod: Allied Artists. Dist: Ivy.
    Cast: Craig Stevens, Joyce Holden.
    A series of murders keeps detective Stevens busy.

PALMER, STUART

The Riddle of the Dangling Pearl
    The Plot Thickens
    7 reels   b&w   1936
    Dir: Ben Homes. Sp: Clarence Upson Young, Jack Townley. Prod: RKO.
    Cast: ZaSu Pitts, Louise Latimer.
    An unmarried schoolteacher foils the theft of a priceless museum piece.

The Riddle of the 40 Naughty Girls
    Forty Naughty Girls
    7 reels   b&w   1937
    Dir: Edward Cline. Sp: John Grey. Prod: RKO.
    Cast: James Gleason, Joan Woodbury.
    A schoolteacher's friend solves two murders blundered by the police.

PARKER, DOROTHY see Horsie under ASHWORTH, JOHN

PARKER, GILBERT

The Lodge in the Wilderness in *Northern Lights* (New York, 1909)
    The Lodge in the Wilderness
    6 reels   sil.   b&w   1926
    Dir: Henry McCarthy. Prod: Tiffany Prod.
    Cast: Anita Stewart, Edmund Burns.
    Jim, a young engineer in a Northwest logging camp, is convicted and jailed for
a murder though he is innocent. His sweetheart clears him.

PARKER, GILBERT (cont'd)

She of the Triple Chevron in *Pierre and His People: Tales of the Far North* (New York, 1893)
Over the Border
7 reels   sil.   b&w   1922
Dir: Penrhyn Stanlaws. Prod: Famous Players—Lasky.
Cast: Betty Compson, Tom Moore.
The daughter of a whiskey smuggler falls in love with a Canadian Mountie and must cope with divided loyalties.

PARKER, LOUIS NAPOLEON see Monkey's Paw under JACOBS, WILLIAM W.

PARKER, NORTON S.

The Walls of San Quentin
Prison Break
72 min.   b&w   1938
Dir: Arthur Lubin. Sp: Parker, Dorothy Reid. Prod: Trem Carr.
Cast: Barton MacLaine, Glenda Farrell.
A tuna fisherman takes the blame for a murder even though he is innocent.

PARKER, PHYLLIS

Unidentified story
Steel Fist
72 min.   b&w   1952
Dir: Wesley Barry. Prod: Monogram. Dist: Hurlock Cine World.
Cast: Roddy McDowall, Kristine Miller.
A United States student is trapped in an Iron Curtain country.

PARROTT, URSULA

Love Affair
Love Affair
6,299'   b&w   1932
Dir: Thornton Freeland. Adap: Jo Swerling. Prod: Columbia.
Cast: Humphrey Bogart, Dorothy Mackaill.

Unidentified story
Strangers May Kiss
85 min.   b&w   1931
Dir: George Fitzmaurice. Prod: M-G-M.
Cast: Irene Rich, Robert Montgomery, Norma Shearer, Neil Hamilton.
The heroine (Shearer) toys with lovers around the world.

PATTEN, LEWIS B.

Back Trail
    Red Sundown
    81 min.   color   1956
    Dir: Jack Arnold. Prod: Universal. Dist: Universal.
    Cast: Rory Calhoun, Martha Hyer, Dean Jagger.
    Western. A former gunslinger becomes a deputy.

PATTERSON, NEIL

International Incident
    Man on a Tightrope
    105 min.   b&w   1953
    Dir: Elia Kazan. Prod: 20th Century Fox. Dist: Films Inc
    Cast: Fredric March, Gloria Grahame.
    In a small traveling circus, a man loves an unfaithful wife.

Scotch Settlement
    The Little Kidnappers (Br.; Br. title The Kidnappers)
    93 min.   b&w   1954
    Dir: Philip Leacock. Prod: United Artists. Dist: Janus.
    Cast: Adrienne Corri, Duncan MacRae.
    Two boys, who can't have a dog, kidnap a baby.

PATTERSON, ROBERT

Unidentified story
    Brute Force
    96 min.   b&w   1947
    Dir: Jules Dassin. Prod: Universal-International. Dist: Ivy.
    Cast: Burt Lancaster, Hume Cronyn, Charles Bickford.
    Drama. A sadistic guard and a potential prison break set the scene for the story
of each inmate's reason for wanting out.

PATULLO, GEORGE

The Ledger of Life in *Saturday Evening Post* (March 4, 1922)
    Private Affairs
    6 reels   sil.   b&w   1925
    Dir: Renaud Hoffman. Prod: Renaud Hoffman Prod.
    Cast: Gladys Hulette, Robert Agnew.
    The discovery of a 5-year-old package of undelivered letters in a small town post
office disrupts the lives of the addressees.

PAYNE, STEPHEN

Tracks
  Swifty
  61 min.   b&w   1936
  Prod: Walter Futter. Dist: United Films.
  Cast: Hoot Gibson.

PAYNE, WILL J.

Black Sheep in *Saturday Evening Post*
  The Family Closet
  6 reels   sil.   b&w   1921
  Dir: John B. O'Brien. Prod: Ore-Col Film Corp.
  Cast: Holmes Herbert, Alice Mann, Kempton Greene.
  Mystery melodrama. An editor hires McMurty to obtain evidence against a man
suing him for libel.

PAYNTER, ERNEST

Maskee
  Shipmates
  6 reels   b&w   1931
  Dir: Harry Pollard. Sp: Delmer Davis, Lou Edelman. Prod: M-G-M.
  Cast: Robert Montgomery, Dorothy Jordan.
  A formula Navy story of a young sailor who falls for the admiral's daughter.

PELLEY, WILLIAM DUDLEY

The Sunset Derby in *American Magazine* (January 1926)
  The Sunset Derby
  6 reels   sil.   b&w   1927
  Dir: Albert Rogell. Prod: First National Pictures.
  Cast: Mary Astor, William Collier, Jr.
  Melodrama. Former partners in a livery business have a falling out when one opens
a service station.

PENTECOST, HUGH

If I Should Die
  Appointment with a Shadow
  72 min.   b&w   1958
  Dir: Richard Carlson. Sp: Alex Coppel, Norman Jolley. Prod and Dist: Universal.
  Cast: George Nader, Joanna Moore.
  Drama. The downfall of a former top reporter who becomes an alcoholic.

PERKINS, KENNETH

Bow Tamely to Me
    Escape to Burma
    87 min.   color   1955
    Dir: Allan Dwan. Prod: RKO. Dist: Macmillan.
    Cast: Barbara Stanwyck, Robert Rayn.
    Melodrama. The mistress of a Burmese teak plantation gives refuge to a murder
suspect.

The Devil's Saddle in *Argosy All-Story Weekly*
    The Devil's Saddle
    6 reels   sil.   b&w   1927
    Dir: Albert Rogell. Adap: Marion Jackson. Prod: Charles R. Rogers Prod.
    Cast: Ken Maynard, Kathleen Collins.
    Western melodrama. The Hopi Indians' land is invaded.

PEARLMAN, VAN TERRYS

Scoop
    That's My Story
    63 min.   b&w   1937
    Dir: Sidney Salkow. Prod: Universal.
    Cast: Claudia Morgan, William Lundigan.
    Comedy drama. A fired reporter finds the only way to get a job is to interview a
gangster's moll, who is jailed in a small town. He gets himself thrown in jail and
mistakes a female reporter for the moll.

PEROWNE, BARRY

Blind Spot
    Blind Spot
    73 min.   b&w   1947
    Dir: Robert Gordon. Prod: Columbia.
    Cast: Chester Morris, Constance Dowling.
    A writer on a drunk is accused of the murder of his publisher.

PESTRINIERO, RENATO

One Night of 21 Hours
    Planet of the Vampires
    86 min.   color   1965
    Dir: Mario Bava. Prod: American International. Dist: Kerr.
    Cast: Barry Sullivan, Norma Begell, Angela Aranda.
    The Argos and the Galliot space ships land on the strange planet Aura in an
effort to contact the inhabitants.

PETRACCA, JOSEPH

Four Eyes
It's a Big Country (a film in eight segments; three based on short stories)
s.m. "Interruptions, Interruptions," by Edgar Brooke; "Rosika the Rose," by
  Claudia Cranston
89 min.   1952
Dir: several. Prod: M-G-M.
Cast: Gene Kelly, Janet Leigh, Frederic March.
The stories show America's greatness.

PFALZGRAF, FLORENCE LEIGHTON see LEIGHTON, FLORENCE (pseud.)

PHILIPS, JUDSON P.

The House of Death
House of Mystery
s.m. radio show Street and Smith's Detective Story Magazine Hour
20 min.   b&w   1931
Dir: Kurt Neumann. Sp: Samuel Freedman. Prod: Universal.
A mystery fantasy Shadow-Detective short—number four.

PHILLIPI, ERICH

Secret of the Blue Room
The Missing Guest
68 min.   b&w   1938
Dir: John Rawlins. Sp: Charles Martin, Paul Perez. Prod: Universal.
Cast: Paul Kelly, Constance Moore, William Lundigan.
A reporter poses as a psychic when a family re-opens the mansion where a man
was killed 20 years earlier.

Murder in the Blue Room
61 min.   b&w   1944
Dir: Leslie Goodwins. Sp: I. A. L. Diamond, Stanley Davis. Prod: Universal. Dist:
  Mogull's.
Cast: Anne Gwynne, Donald Cook.
Mystery comedy. A man tries to solve the mystery of his wife's first husband,
who was killed in the Blue Room. As a result, more murders occur.

Secrets of the Blue Room
66 min.   b&w   1933
Dir: Kurt Neumann. Sp: William Hurlbut. Prod and Dist: Universal.
Cast: Lionel Atwill, Gloria Stuart, Paul Lukas.

PHILLIPI, ERICH (cont'd)

Secrets of the Blue Room (cont'd)
Mystery. Twenty-three years after deaths occur in the castle's Blue Room, a beautiful girl's three suitors decide to spend the night there to prove their bravery to the girl.

PIRANDELLO, LUIGI

The Fan see Of Life and Love

The Jar in *Better Think Twice About It*
Of Life and Love (It.)
s.m. "The Fan," "The Lap Dog," "The Night Tuxedo"
103 min.   b&w   1958
Dir: Aldo Babrizi. Prod: Distributors' Corp.
Cast: Anna Magnani.
Several unrelated romantic plots.

The Lap Dog see Of Life and Love

The Night Tuxedo see Of Life and Love

POE, EDGAR ALLAN

See also The Haunted Palace under LOVECRAFT, H. P.

The Black Cat see also Tales of Terror under Facts on the Case of M. Valdemar

The Black Cat
The Black Cat (Br. title House of Doom)
65 min.   b&w   1934
Dir: Edgar G. Ulmer. Prod: E. M. Asher. Dist: Swank, Twyman.
Cast: Boris Karloff, Bela Lugosi.
A mad architect-soldier builds a fantastic structure on the ruins of a castle he betrayed in the first World War, and stashes the corpses of young girls in glass cases in its underground passages. The re-release title was The Vanishing Body.

The Black Cat
70 min.   b&w   1941
Dir: Albert S. Rogell. Prod: Universal. Dist: Universal.
Cast: Basil Rathbone, Bela Lugosi, Broderick Crawford.
A real estate promoter and a goofy antique collector intrude upon the reading of a will in a gloomy old mansion, and murder ensues.

POE, EDGAR ALLAN (cont'd)

The Black Cat
  The Black Cat
  77 min.   b&w   1966
  Dir: Harold Hoffman. Prod: Falcon International.
  Cast: Robert Frost, Robyn Baker, Scotty McKay.
  A man believes that a cat is the reincarnation of his murdered father.

  The Living Dead
  s.m. "The System of Doctor Tarr and Professor Feather"; "The Suicide Club"
      by Robert Louis Stevenson.
  70 min.   b&w   1940
  Dir: Thomas Bentley. Dist: Thunderbird.
  Cast: Sir Gerald du Maurier.

  Maniac
  s.m. based partly on this story
  52 min.   b&w   1934
  Dir: Dwain Esper. Dist: Budget.
  Cast: Bill Woods, Horace Carpenter.
  A sub-Z, low-budget horror film. A mad doctor's assistant murders his boss, then
impersonates the doctor and treats a patient. As the patient's horrified wife watches,
the wrong injection makes this victim literally go "ape" and he begins his own
murder spree.

The Cask of Amontillado see also Tales of Terror under Facts in the Case of M.
    Valdemar

  The Cask of Amontillado
  15 min.   b&w   1955
  Prod: Dynamic Films. Dist: Audio Brandon.
  Cast: Monty Woolley.
  Montressor lures Fortunato to his death in a walled-in wine cellar.

  The Edgar Allan Poe Special
  s.m. "The Tell-Tale Heart," "The Sphinx," "The Pit and the Pendulum"
  56 min.   color   1970
  Dir: Ken Johnson. Prod: Roger Corman. Dist: Wholesome Film Center.
  Four of Poe's stories, narrated and interpreted by Vincent Price.

POE, EDGAR ALLAN (cont'd)

A Descent Into the Maelstrom
   War-Gods of the Deep
   s.m. The Doomed City, a poem
   85 min.   color   1965
   Dir: Jacques Tourneur. Sp: Charles Bennett. Dist: Kerr, Macmillan, Modern,
      Wholesome Film Center.
   Cast: Vincent Price, Tab Hunter, Susan Hart.
   A girl is kidnapped from her home on the Cornish coast and two friends go to
her rescue. Their search for her leads through secret doorways and subterranean
passages to a strange city under the sea ruled by Price.

Facts in the Case of M. Valdemar
   Tales of Terror
   s.m. "Morella," "The Black Cat," "Cask of Amontillado"
   90 min.   color   1961
   Dir: Roger Corman. Prod: American International. Dist: Audio Brandon.
   Cast: Vincent Price, Peter Lorre, Basil Rathbone, Debra Paget.
   Three tales: Morella is a brief, morbid study of obsession. Leonara, a young student, returns to her brooding family estate by the sea. Her father has preserved the
mummified body of his wife Morella. In the second tale a stumbling drunk and an
effete wine taster have two loves in common: fine spirits and the drink's wife. Freely
adapted. The Case of M. Valdemar pits a medical hypnotist against a dying patient.
At the moment of Valdemar's death the hypnotist forbids his soul to depart.

The Fall of the House of Usher
   Fall of the House of Usher
   55 min.   sil.   b&w   1927
   Dir: Jean Edstein.
   Cast: Margaret Gance, Jean Dubencourt, Charles Lamay.
   A Caligari approach to the tale.

The Fall of the House of Usher
   12 min.   sil. (sd. added later)   1928
   Dir: James Sibley Watson, Jr. Dist: Museum of Modern Art.
   One of the first American avant-garde adaptations.

The Fall of the House of Usher (Br.)
   70 min.   b&w   1952
   Dir: Ivan Barnett. Prod: L. Barry Bernard, Arthur Mason.
   Cast: Kay Tendeter, Irving Steen, Lucy Pavey.
   Horror. A lord's sister is revived after being buried alive. Re-issued in 1955 and
1961.

POE, EDGAR ALLAN (cont'd)

The Fall of the House of Usher (cont'd)
House of Usher
81 min.   color   1960
Dir: Roger Corman. Prod: American International. Dist: Audio Brandon.
Cast: Vincent Price, Mark Damon, Myrna Fahey.
Roderick Usher, a man who fears being buried alive more than anything else, has accidently buried his sister alive. Her spirit beckons him from the crypt where she still lives.

The Fall of the House of Usher
30 min.   color   1969
Prod and Dist: Encyclopaedia Britannica.
The events surrounding the mysterious Usher twins, the last survivors of an ancient family, build to a violent climax.

Gold Bug
Manfish
s.m. "The Tell-Tale Heart"
76 min.   color   1956
Dir: W. Lee Wilder. Prod: United Artists.
Cast: John Bromfield, Lon Chaney, Jr., Victor Jory.
Mystery horror. Bubbles reveal the location of a murdered diver.

Hop-Frog see Masque of the Red Death

Ligeia
Tomb of Ligeia
81 min.   color   1965
Dir: Roger Corman. Prod: American International. Dist: Audio Brandon.
Cast: Vincent Price, Elizabeth Shepherd, John Westbrook.
A fight for the possession of the body of Ligeia, the reluctantly deceased wife.

The Masque of the Red Death
Masque of the Red Death
s.m. "Hop-Frog"
89 min.   color   1961
Dir: Roger Corman. Prod: American International. Dist: Budget, Macmillan, Roa's, Wyman.
Cast: Vincent Price, Hazel Court.
Prince Prospero, advocate and leader of a devil cult, stays in his castle with his houseguests while the Red Death, a plague, claims victims on the outside. Finally, the Red Death enters the castle.

POE, EDGAR ALLAN (cont'd)

The Masque of the Red Death (cont'd)
  The Masque of the Red Death
  10 min.   color   1970
  Dir and Sp: Pavao Stalter. Dist: McGraw-Hill.
    Animated. Count Prospero locks himself and his court inside his castle as protection against the plague which is devastating the countryside. A seductive woman entices the count and he finds out she is really the plague.

Metzengerstein
  Spirits of the Dead
  s.m. "William Wilson," "Never Bet the Devil Your Head"
  118 min.   color   1969
  Dir: Roger Vadim, Louis Malle, Federico Fellini. Sp: Vadim, Pascal Cousin Malle, Fellini, Bernadino Zapponi. Dist: Kit Parker, Wholesome.
    In William Wilson a medical student is involved in a game for his life against a Don Juan double who returns to embarrass and taunt him. In Toby Dammit (based on "Never Bet the Devil Your Head"), the hero makes a small bet with the devil, in order to escape the world of cameras and microphones.

Morella see Tales of Terror under Facts in the Case of M. Valdemar

The Murders in the Rue Morgue
  Murders in the Rue Morgue
  62 min.   b&w   1932
  Dir: Robert Florey. Sp: Tom Reed, Dale Van Every. Prod: Universal.
  Cast: Bela Lugosi, Sidney Fox.
    Dr. Mirakle, a fanatically dedicated scientist, supports his experiments in evolution by his activities as a sideshow concessionaire in the Paris circus. He requires the blood of selected young women to prove his theory of man's kinship with the ape.

  Murders in the Rue Morgue
  86 min.   color   1973
  Dir: Gordon Hessler. Prod: American International. Dist: Swank.
  Cast: Jason Robards, Jr., Herbert Lom, Christine Kaufmann.
    The only clue to a series of murders is that all the victims were business associates of a theater owner.

  Phantom of the Rue Morgue
  84 min.   color   1953
  Dir: Roy Del Ruth. Prod: Warner Bros. Dist: Budget, Macmillan, Modern, Wholesome.
  Cast: Karl Malden, Claude Dauphin, Patricia Medina.

POE, EDGAR ALLAN (cont'd)

The Murders in the Rue Morgue (cont'd)
  Phantom of the Rue Morgue (cont'd)
  A series of unexplained murders occurs in the Rue Morgue section of Paris and
the police are baffled. An amateur detective, Dupin, discovers the culprit.

The Mystery of Marie Roget
  The Mystery of Marie Roget
  60 min.   b&w   1942
  Dir: Phil Rosen. Sp: Michael Jacoby. Prod and Dist: Universal.
  Cast: Maria Montez, Maria Ouspenskaya, John Litel, Patric Knowles.
  Murder mystery. A detective investigates the disappearance of a beautiful actress.

Never Bet the Devil Your Head see Spirits of the Dead under Metzengerstein

The Oblong Box
  The Oblong Box
  95 min.   b&w   1969
  Dir: Gordon Hessler. Dist: Wholesome.
  Cast: Vincent Price, Christopher Lee.
  His face distorted by the curse of an African witch doctor, Sir Edward Markham
is kept in cruel imprisonment in a dark English mansion by his tyrannical older
brother. He is driven to the brink of insanity and devises a rash, bizarre plan to secure
an exotic drug that induces a deep coma.

The Pit and the Pendulum see also The Edgar Allan Poe Special under The Cask
  of Amontillado

  The Blood Demon (W. Ger.)
  85 min.   color   1967
  Dir: Harold Reinl. Sp: Manfred R. Kohler.
  Cast: Christopher Lee, Lex Barber.
  Lee is revived from the dead.

  The Pit and the Pendulum
  85 min.   color   1961
  Dir: Roger Corman. Prod: American International. Dist: Audio Brandon, Swank.
  Cast: Vincent Price, John Kerr, Barbara Steele.
  Driven mad by hereditary insanity, Nicholas Medina reverts to the period of the
Spanish Inquisition and uses instruments of torture perfected by his father and
the sadistic inquisitors.

POE, EDGAR ALLAN (cont'd)

The Pit and the Pendulum (cont'd)
  The Raven
  s.m. The Raven, a poem
  62 min.   b&w   1935
  Dir: Louis Friedlander (later Lew Landers). Sp: David Boehm. Prod: Universal.
  Cast: Boris Karloff, Bela Lugosi.
    Thriller. Obsessed with the writings of Poe, a mad doctor creates his own
torture machines.

The Premature Burial
  The Crime of Doctor Crespi
  63 min.   b&w   1935
  Dir: John H. Auer. Prod: Liberty Pictures. Dist: Budget, Kit Parker.
    Horror. Dr. Andre Crespi—master surgeon, hospital saint, and full-time
madman—is embittered by the loss to a former assistant of the woman he loved.
Crespi gets his chance to exact a warped revenge. When his rival is seriously injured
in an auto accident, Crespi injects him with a drug that will make him appear dead.

  Premature Burial
  81 min.   color   1962
  Dir: Roger Corman. Prod: American International. Dist: Budget, Macmillan,
       Modern, Twyman.
  Cast: Ray Milland, Hazel Court.
    Set in London during the 1860s, a medical student, suffering from a cataleptic
fit, is haunted by a fear of being buried alive. He is treated by a friend who suggests
that they open the father's coffin to prove he was not buried alive. But he was.

The Sphinx see The Edgar Allan Poe Special under The Cash of Amontillado

The System of Doctor Tarr and Professor Feathertop see The Living Dead under
    The Black Cat

The Tell-Tale Heart see also The Edgar Allan Poe Special under The Cask of
    Amontillado; Manfish under Gold Bug

  The Avenging Conscience
  60-80 min.   sil.   b&w   1914
  Dir: D. W. Griffith. Prod: Reliance/Majestic. Dist: Museum of Modern Art.
  Cast: Henry B. Walthall, Blanche Sweet.
    Drawn from various works of Poe, primarily The Tell-Tale Heart, this film is
considered significant for showing the development of Griffith as a director.

POE, EDGAR ALLAN (cont'd)

The Tell-Tale Heart (cont'd)
Bucket of Blood (Br. title Telltale Heart)
49 min.   b&w   1934
Dir: Brian Desmond Hurst. Sp: David Plunkett Greene. Prod: Du World.
Cast: Norman Dryden, John Kelt.
Horror.

Heartbeat
2 reels   b&w   1949
Dir: William Cameron Menzies. Prod: General TV Enterprises.
Made for TV and theatrical distribution.

The Tell-Tale Heart
8 min.   color
Prod: Stephen Bosustow. Dist: Learning Corp.
Animated; narrated by James Mason. "That eye, that eye"—he saw it everywhere.
He couldn't rest until he had killed it, but that was not the end. Day and night, the
heartbeat of the murdered man continued its insistent throbbing, haunting him.

The Tell-Tale Heart (Br.)
81 min.   b&w   1962
Dir: Ernest Morris. Prod: Danziger. Dist: Macmillan, Select.
Cast: Laurence Payne, Adrienne Corri.
An author dreams he killed his rival and is driven mad. Re-issued in 1972.

The Tell-Tale Heart
20 min.   b&w   1953
Prod: M-G-M. Dist: Films Inc.
An excerpt. An apprentice kills his master and then is driven mad by the sound
of the dead man's heart beating.

The Tell-Tale Heart
26 min.   b&w   1973
Dir: Steve Carver. Prod: American Film Institute. Dist: Time-Life.
Cast: Alex Cord.
A live-action interpretation of a manservant driven to murder his elderly
employer because of the man's sinister, clouded eye.

William Wilson see Spirits of the Dead under Metzengerstein

POLIDORI, JOHN

The Vampyre (suggestion for)
  The Vampire's Ghost
  54 min.   b&w   1945
  Dir: Leslie Selander. Dist: Ivy.
  Cast: Charles Gordon, Adele Mara.
  A leader of the underworld on the West Coast of Africa is revealed to be a vampire 400 years old, and not a traditional vampire at that.

PONTSEVREZ

The Ingenious Reporter
  The Ingenious Reporter
  25 min.   color   1977
  Prod: 20th Century Fox. Dist: Encyclopaedia Britannica.
  A brash, young American reporter who works for a Paris scandal sheet devises a clever way to improve his paper's circulation. Learning of a murder in which neither the victim nor the murderer has been identified, he decides to pose as the suspect. The victim is later identified as his sweetheart! Orson Welles introduces the film.

PORTER, ELEANOR H.

Unidentified story
  Has Anybody Seen My Gal?
  89 min.   color   1952
  Dir: Douglas Sirk. Prod and Dist: Universal.
  Cast: Charles Coburn, Piper Laurie, Rock Hudson.
  A wealthy man bestows a fortune on a typical family, moves in (incognito) with them, and watches the family relations fall apart.

POZNER, VLADIMIR

The Dark Mirror in *Good Housekeeping*
  The Dark Mirror
  85 min.   b&w   1946
  Dir: Robert Siodmak. Sp: Nunnally Johnson. Prod: Universal. Dist: Ivy.
  Cast: Olivia De Havilland, Lew Ayres.
  Drama. A story about twins, one good and one evil.

PRATT, THEODORE

Unidentified story
  Juke Girl
  90 min.   b&w   1942
  Dir: Curtis Bernhardt. Prod: Warner Bros. Dist: United Artists.

PRATT, THEODORE (cont'd)

Juke Girl (cont'd)
Cast: Ronald Reagan, Ann Sheridan, Gene Lockhart.
A dramatic account of Florida itinerant fruit pickers who become involved in a marketing war.

PRESSBURGER, EMERIC

Breach of Promise
    Adventure in Blackmail
    8 reels   b&w   1943
    Dir: Harold Huth. Prod: Mercury.
    Cast: Clive Brook, Judy Campbell.
    Comedy of a girl more interested in money than marriage.

PUSHKIN, ALEXANDER

The Captain's Daughter in *The Captain's Daughter and Other Stories* (N.Y., Dutton, 1933)
    The Captain's Daughter
    1959
    Prod: Mosfilm Studios.

Mozart and Salieri in *Complete Prose Tales* (Norton, 1966)
    Requiem for Mozart (U.S.S.R.)
    47 min.   b&w   1967
    Prod: Riga Film Studio.
    Cast: Innokentity Smoktunovskiy, Pyotr Glebov.
    An opera film. Composer Salieri envies Mozart.

Postmaster in *Great Russian Short Stories*, ed. by S. Graham (Liveright, 1929)
    Postmaster's Daughter
    1946
    Prod: Vog Films.

Queen of Spades*
    Pikovaya Dama (U.S.S.R.)
    100 min.   color   1960
    Dir: Roman Tikhomirov. Sp: Georgy Vassiliev. Prod: Artkino.
    Cast: Oleg Strizhenov, Olga Krasina.
    An operatic version adapted from Tchaikovsky. *Note: A number of silent foreign films were based on this story including Pique Dame (Ger., 1927); Queen of Spades (U.S.S.R., 1916).

PUSHKIN, ALEXANDER (cont'd)

Queen of Spades (cont'd)
Pique Dame (Fr.)
100 min.   b&w   1937
Dir: Fedor Ozep. Sp: Bernard Zimmer.
Cast: Pierre Blanchar, Andre Luquet.

The Queen of Spades (Br.)
95 min.   b&w   1953
Dir: Thorold Dickinson. Prod: Stratford Pictures. Dist: Janus.
Cast: Antor Walbrook, Dame Edith Evans, Yvonne Mitchell, Ronald Howard.
An Army captain learns the art of gambling at the expense of his soul.

The Queen of Spades
15 min.   b&w   1954
Prod: Dynamic Films. Dist: Audio Brandon.
Cast: Monty Woolley.
A clerk's eagerness for success at the gambling tables makes him force a supernatural secret out of an ancient countess. Her death is the clerk's undoing.

PUTNAM, NINA WILCOX

Doubling for Cupid in *Saturday Evening Post* (December 13, 1924)
The Beautiful Cheat
7 reels   sil.   b&w   1926
Dir: Edward Sloman. Prod: Universal.
Cast: Laura La Plante, Harry Myers, Bertram Grassby.
Comedy drama. Press agent Jimmy Austin takes Mary Callahan, a shop girl, to Europe. She returns as Maritza Callahansky, a Russian actress.

The Grandflapper in *Saturday Evening Post* (October 23, 1926)
Slaves of Beauty
5,412'   sil.   b&w   1927
Dir: J. G. Blystone. Prod: Fox.
Cast: Olive Tell, Holmes Herbert.
Science fiction. A "clay" operation makes a woman beautiful.

Two Weeks with Pay in *Saturday Evening Post* (October 9, 1920)
Two Weeks with Pay
5 reels   sil.   b&w   1921
Dir: Maurice Campbell. Prod: Realart Pictures.
Cast: Bebe Daniels, Jack Mulhall.

PUTNAM, NINA WILCOX (cont'd)

Two Weeks with Pay (cont'd)
Comedy. At a resort hotel a clerk mistakes Patsy for a movie star, and Patsy goes along with the deception.

RAINE, NORMAN REILLY

Stories about Tugboat Annie in *Saturday Evening Post*
Tugboat Annie
88 min.   b&w   1933
Dir: Mervyn LeRoy. Sp: Zelda Sears, Eve Greene. Prod: M-G-M. Dist: Films Inc.
Cast: Wallace Beery, Marie Dressler.
Slapstick. A story about husband-and-wife brawling and mother-son sentiment.
Later films based on the character Tugboat Annie include Tugboat Annie Sails Again (Warner Bros., 1940) and Capt. Tugboat Annie (Republic, 1945).

RANKIN, WILLIAM (jt. author) see Be It Ever So Humble and Hi, Beautiful under GRIFFIN, ELEANOR

RAPHAELSON, SAMSON

The Day of Atonement
The Jazz Singer
s.m. the film was based on the play The Jazz Singer, in turn based on the story
89 min.   b&w   1927
Dir: Alan Crosland. Prod: Warner Bros. Dist: United Artists.
Cast: Al Jolson, Warner Oland, May McAvoy.
The first sound film which won a Special Academy Award for "Marking an Epoch in Motion Picture History." The story of a singer who chooses show business rather than following the wishes of his orthodox Jewish father to become a cantor.

A Rose Is Not a Rose
Bannerline
81 min.   b&w   1951
Dir: Don Weiss. Sp: Charles Schnee. Prod: M-G-M. Dist: Films Inc.
Cast: Keefe Brasselle, Lionel Barrymore.
The story of a cub reporter.

REILLY, PATRICIA

Big Business Girl in *College Humor* (jt. author H. N. Swanson)
  Big Business Girl
  8 reels   b&w   1931
  Sp: Robert Lord. Prod: First National Pictures.
  Cast: Loretta Young, Frank Albertson, Ricardo Cortez, Joan Blondell.
  Comedy about a secretary's adventures in New York.

REYNOLDS, QUENTIN

West Side Miracle
  Secrets of a Nurse
  75 min.   b&w   1938
  Dir: Arthur Lubin. Sp: Tom Lennon, Lester Cole. Prod: Universal Pictures.
  Cast: Edmund Lowe, Helen Mack, Dick Foran.
  Mystery drama. An ex-prisefighter is convicted of a murder he didn't commit.

RICE, ALBERT (jt. author) see Gay Blades under GOODMAN, JACK

RICHARDS, LAURA E.

Captain January
  Captain January
  75 min.   b&w   1936
  Dir: David Butler. Prod: Fox. Dist: Films Inc.
  Cast: Shirley Temple, Guy Kibbee.
  The law wants to take Shirley away from her loving guardians.

RICHLER, MORDECAI

The Summer My Grandma Was Supposed to Die
  The Street
  10 min.   color   1976
  Dir: Caroline Leaf. Prod and Dist: National Film Board of Canada.
  Watercolor and ink animation. Family reactions to a dying grandmother are seen from a child's point of view.

RIGDON, GERTRUDE

The Department Store
  Hold Me Tight
  6,484'   b&w   1933
  Dir: David Butler. Sp: Gladys Lehman. Prod: Fox.
  Cast: James Dunn, Sally Eilers.
  Romance. Trouble begins when a husband is fired from his job without cause.

RILEY, J. W.

An Old Sweetheart of Mine
  An Old Sweetheart of Mine
  6 reels   sil.   b&w   1923
  Dir: Harry Garson. Adap: Louis Duryea Lighton.
  Cast: Pat Moore, Elliott Dexter.
  A man reminisces about his first sweetheart, a woman business associate who prevented oil swindlers from cheating the town out of profits from its oil wells.

RINEHART, MARY ROBERTS

Affinities in *Affinities and Other Stories*
  Affinities
  6 reels   sil.   b&w   1922
  Dir: Ward Lascelle. Prod: Ward Lascelle Prod.
  Cast: John Bowers, Colleen Moore, Joe Bonner, Grace Gordon.
  Comedy drama. Two couples spend a lot of time at a country club. Fanny's spouse and Fred's spouse leave them alone so often that Fred suggests an "affinity" party.

Babs
  Rinehart's character Babs was used in several films produced prior to 1920 by Famous Players Film Co.

Her Majesty, the Queen in *Tempermental People* (1924)
  Her Love Story
  7 reels   sil.   b&w   1924
  Dir: Allan Dwan. Prod: Famous Players—Lasky.
  Cast: Gloria Swanson, Ian Keith.
  Romantic drama. Princess Marie of the Balkan kingdom of Viatavia falls in love with the captain of the guards and they secretly marry. Then her father forces her to marry the king of another country.

In the Pavilion in *Love Stories* (New York, 1919)
  The Glorious Fool
  s.m. "Twenty-Two" in *Love Stories*
  6 reels   sil.   b&w   1922
  Dir: E. Mason Hopper. Adap: J. G. Hawks. Prod: Goldwyn Pictures.
  Comedy drama. Billy Grant persuades his nurse to marry him so that his property will not be inherited by his relatives.

Mind Over Motor in *Saturday Evening Post* (October 5, 1912)
  Mind Over Motor
  5 reels   sil.   b&w   1923
  Dir and Prod: Ward Lascelle.

RINEHART, MARY ROBERTS (cont'd)

Mind Over Motor (cont'd)
Cast: Trixie Friganza, Ralph Graves.
Tish unknowingly finances a crooked promoter of an auto race.

Mr. Cohen Takes a Walk in *Familiar Faces* (N.Y., Farrar & Rinehart, 1941)
Mr. Cohen Takes a Walk
81 min.   b&w   1936
Dir: William Beaudine. Prod: Warner Bros.
Cast: Paul Graetz, Violet Farebrother.
A story of a loveable London merchant prince.

Seven Days in *Lippincott's Magazine* (December 1908)
Seven Days
7 reels   sil.   b&w   1925
Dir: Scott Sidney. Prod: Christie Film Co.
Cast: Lillian Rich, Creighton Hale.
Farce. A divorced couple, assorted friends, and a cop are trapped inside a
quarantined house.

Tish stories
Tish
8 reels   1942
Dir: S. Sylvan Simon. Sp: Harry Ruskin. Prod: M-G-M.
Cast: Susan Peters, Marjorie Main, ZaSu Pitts, Aline MacMahon.
Comedy. Village spinsters adopt a baby.

Twenty-Three and a Half Hour's Leave (novellette)
Twenty-Three and a Half Hour's Leave
5 reels   sil.   b&w   1919
Dir: Henry King. Prod: Thomas H. Ince for Para-Artcraft.
Cast: Douglas MacLean, Doris May.
A light comedy. A disgraced soldier vindicates himself by uncovering a spy ring,
thereby winning the colonel's daughter.

23½ Hours Leave
8 reels   b&w   1937
Dir: John G. Blystone. Sp: Harry Ruskin, Henry McCarty. Prod: Grand National
    Films.

Twenty-Two see The Glorious Fool under In the Pavilion

RINEHART, MARY ROBERTS (cont'd)

What Happened to Father in *Lippincott's Magazine* (September 1909)
  What Happened to Father
  6 reels   sil.   b&w   1927
  Dir: John G. Adolfi. Prod: Warner Bros.
  Cast: Warner Oland, Flobelle Fairbanks.
  Farce. An absent-minded professor is cowed by his wife who is trying to arrange
a marriage between their daughter and a wealthy man.

RITCHIE, JACK

The Green Heart
  A New Leaf
  102 min.   color   1971
  Dir: Elaine May. Sp: Elaine May. Prod: Paramount. Dist: Films Inc.
  Cast: Walter Matthau, Elaine May, Jack Weston.
  Fastidious middle-aged bachelor playboy, running out of his inheritance, is forced
to go to work or to acquire a rich wife. The wealthy source he finds is awkward Miss
May, as unsexy as the Alsophipila Grahamicus, a new leaf she cultivated.

ROBERTS, STANLEY

Riding Monte Christo
  Galloping Dynamite
  1936
  Prod: Maurice Conn Prod.

ROCHE, ARTHUR SOMERS

Penthouse in *Cosmopolitan*
  Penthouse
  90 min.   b&w   1933
  Dir: W. S. Van Dyke. Sp: Frances Goodrich, Albert Hackett. Prod: M-G-M.
    Dist: Films Inc.
  Cast: Phillips Holmes, Mae Clarke, Myrna Loy.
  Story about a murder frame-up.

  Society Lawyer
  77 min.   b&w   1939
  Dir: Edwin Marin. Sp: Frances Goodrich, Albert Hackett, Leon Gordon, Hugo
    Butler. Prod: M-G-M.
  Cast: Walter Pidgeon, Edvardo Ciannelli.
  Crime drama, a re-make of Penthouse.

ROCHE, ARTHUR SOMERS (cont'd)

Rich But Honest in *Hearst's International Cosmopolitan* (November 1926)
Rich But Honest
6 reels   sil.   b&w   1927
Dir: Albert Ray. Prod: Fox.
Cast: Nancy Nash, Clifford Holland.
A department store clerk who wins a Charleston contest gets a job on the stage,
only to alienate her steady sweetheart.

A Scrap of Paper in *Saturday Evening Post*
Living Lies
5 reels   sil.   b&w   1922
Dir: Emile Chautard. Prod: Mayflower Photoplay Corp.
Cast: Edmund Lowe, Mona Kingsley.
A reporter obtains documented evidence of the crooked deals of a band of high
financiers. He and his sweetheart are kidnapped and tortured.

Wolf's Clothing in *Hearst's International Cosmopolitan* (May-October 1926)
Wolf's Clothing
7,068'   sil.   b&w   1927
Dir: Roy Del Ruth. Prod: Warner Bros.
Cast: Monte Blue, Patsy Ruth Miller.
In a dream, a man imagines himself being very tiny in a huge world.

ROECCA, SAMUEL

Salem Came to Supper
The Night Visitor
106 min.   color   1971
Dir: Laslo Benedek. Prod: Mel Ferrer. Dist: Audio Brandon.
Cast: Max Van Sydow, Liv Ullmann, Trevor Howard.
A man escapes from a prison for the criminally insane, and sets out to avenge
himself on the husband and wife who committed the murder for which he was
convicted.

ROONEY, FRANK

The Cyclists Raid
The Wild One
79 min.   b&w   1953
Dir: Laslo Benedek. Prod: Stanley Kramer Prod. Dist: Budget, Macmillan,
    Modern, Twyman.
Cast: Marlon Brando.
A leather-jacketed motorcycle gang vandalizes and terrorizes a small town;
Brando, as the leader of the gang, is attracted to a nice girl.

ROSTEN, LEO

The Dark Corner
   The Dark Corner
   99 min.   b&w   1946
   Dir: Henry Hathaway. Prod: Fox. Dist: Films Inc.
   Cast: Lucille Ball, Clifton Webb, Mark Stevens.
   Melodrama. A detective is framed for murder.

Unidentified story
   Mr. Cory
   95 min.   color   1957
   Dir: Blake Edwards. Prod: Universal International. Dist: Universal.
   Cast: Tony Curtis, Martha Hyer.
   Drama. A boy from the Chicago slums becomes a big-time gambler.

ROTH, PHILIP

Goodbye, Columbus (novella) in *Goodbye, Columbus and Five Short Stories*
   Goodbye, Columbus
   105 min.   color   1969
   Dir: Larry Peerce. Prod: Paramount. Dist: Films Inc.
   Story about the romance between a poor boy from the Bronx who works in a
local library, and a rich girl from Westchester.

RUNYON, DAMON

The Big Mitten
   No Ransom
   8 reels   b&w   1934
   Dir: Fred Newmeyer. Prod: Liberty Pictures.

Bloodhounds of Broadway
   Bloodhounds of Broadway
   90 min.   color   1952
   Dir: Harmon Jones. Prod: Fox. Dist: Films Inc.
   Cast: Mitzi Gaynor, Scott Brady.
   Mitzi Gaynor plays a hillbilly who comes to the city and turns into a curvaceous
Broadway babe. The plot involves a crime being investigated by a committee.

Butch Minds the Baby in *Box Office*
   Butch Minds the Baby
   75 min.   b&w   1942
   Dir: Albert S. Rogell. Sp: Leonard Spigelgass. Prod: Mayfair Prod.
   Cast: Virginia Bruce, Broderick Crawford.
   Comedy. Zany things happen when a thug is forced to watch a small child.

RUNYON, DAMON (cont'd)

A Call on the President
  Joe and Ethel Turp Call on the President
  7 reels   b&w   1939
  Dir: Robert Sinclair. Prod: M-G-M.
  Cast: Walter Brennan, Ann Sothern, William Gargan.
  A B-picture. A couple takes its troubles right up to the White House.

Guys and Dolls
  Guys and Dolls
  s.m. the musical by Jo Swerling and Abe Burrows in turn based on this story.
  100 min.   b&w   1955
  Dir: Joseph L. Mankiewicz. Prod: Samuel Goldwyn. Dist: Wholesome.
  Cast: Marlon Brando, Frank Sinatra, Jean Simmons, Vivian Blaine.
  A fable about gamblers and gangsters and the women who take them from their
crap games to the marriage altar. Score by Frank Loesser.

Hold'em Yale in *The Best of Damon Runyon* (Stokes, 1938)
  Hold'em Yale
  7 reels   b&w   1935
  Dir: Sidney Lanfield. Sp: Paul Gerard Smith, Eddie Welch. Prod: Paramount.
  Cast: Patricia Ellis, Cesar Romero.
  Comedy. Ticket scalpers are double-crossed.

Johnny One-Eye
  Johnny One-Eye
  78 min.   b&w   1950
  Prod: Cahuenga Prod.
  Cast: Pat O'Brien, Wayne Morris, Dolores Moran.
  A gangster with a heart of gold is on the lam.

The Lemon Drop Kid
  The Lemon Drop Kid
  8 reels   b&w   1934
  Dir: Marshal Neilan. Sp: Howard J. Green. Prod: Paramount.
  Cast: Lee Tracy.

  The Lemon Drop Kid
  91 min.   b&w   1951
  Dir: Sidney Lanfield. Prod: Paramount. Dist: Budget, Ivy, Macmillan, Twyman.
  When gangster Moose Moran loses $10,000 following a bad tip from a racetrack
tout, the heat is on. The Lemon Drop Kid schemes to raise the money.

RUNYON, DAMON (cont'd)

Little Miss Marker
   Little Miss Marker
   80 min.   b&w   1934
   Dir: Alexander Hall. Prod: Paramount. Dist: Universal.
   Cast: Shirley Tample, Adolphe Menjou.
   A sentimental tale of a little girl who reforms a bookie.

   Sorrowful Jones
   s.m. the screen play of the 1934 film, Little Miss Marker
   88 min.   b&w   1949
   Dir: Sidney Lanfield. Prod: Paramount. Dist: Universal.
   Cast: Bob Hope, Lucille Ball, William Demarest, Bruce Cabot.
   A small-time bookie adopts a little girl and gets involved with racketeers trying
to fix a horse race.

Little Pinks in *Collier's* (January 27, 1940)
   The Big Street
   88 min.   b&w   1942
   Dir: Irving Reis. Prod: RKO. Dist: Films Inc.
   Cast: Henry Fonda, Lucille Ball.
   Gloria, a selfish singer, is loved by Little Pinks, who takes care of her when she
becomes incurably crippled.

Madame La Gimp
   Lady for a Day
   95 min.   b&w   1933
   Dir: Frank Capra. Prod: Columbia.
   Cast: May Robson, Warren William, Walter Connolly, Hobart Bosworth.
   Apple Annie, a ragpicker, is put into a mansion for a week by gambler Dave the
Dude to convince Louise, her daughter, that she has a stately position in life.
Nominated for four Academy Awards: Best Picture, Best Writing, Best Directing,
Best Actress.

   Pocketful of Miracles
   s.m. the screenplay of Lady for a Day
   136 min.   color   1961
   Dir: Frank Capra. Sp: Hal Kantor, Harry Tugend (uncredited). Prod: Franton.
     Dist: United Artists.
   Cast: Glenn Ford, Bette Davis.

RUNYON, DAMON (cont'd)

Money from Home
  Money from Home
  100 min.   color   1954
  Dir: George Marshall. Sp: Hal Kanter. Prod: Paramount.
  Cast: Dean Martin, Jerry Lewis.
  A slapstick comedy. Gangsters complicate a gambler's effort to recoup his losses at the track by arranging an illegal race.

The Old Doll's House
  Midnight Alibi
  59 min.   b&w   1934
  Dir: Alan Crosland. Prod: First National Pictures.
  Cast: Richard Barthelmess, Ann Dvorak.
  A sweet old lady befriends a fleeing gambler.

Princess O'Hara
  It Ain't Hay
  80 min.   b&w   1943
  Dir: Erle C. Kenton. Sp: Allen Boretz, John Grant. Prod: Universal.
  Cast: Bud Abbott, Lou Costello.
  Comedy. A championship horse is mistakenly given away. A re-make of Princess O'Hara.

  Princess O'Hara
  74 min.   b&w   1935
  Dir: David Burton. Sp: Doris Malloy, Harry Clork. Prod: Universal.
  Drama comedy. A man tries to help the four children of a taxi driver who was killed.

Three Wise Guys in *The Damon Runyon Omnibus* (Blue Ribbon Books)
  Three Wise Guys
  8 reels   b&w   1936
  Dir: George B. Seitz. Sp: Elmer Harris. Prod: M-G-M.
  Cast: Robert Young, Betty Furness.
  A story about Broadway sharpies.

Tight Shoes in *Take It Easy*
  Tight Shoes
  68 min.   b&w   1941
  Dir: Albert S. Rogell. Prod: Mayfair Prod.
  Cast: John Howard, Binnie Barnes, Broderick Crawford.
  Comedy. A gangster gets a shoe clerk started in a political career.

RUSSELL, JOHN

The Fire-Walker in *Far Wandering Men* (New York, 1929)
 Girl of the Port
 8 reels   sd. or sil.   b&w   1930
 Dir: Bert Glennon. Sp: Beulah Marie Dix. Prod: RKO.
 Cast: Sally O'Neil, Reginald Sharland.
 Romantic melodrama. Love between a showgirl and an English war veteran.

The Lost God in *Where the Pavement Ends* (London, 1921)
 The Sea God
 9 reels   b&w   1930
 Dir: George Abbott. Prod: Paramount Publix.
 Cast: Richard Arlen, Fay Wray.
 Adventure melodrama. Two traders seek the attentions of Daisy.

The Passion Vine in *The Red Mark, and Other Stories* (New York, 1919)
 Where the Pavement Ends
 8 reels   sil.   b&w   1923
 Dir: Rex Ingram. Prod: Metro Pictures.
 Cast: Edward Connelly, Alice Terey.
 Melodrama. Pastor Spencer, trying to convert the natives, contends with Hull,
who operates a saloon.

The Red Mark in *Short Stories by Present Day Authors*, ed. by W. Pence
 (N.Y., Macmillan, 1922)
 The Red Mark
 8 reels   sil.   b&w   1928
 Dir: James Cruze. Adap: Julien Josephson. Prod: James Cruze, Inc.
 Cast; Nina Quartaro, Gaston Glass.
 Melodrama. The rival of Bibi-Ri on the penal island of Noumea is the
executioner whom Bibi-Ri fears.

RYERSON, FLORENCE

Willie the Worm in *American Magazine* (September 1926)
 Love Makes 'em Wild
 6 reels   sil.   b&w   1927
 Dir: Albert Ray. Prod: Fox.
 Cast: Johnny Harron, Sally Phipps.
 A spineless office plodder known as Willie the Worm is told by quack doctors
that he has only six months to live, so he proceeds to get even with those who have
bullied him.

ST. JOHN, ADELA ROGERS

Great God Fourflush
  Woman's Man
  80 min.   b&w   1934
  Dir: Edward Ludwig. Prod: Monogram. Dist: Mogull's.
  Cast: John Halliday, Wallace Ford.
  A spoiled Hollywood movie star meets a prizefighter.

The Haunted Lady in *Hearst's International Cosmopolitan* (May 1925)
  Scandal
  7 reels   sil.   b&w   1929
  Dir: Wesley Ruggles. Prod: Universal.
  Cast: Laura La Plante, Huntley Gordon.
  Melodrama. When her family wealth is dissipated, socialite Laura Hunt goes to work and marries for money.

Love o' Women in *Hearst's International Cosmopolitan* (February 1926)
  Singed
  6 reels   sil.   b&w   1927
  Dir: John Griffith Wray. Prod: Fox.
  Cast: Blanche Sweet, Warner Baxter.
  Society melodrama. Because dancer Dolly loves Royce Wingate, an irresponsible chap, she backs an oil well in which he has an interest. When he becomes wealthy, he leaves her.

Pretty Ladies in *Cosmopolitan Magazine*
  Pretty Ladies
  6 reels   sil.   b&w   1925
  Dir: Monta Bell. Adap: Alice D. G. Miller. Prod: M-G-M.
  Cast: ZaSu Pitts, Tom Moore, Ann Pennington, Lilyan Tashman.
  A star comedienne helps a drummer become a successful songwriter and gives up her career to marry him.

ST. JOHN, ADELA ROGERS (cont'd)

Unidentified story
    Back in Circulation
    82 min.   b&w   1937
    Dir: Ray Enright. Sp: Warren Duff. Prod: Warner Bros. Dist: United Artists.
    Cast: Pat O'Brien, Joan Blondell.
    Comedy story about an editor and top reporter who get mixed up in a murder.

The Worst Woman in Hollywood in *Cosmopolitan* (February 1924)
    Inez from Hollywood
    7 reels   sil.   b&w   1924
    Dir: Alfred E. Green. Adap: J. G. Hawks. Prod: Sam E. Rork Prod.
    Drama. Inez, a vamp and Hollywood star, tries to protect her sister from men
she considers dishonorable.

SAKI

Open Window
    Open Window
    12 min.   color   1971
    Dir: Richard Patterson. Prod: American Film Institute. Dist: Pyramid.
    A young girl tells a ghost story to a visitor who then flees.

SALE, RICHARD

The Doctor Doubles in Death
    Embraceable You
    80 min.   b&w   1948
    Dir: Felix Jacoves. Prod: Warner Bros. Dist: United Artists.
    Cast: Dane Clark, Geraldine Brooks.
    A small-time crook falls for a girl he injured.

    This Side of the Law
    74 min.   b&w   1950
    Dir: Richard L. Bare. Prod: Warner Bros.
    Cast: Viveca Lindfors, Kent Smith, Janis Paige.
    A contrived plot in which a shady lawyer hires a man to impersonate a missing
wealthy man.

Several unidentified stories
    Torpedo Run
    96 min.   color   1958
    Dir: Joseph Pevnay. Prod: M-G-M. Dist: Films Inc.
    Cast: Glenn Ford, Ernest Borgnine, Dean Jones, Diane Brewster.

SALE, RICHARD (cont'd)

Torpedo Run (cont'd)
A terrible decision faces an American submarine commander when he learns his wife and child are prisoners aboard a transport shielding his prime target—the Japanese carrier *Shinaru*.

SALINGER, J. D.

Uncle Wiggily in Connecticut in *New Yorker*
My Foolish Heart
98 min.   b&w   1949
Dir: Mark Robson. Sp: Julius and Philip Epstein. Prod: Samuel Goldwyn Prod.
    Dist: Macmillan.
Cast: Susan Hayward, Dana Andrews.
A wartime romance between a lonely girl and a pilot. Hollywood transformed this story of a suburban lush into that of a wronged, lonely woman.

SANTLEY, JOSEPH

Murder in a Chinese Theatre
Mad Holiday
8 reels   b&w   1936
Dir: George B. Seitz. Sp: Florence Ryerson, Edgar Allan Woolf. Prod: M-G-M.
Cast: Elissa Landi, Edmund Lowe, ZaSu Pitts.
A comedy whodunit in Thin Man style.

SAPPER (pseud. of H. C. McNeile)

Challenge*
Bulldog Drummond in Africa
70 min.   b&w   1938
Dir: Louis King. Prod: Paramount. Dist: Kit Parker.
Cast: John Howard, Heather Angel.
Col. Nielson is kidnapped and Drummond chases after him to Africa. *Note: The character of Bulldog Drummond appeared in many novels and some stories.

The Female of the Species
Bulldog Drummond Comes Back
70 min.   b&w   1937
Dir: Louis King. Prod: Paramount. Dist: Budget.
Cast: John Howard, Heather Angel.
Bulldog Drummond is hot on the trail of a clever criminal who has kidnapped Drummond's fiancé.

SAPPER (pseud. of H. C. McNeile) (cont'd)

Thirteen Lead Soldiers in *Boys' Second Book of Great Detective Stories*
(N.Y., Harper, 1938)
Thirteen Lead Soldiers
64 min.   b&w   1948
Dir: Frank McDonald. Sp: Irving Elman. Prod: Reliance Pictures.
Cast: Tom Conway, Maria Palmer.
Bulldog Drummond solves three murders with the aid of thirteen lead soldiers
that hold the key to hidden treasure.

SAUNDERS, JOHN MONK

A Maker of Gestures in *Cosmopolitan* (April 1923)
Too Many Kisses
6 reels   sil.   b&w   1925
Dir: Paul Sloane. Prod: Famous Players—Lasky.
Cast: Richard Dix, Frances Howard.
Romantic comedy. Because he puts pleasure before business, Richard's father
sends him to Spain, where he falls in love with a Spanish girl.

SAUNDERS, KENNETH J.

The Devil's Playground
The Lady Who Dared
55 min.   b&w   1931
Dir: William Beaudine. Prod: First National Pictures. Dist: United Artists.
Cast: Billie Dove, Conway Tearle.
A diamond smuggler is forced to join in a crooked scheme.

SAYERS, DOROTHY L.

The Inspiration of Mr. Budd
The Inspiration of Mr. Budd
25 min.   color   1976
Prod: 20 Century Fox. Dist: Encyclopaedia Britannica.
A meek, unsuccessful barber meets adventure when a fierce-looking, red-haired
man demands his hair be dyed and talks as though he has murdered his wife. The
barber dyes his hair brown—but with a slow-working chemical that turns it green.

SAYRE, JOEL

Man on the Ledge
Fourteen Hours
91 min.   b&w   1951
Dir: Henry Hathaway. Prod: 20th Century Fox. Dist: Films Inc.
Cast: Paul Douglas, Richard Basehart, Grace Kelly.

SAYRE, JOEL (cont'd)

Fourteen Hours (cont'd)
The fourteen hours a man spends on a 15th floor New York window ledge, threatening to jump, pivot the related dramas of his parents, sweetheart, the cop, and the street crowd.

SCHAEFER, JACK

Jeremy Rodock
Tribute to a Bad Man
95 min.   color   1956
Dir: Robert Wise. Prod: M-G-M. Dist: Films Inc.
Cast: James Cagney, Irene Papas.
Set in Wyoming in 1875. A vengeful rancher takes the law into his own hands when horse thieves steal some of his breeding stock, but a young man tries to convince the rancher that justice is the better course.

SCOTT, EWING

Arctic Manhunt
Narana of the North
b&w   1948
Prod: Universal (?).
Cast: Mikel Conrad, Carol Thurston.
Story about an ex-convict's flight to Alaska to cash in on some armored car loot.

Gaitor Bait
Untamed Fury
65 min.   b&w   1947
Dir: Ewing Scott. Prod: Pathe Industries. Dist: Institutional Cinema.
Cast: Mikel Conrad, Leigh Whipper.

Shadow of the Curtain
Arctic Flight
75 min.   b&w   1952
Prod: Monogram.
Cast: Wayne Morris, Lola Albright.
Bush pilot battles foreign agents in the Arctic.

SCOTT, LEROY

In Borrowed Plumes in *Smart Set*
In Borrowed Plumes
6 reels   sil.   b&w   1926
Dir: Victor Hugo Halperin. Prod: Welcome Pictures.

SCOTT, LEROY (cont'd)

In Borrowed Plumes (cont'd)
Cast: Marjorie Daw, Niles Welch.
Society melodrama. A penniless society girl passes herself off as the Countess
D'Autreval.

Little Angel
Lady of Chance
8 reels   b&w   sil.   1928
Dir: Robert Z. Leonard. Sp: A. P. Younger. Prod: M-G-M.
Cast: Norma Shearer, Lowell Sherman.
The heroine lures men to her apartment in order to blackmail them.

The Mother in *Cosmopolitan* (February 1914)
The Poverty of Riches
6 reels   sil.   b&w   1921
Dir: Reginald Barker. Prod: Goldwyn.
Cast: Richard Dix, Leatrice Joy.
A woman yearns to have children but her husband wants to achieve financial
and social success first.

SHAFFER, ROSALIND KEATING

Finger Man
Lady Killer
76 min.   b&w   1933
Dir: Roy Del Ruth. Prod: Warner Bros. Dist: United Artists.
Cast: James Cagney, Margaret Lindsay, Mae Clark.
A mobster becomes a Hollywood actor.

SHAFTEL, JOSEPH

The Bliss of Mrs. Blossom
The Bliss of Mrs. Blossom
s.m. the film was based on A Bird in the Nest, a play by Alec Coppel in turn based
    on this story
93 min.   color   1968
Dir: Joseph McGrath. Prod: Paramount. Dist: Films Inc.
Cast: Shirley MacLaine, Richard Attenborough.
Farce. A brassiere manufacturer keeps a lover in the attic.

SHARP, MARGERY

Notorious Tenant in *Collier's* (February 3, 1956)
    Notorious Landlady
    123 min.   b&w   1962
    Dir: Richard Quine. Prod: Columbia. Dist: Budget, Macmillan, Roa's.
    Cast: Kim Novak, Jack Lemmon.
    A young American diplomat stationed in London rents an apartment in the
fashionable private home of a beautiful young woman suspected by Scotland Yard
of having murdered her husband.

SHAW, DAVID (jt. author) see Take One False Step under SHAW, IRWIN

SHAW, IRWIN

In the French Style
    In the French Style
    s.m. "A Year to Learn the Language"
    105 min.   1963
    Dir: Robert Parrish. Prod: Gasanna-Orsay Films.
    Cast: Jean Seberg, Stanley Baker.
    A post-World War II female expatriate becomes involved in a series of brief,
meaningless love affairs.

Night Call (jt. author David Shaw)
    Take One False Step
    94 min.   b&w   1947
    Dir: Chester Erskine. Prod: Universal. Dist: Universal.
    Cast: William Powell, Shelley Winters.
    An innocent college professor becomes entangled with the police when a blonde
from his past runs into him.

Then There Were Three in *Selected Short Stories of Irwin Shaw* (Random, 1961)
    Three
    102 min.   1969
    Dir and Sp: James Salter. Prod and Dist: United Artists.
    Three Americans, just out of college during the 1950s, wind up a vacation in
Europe.

Tip on a Dead Jockey in *New Yorker* (March 6, 1954)
    Tip on a Dead Jockey
    129 min.   b&w   1957
    Dir: Richard Thorpe. Prod: M-G-M. Dist: Films Inc.
    Cast: Robert Taylor, Dorothy Malone.
    Drama. A pilot is involved with smugglers.

SHAW, IRWIN (cont'd)

A Year to Learn the Language see In the French Style

SHER, JACK

Memo to Kathy O'Rourke in *Saturday Evening Post* (November 23, 1946)
  Kathy-O
  99 min.   color   1958
  Dir: Jack Sher. Prod and Dist: Universal.
  Cast: Patty McCormack, Dan Duryea, Jan Sterling.
A tempermental child star who makes life miserable for her public relations man is kidnapped.

SHERDEMAN, TED

Latitude Zero stories
  Latitude Zero (Japan)
  99 min.   color   1970
  Dir: Ishiro Hondo.
  Cast: Joseph Cotten, Cesar Romero.
Sci-fi adventure of an underwater civilization. Benevolent geniuses battle the legions of Malic, who are out to rule the world.

SHEW, EDWARD SPENCER

Hands of the Ripper
  Hands of the Ripper (Br.)
  85 min.   1972
  Dir: Peter Sasdy. Sp: L. W. Davidson. Rel., Universal.
  Cast: Eric Porter, Angharad Rees.
Thriller. In Victorian England a series of murders occur soon after a psychiatrist takes custody of a 17-year-old.

SHIPMAN, SAMUEL (jt. author) see Law of the Underworld under HYMER,
    JAMES

SHORE, VIOLA BROTHERS

On the Shelf in *Saturday Evening Post* (July 22, 1922)
  Let Women Alone
  6 reels   sil.   b&w   1925
  Dir: Paul Powell. Adap: Frank Woods. Prod: Peninsula Studios.
  Cast: Pat O'Malley, Wanda Hawley, Wallace Beery.
Beth, an interior decorator whose husband was lost at sea, plans to marry Tom, but her husband re-appears.

SHORE, VIOLA BROTHERS (cont'd)

The Prince of Headwaiters in *Liberty Magazine* (April 9, 1927) (jt. author Garrett
  Fort)
  The Prince of Headwaiters
  7 reels   sil.   b&w   1927
  Dir: John Francis Dillon. Prod: Sam E. Rork Prod.
  Cast: Lewis Stone, Priscilla Bonner.
  The headwaiter at the Ritz Hotel saves a college boy from a notorious gold
digger and finds out the boy is his son.

SHORT, LUKE (pseud. of Fred Dilley Glidden)

Hurry, Charlie, Hurry
  Hurry, Charlie, Hurry
  65 min.   b&w   1941
  Dir: Charles E. Roberts. Prod: RKO. Dist: Films Inc.
  Cast: Leon Errol.
  A henpecked husband who gets into trouble is abbetted by his Indian friends.

Unidentified story in *Saturday Evening Post*
  Ride the Man Down
  90 min.   b&w   1952
  Dir: Joseph Kane. Prod: Republic. Dist: Ivy.
  Cast: Rod Cameron, Brian Donlevy, Ella Raines.
  Western. A foreman keeps the ranch from land grabbers while waiting for the
new owners.

SHRANK, JOSEPH see He Couldn't Say No under MATSON, NORMAN

SIMENON, GEORGE

A Life in the Balance
  A Life in the Balance
  74 min.   b&w   1955
  Dir: Harry Horner. Prod: 20th Century Fox. Dist: Films Inc.
  Cast: Ricardo Montalban, Anne Bancroft.
  Mystery. Murders in Mexico.

SINGER, ISAAC

The Beard
  Isaac Singer's Nightmare and Mrs. Pupko's Beard
  30 min.   color   1973
  Dir: Bruce Davidson. Dist: New Yorker.
  The story features the famous writer, intercut with a dramatization of his own

SINGER, ISAAC (cont'd)

Isaac Singer's Nightmare and Mrs. Pupko's Beard (cont'd)
story about a writer married to a bearded woman. The writer invests in the stock
market and becomes rich. Pupko urges Singer to write about him, but Singer
refuses, accusing Pupko of having stooped to bribing the critics. Pupko falls very
ill and Mrs. Pupko asks Singer to confront him.

SLESINGER, TESS

The Answer on the Magnolia Tree in *Time the Present, a Book of Short Stories*
   (N.Y., Simon and Schuster, 1935)
   Girl's School
   8 reels   b&w   1938
   Dir: John Brahm. Sp: Tess Slesinger. Prod: Columbia.
   Cast: Anne Shirley, Nan Grey.
   Two roommates clash over romance and school rules.

SLODE, CHRISTINE J.

Caretakers Within in *Saturday Evening Post* (February 5, 1921)
   Life's Darn Funny
   6 reels   sil.   b&w   1921
   Dir: Dallas M. Fitzgerald.
   Cast: Viola Dana, Gareth Hughes.
   Comedy. A young couple goes into business designing clothes.

SMITH, FRANK LEON

Bells of Waldenbruck
   Melody in Spring
   8 reels   b&w   1934
   Dir: Norman McLeod. Sp: Benn W. Levy. Prod: Paramount.
   Cast: Lanny Ross, Charles Ruggles.
   Musical romance. A young man who wants a job as a soloist on the Blodgett
Radio Hour, agrees to elope with Blodgett's daughter.

SMITH, GARRETT

Old Hutch Lives Up to It
   Old Hutch
   8 reels   b&w   1936
   Dir: J. Walter Ruben. Prod: M-G-M.
   Cast: Wallace Beery, Cecilia Parker.
   Comedy. A ne'er-do-well finds $100,000 but can't spend it because everyone
knows he has never earned a penny.

SMITH, HAROLD JACOB

The Highest Mountain
The River's Edge
87 min.   color   1957
Dir: Allan Dwan. Prod: Fox. Dist: Films Inc.
Cast: Anthony Quinn, Ray Milland, Debra Paget.
Crime melodrama. A killer menaces his old girlfriend and her husband.

SMITH, MAXWELL

Dated in *Saturday Evening Post* (July 3, 1920)
The Last Card
6 reels   sil.   b&w   1921
Dir: Bayard Veiller. Prod: Metro Pictures.
Cast: May Allison, Albert Roscoe.
A criminal lawyer murders his wife's lover and frames a friend. The friend hires
the lawyer to defend him but is found guilty. The friend's wife eventually finds out
the truth.

SMITH, WALLACE

The Grouch Bag in *Hearst's International Cosmopolitan*
Not Quite Decent
5 reels   talking sequences and sd. effects   b&w   1929
Dir: Irving Cummings. Prod: Fox.
Cast: Louise Dresser, Jane Collyer.
An aging nightclub singer meets an actress who turns out to be the daughter
from whom she had been separated years before.

Little Ledna in *Are You Decent* (N.Y., Putnam, 1927)
Big Time
8 reels   b&w   1930
Dir: Kenneth Hawks. Adap: Sidney Lanfield. Prod: Fox.
Cast: Lee Tracy, Mae Clarke.
Melodrama. A vaudeville husband and wife team breaks up when a schemer
named Gloria slips into the act.

New York West in *Blue Book Magazine* (March 1926)
West of Broadway
6 reels   sil.   b&w   1926
Dir: Robert Thornby. Adap: Harold Shumate. Prod: Metro Pictures.
Cast: Priscilla Dean, Arnold Gray.
Western romantic comedy. The golf instructor hired by a rancher turns out to
be a woman.

SMITH, WALLACE (cont'd)

The Snake's Wife in *Hearst's International Cosmopolitan* (May 1926)
Upstream
6 reels   sil.   b&w   1927
Dir: John Ford. Prod: Fox.
Cast: Nancy Nash, Earle Foxe.
Comedy drama. An actor becomes the victim of his own conceit.

A Woman Decides in *Cosmopolitan*
The Delightful Rogue
7 reels   sil. or sd.   b&w   1929
Dir: Lynn Shores. Prod: RKO.
Cast: Rod La Rocque, Rita La Roy, Charles Byer.
Romantic melodrama. A tropical seas romance between a pirate and an American dancer.

SOMERVILLE, A. W.

No Brakes in *Saturday Evening Post* (December 8, 1928)
Oh, Yeah!
85 min.   b&w   1930
Dir: Tay Garnett. Prod: Pathe Exchange. Dist: Film Classic Exchange.
Cast: James Gleason, ZaSu Pitts.
Comedy melodrama. Two drifters blow into town and each finds a sweetheart.

SOUTAR, ANDREW

On Principle in *Snappy Stories* (April 2, 1918)
Love's Redemption
6 reels   sil.   b&w   1921
Dir: Albert Parker. Prod: Norma Talmadge Prod.
Cast: Norma Talmadge, Harrison Ford.
A young woman raised in Jamaica marries a rich Englishman and returns with him to England only to become disillusioned with the upper crust.

SPAULDING, SUSAN MARR

Two Shall Be Born in *An American Anthology, 1787-1900* (Boston, 1900)
Two Shall Be Born
6 reels   sil.   b&w   1924
Dir: William Bennett. Prod: Twin Pictures.
Cast: Jane Novak, Kenneth Harlan.
Melodrama. Mayra is entrusted with important international papers and is then kidnapped.

SPEARMAN, FRANK HAMILTON

The Nerve of Folly in *The Nerve of Folly and Other Railroad Stories* (New York, 1900)
    The Runaway Express
    6 reels   sil.   b&w   1926
    Dir: Edward Sedgwick. Dist: Mogull's.
    Cast: Jack Daugherty, Blanche Mehaffey.
    Melodrama. Joe commandeers an engine to get cattle to market and is offered a job on the railroad.

Whispering Smith Rides
    The Lightning Express (serial)
    2 reels each   b&w   1930
    Dir: Henry McRae. Prod: Universal.
    Cast: Lane Chandler, Louise Lorraine.
    Ten chapters. The Lightning Express is a train which needs the rights to cross land owned by a pretty girl, whose unscrupulous guardian fights the railroad.

    Whispering Smith*
    88 min.   b&w   1949
    Dir: Leslie Fenton. Prod: Universal.
    Cast: Alan Ladd, Robert Preston, Brenda Marshall.
    A western re-make of the serial The Lightning Express. A railroad detective finds his best friend mixed up with bandits. *Note: The stories of Whispering Smith were published in a book of the same title by Scribner (New York, 1914).

SPRINGER, NORMAN

Then Hell Broke Loose
    Shanghaied Love
    7 reels   b&w   1931
    Dir: George B. Seitz. Adap: Roy Chanslor, Jack Cunningham. Prod: Columbia.

SPRINGS, ELLIOT WHITE

The One Who Was Clever in *Redbook* (August 1929)
    Young Eagles
    s.m. "Sky-High," in *Redbook* (July 1929)
    6 reels   sil. or sd.   b&w   1930
    Dir: William A. Wellman. Prod: Paramount. Dist: Universal.
    Cast: Charles Rogers, Jean Arthur.
    War melodrama. The romance of a lieutenant and an American is cut short when he must return to the front.

SQUIER, EMMA LINDSAY

The Angry God and the People of Corn in *Sacred Well and Other Tales of Ancient Mexico*
  The Angry God
  57 min.   color   1948
  Dir: Van Campel Heilner. Prod: Arlisle Prod.
  Cast: Alicia Parla, Casimiro Ortega.
  The god of the Mexican Indians is personified.

Glorious Buccaneer
  Dancing Pirate
  80 min.   color   1936
  Dir: Lloyd Corrigan. Prod: RKO. Dist: Ivy, Mogull's.
  Cast: Charles Collins, Frank Morgan.
  Musical. The romantic adventures of a dancing instructor shanghaied in Boston
in the early part of the 19th century.

STARRET, VINCENT

Recipe for Murder
  Great Hotel Murder
  5,250'   b&w   1935
  Dir: James Tinling. Sp: Bess Meredyth. Prod: Fox.
  Cast: Edmund Lowe, Victor McLaglen.
  McLaglen plays a detective in a hotel where a dead man is discovered.

STEELE, WILBUR DANIEL

Ropes in *Harper's Monthly* (January 1921)
  Undertow
  60 min.   b&w   1930
  Dir: Harry A. Pollard. Adap: Winnifred Reeve, Edward T. Lowe. Prod: Universal.
  Cast: Mary Nolan, Johnny Mack Brown.
  Drama. A young man in the Coast Guard steals away the wife of the lighthouse
keeper.

STEINBECK, JOHN

Flight in *Masters of the Modern Short Story*, ed. by W. Havinghurst (N.Y., Harcourt, 1945)
  Flight
  Prod: San Francisco Films; rel. Columbia.

STELLA, ENRICO

A Girl Named Francesca
Crazy Desire (It.)
108 min.   b&w   1962
Dir: Luciano Salce. Prod: Isidoro Broggi, Renato Libassi. Dist: Macmillan.
Cast: Ugo Tognazzi, Catherine Spaak.
A 40-year-old businessman falls prey to the teasing of a 16-year-old girl and
willingly undergoes all sorts of indignities.

STEPHENSON, CARL

Leiningen Versus the Ants
The Naked Jungle
95 min.   color   1953
Dir: Byron Haskin. Prod: Paramount. Dist: Films Inc.
Cast: Charlton Heston, Eleanor Parker.
Convinced that his mail order bride was too beautiful to be useful, Christopher
urges her to leave his South American plantation, but she refuses, then helps him
in a struggle to survive.

STERN, PHILIP VAN DOREN

The Greatest Gift
It's a Wonderful Life
130 min.   b&w   1947
Dir: Frank Capra. Sp: Frances Goodrich, Albert Hackett, Capra. Prod: RKO.
     Dist: Ivy, Kit Parker.
Cast: James Stewart, Donna Reed.
A hard-working man whose business fails attempts to commit suicide, but is
shown the value of life by a loveable guardian angel.

STEVENSON, ROBERT LOUIS

The Body Snatcher
The Body Snatcher
77 min.   b&w   1945
Dir: Robert Wise. Sp: Philip MacDonald, Carlos Keith. Prod: RKO. Dist: Films
     Inc.
Cast: Boris Karloff, Bela Lugosi.
Set in 19th century Edinburgh, a distinguished surgeon falls into the power of
the man who supplies cadavers for his medical classes.

The Rajah's Diamond
The Tame Cat
4,943'   sil.   b&w   1921
Dir: William Bradley. Prod: Dramafilms.

STEVENSON, ROBERT LOUIS (cont'd)

The Tame Cat (cont'd)
Cast: Ray Irwin, Marion Harding.
A story about a fabulous gem, and the people who desperately want to possess it.

Silverado Squatters
Adventures in Silverado
75 min.   b&w   1948
Dir: Phil Karlson. Prod: Columbia. Dist: International Cinema Service, Modern.
Cast: William Bishop, Forrest Tucker.
A drama of the California frontier in 1880. Honest citizens try to build a home
in the new frontier.

Sire de Malétroit's Door
The Strange Door
81 min.   b&w   1951
Dir: Joseph Pevney. Prod: Universal International. Dist: Universal.
Cast: Boris Karloff, Charles Laughton, Sally Forrest.
An insane French nobleman vows revenge on his dead sweetheart by imprisoning
members of her family.

The Suicide Club* see also The Living Dead under POE, EDGAR ALLAN
*Note: Three silent versions were made of this story, one in 1910, another in
France in 1912, a third in Britain in 1914.

Suicide Club (Br.)
1932
Dir: Maurice Elvey.

Trouble for Two
s.m. "The Young Man with the Cream Tart"
80 min.   b&w   1936
Dir: J. Walter Ruben. Sp: Manuel Seff, Edward Paramore, Jr. Prod: M-G-M. Dist:
    Films Inc.
Cast: Robert Montgomery, Rosalind Russell.
Chilling adventure tale.

The Treasure of Franchard in *The Strange Case of Dr. Jekyll and Mr. Hyde: The
    Merry Men and Other Tales and Fables* (New York, 1909)
The Treasure of Lost Canyon
82 min.   color   1951
Dir: Ted Tetzlaff. Sp: Brainerd Duffield, Emerson Crocker. Prod: Universal.
    Dist: Universal.

STEVENSON, ROBERT LOUIS (cont'd)

The Treasure of Lost Canyon (cont'd)
Cast: William Powell, Julia Adams.

A young orphan, adopted by a middle-aged couple, stumbles onto a buried treasure and brings havoc into their lives.

The Young Man with the Cream Tart see Trouble for Two under The Suicide Club

STOCKTON, FRANK R.

The Lady or the Tiger
The Lady or the Tiger
10 min.
Dir: Fred Zinnemann. Prod: M-G-M. Dist: Wholesome.

A Roman gladiator, faced with a life and death dilemma, must choose his fate. Behind one door is a beautiful woman—behind the other a ferocious tiger.

The Lady, or the Tiger?
16 min.   color   1969
Prod and Dist: Encyclopaedia Britannica.
Re-set in the space age.

STONE, PETER

The Unsuspecting Wife*
Charade
113 min.   color   1963
Dir: Stanley Donen. Prod: Universal. Dist: Twyman, Universal.
Cast: Cary Grant, Audrey Hepburn.

A suspenseful, elegant thriller that also manages to spoof its genre. A preposterous and deadly chase through Parisian environs complete with five corpses and red-herrings. *Note: According to the American Film Institute publication of this story was undetermined; the Writers' Guild claims the story was published.

STRAKOSCH, AVERY

I Married an Artist
She Married an Artist
8 reels   b&w   1938
Dir: Marion Gering. Sp: Gladys Lehman, Delmar Davies. Prod: Columbia.

STREET, JAMES

The Biscuit Eater in *Box Office*, by Marjorie Barrows (N.Y., Ziff-Davis, 1943)
The Biscuit Eater
83 min.   b&w   1942

STREET, JAMES (cont'd)

The Biscuit Eater (cont'd)
Dir: Stuart Heisler. Prod: Paramount. Dist: Universal.
Cast: Billy Lee, Cordel Hickman, Helen Millard, Richard Lee.
A Georgia youngster takes an outcast puppy, names him Promise, and tries to
make him a champion hunting dog. One night the pointer is found raiding the
chicken coop, and the boy fears that Promise will be a biscuit eater, an ornery dog.

The Biscuit Eater
90 min.   color   1972
Dir: Vincent McEveety. Prod: Walt Disney Prod.
Cast: Earl Holliman, Johnny Whitaker, Lew Ayres, Godfrey Cambridge.

Letter to the Editor
Living It Up
s.m. screenplay of Nothing Sacred and the play Hazel Flagg by Ben Hecht in
    turn based on the story
94 min.   color   1954
Dir: Norman Taurog. Prod: York Pictures Corp. Dist: Films Inc.
Cast: Dean Martin, Jerry Lewis, Janet Leigh.
A story about a railroad attendant with sinus trouble.

Nothing Sacred
80 min.   b&w   1938
Dir: William Wellman. Prod: United Artists. Dist: Cinema 8, Mogull's.
Cast: Carole Lombard, Fredric March.
Drama of a girl with a short time to live, who is given a good time for two weeks
which is nothing but a publicity stunt.

Mr. Bisbee's Princess in *O. Henry Memorial Award Prize Stories of 1930*
So's Your Old Man
6,347'   sil.   b&w   1926
Dir: Gregory La Cava. Prod: Famous Players—Lasky.
Cast: W. C. Fields.
Fields invents unbreakable glass.

You're Telling Me
70 min.   b&w   1934
Dir: Erle C. Kenton. Prod: Paramount. Dist: Swank
Cast: W. C. Fields.
Comedy story about an inventor; a re-make of So's Your Old Man.

STRINGER, ARTHUR

The Coward in *Hearst's International*
    The Coward
    6 reels   sil.   b&w   1927
    Dir: Alfred Raboch. Prod: R-C Pictures.
    Cast: Warner Baxter, Sharon Lynn.
    Society melodrama. A young rich idler must prove his worth.

Fifth Avenue in *Saturday Evening Post* (September 19, 1925)
    Fifth Avenue
    6 reels   sil.   b&w   1926
    Dir: Robert G. Vignola. Sp: Anthony Coldewey. Prod: Belasco Prod.
    Cast: Marguerite De La Motte, Allan Forrest.
    Society drama. When her cotton crop is burned, Barbara Pelham goes to New York, where she is mistaken for a whore.

Manhandled in *Saturday Evening Post* (March 29, 1924)
    Manhandled
    50 min.   sil.   b&w   1924
    Dir and Prod: Allan Dwan. Sp: Frank W. Tuttle. Dist: Macmillan.
    Cast: Gloria Swanson, Tom Moore, Frank Morgan.
    Tessie is a New York department store salesgirl, whose boyfriend, a mechanic, leaves for Detroit to demonstrate his invention of a new carburetor. During his absence, Tessie dresses up as a Russian countess, and becomes casually involved with several rich men.

Snowblind in *Hearst's International Magazine* (March 1921)
    Unseeing Eyes
    9 reels   sil.   b&w   1923
    Dir: E. H. Griffith. Prod: Cosmopolitan Prod.
    Cast: Lionel Barrymore, Seena Owen.
    Northwest melodrama. Miriam flies to Canada to help her brother with his silver mine and the plane crashes.

White Hands in *Saturday Evening Post* (July 30-August 20, 1927)
    Half a Bride
    6,238'   b&w   sil.   1928
    Dir: Gregory La Cava. Sp: Doris Anderson. Prod: Paramount.
    Cast: Esther Ralston, Gary Cooper.
    Drama. Thrill-seeker Patience Winslow enters a trial marriage, which is unconsummated because her father kidnaps her.

STRINGER, ARTHUR (cont'd)

The Wilderness Woman in *Saturday Evening Post* (January 16-30, 1926)
The Wilderness Woman
8 reels   sil.   b&w   1926
Dir: Howard Higgin. Prod: Robert Kane Prod.
Cast: Arleen Pringle, Lowell Sherman.
Comedy. A miner finds gold and heads for New York with his daughter. On
route they run into confidence men.

Womanhandled in *Saturday Evening Post* (May 2, 1925)
Buck Benny Rides Again
86 min.   b&w   1940
Dir: Mark Sandrich. Adap: Zion Myers. Prod: Paramount. Dist: Universal.
Cast: Jack Benny, Ellen Drew.
Comedy. Based on Jack's radio character Buck Benny.

Womanhandled
7 reels   sil.   b&w   1925
Dir: Gregory La Cava. Prod: Famous Players—Lasky.
Cast: Richard Dix, Esther Ralston.
Farce. Society playboy Bill must prove to Mollie he's a man, so he goes out
West.

STRONG, HARRISON

Saddle Mates in *Western Story Magazine* (January 12, 1924)
Saddle Mates
5 reels   sil.   b&w   1928
Dir: Richard Thorpe. Prod: Action Pictures.
Cast: Wally Wales, Hank Bell.
Two ranchers track down the crook who cheated them out of their land.

STUHLDREHER, HARRY

The Gravy Game in *Saturday Evening Post Sport Stories* (N.Y., Barnes, 1949)
The Band Plays On (jt. author Thornton Martin)
s.m. "Backfield," by Byron Morgan.
9 reels   b&w   1934
Dir: Russel Mack. Sp: Bernard Schubert, Ralph Spence, Harvey Gates. Prod:
   M-G-M.
Cast: Una Merkel, Stuart Erwin.
Story of a football player.

SUDERMANN, HERMANN

Trip to Tilsit
  Sunrise
  10 reels   sd. effects or sil.   1927
  Dir: Edgar G. Ulmer, Alfred Metscher.
  Cast: George O'Brien, Janet Gaynor.
  Romantic drama. Infatuated with another woman who encourages him to kill his wife, a farmer tries but cannot commit murder.

SULLIVAN, WALLACE

No Power on Earth
  Behind the High Wall
  85 min.   b&w   1956
  Dir: Abner Biblerman. Prod: Universal.
  Cast: Tom Tully, Sylvia Sidney.
  Drama. A prison warden who has a paraplegic wife finds $100,000 of an escaped prisoner's loot.

  The Big Guy
  80 min.   b&w   1939
  Dir: Arthur Lubin. Prod: Universal.
  Cast: Victor McLaglen, Jackie Cooper, Ona Munson.
  Mystery drama. A prison warden is forced to choose between keeping $250,000 or returning it and saving a man from the electric chair.

SURDEZ, GEORGES

A Game in the Bush in *Adventure Magazine*
  South Sea Love
  5 reels   sil.   b&w   1923
  Dir: David Soloman. Prod: Fox.
  Cast: Shirley Mason, J. Frank Glendon.
  Melodrama. Dolores falls in love with her guardian who is already married.

SWANSON, NEIL H.

The First Rebel
  Allegheny Uprising
  81 min.   b&w   1939
  Dir: William A. Seiter. Prod: RKO. Dist: Films Inc., Modern.
  Cast: John Wayne, Claire Trevor.
  American frontiermen battle the British for their civil rights—a preamble to the American Revolution.

SWARTHOUT, GLENDON F.

A Horse for Mrs. Custer
 Seventh Cavalry
 75 min.   color   1956
 Dir: Joseph Lewis. Prod: Producers Actors Corp. Dist: Modern.
 Cast: Randolph Scott, Barbara Hale.
 "Avenge General Custer" is the order that sent the world-renowned seventh
Cavalry charging against tremendous odds to avenge the defeat at The Little Big
Horn.

SYLVESTER, ROBERT

China Valdez in *Rough Sketch*
 We Were Strangers
 106 min.   b&w   1949
 Dir: John Huston. Prod: Columbia.
 Cast: Jennifer Jones, John Garfield.
 Drama. A story about political intrigue and revolution in Cuba during the 1930s.

TAGORE, RABINDRANATH

The Postmaster in *Mashi and Other Stories* (New York, 1918)
 Two Daughters (India)
 s.m. "The Conclusion"
 114 min.   b&w   1961
 Dir: Satyajit Ray. Prod: Ray. Dist: Janus.
 Cast: Anil Chatterjee, Chandana Bannerjee; in the second part of the film,
    Aparna Dad Gupta, Soumitra Chatterjee.
 A young man, who is assigned as the postmaster in a small village, forms a strong
bond with a 10-year-old orphan. In the second half, Amulya refuses to marry his
chosen wife because he wants to marry a tomboy he loves.

TARKINGTON, BOOTH

Father and Son*
    Father's Son
    b&w   1931
    Dir: William Beaudine. Prod: Warner Bros.
    Cast: Lewis Stone, Leon Janney, Irene Rich.
    A sentimental story of a family. *Note: There are conflicting views on these films. One source lists the story as Old Fathers and Young Sons; still another claims the second film was based on an unpublished story.

    Father's Son
    57 min.   b&w   1941
    Dir: Ross Lederman. Prod: Warner Bros. Dist: United Artists.
    Cast: John Litel, Frieda Inescort.

Penrod stories*
    On Moonlight Bay
    95 min.   b&w   1951
    Dir: Roy Del Ruth. Prod: Warner Bros.
    Cast: Doris Day, Gordon MacRae.
    A musical romance.

    Penrod and Sam
    8 reels   b&w   1931
    Dir: William Beaudine. Prod: Warner Bros.
    Cast: Leon Janney.

    Penrod and Sam
    64 min.   b&w   1937
    Dir: William McGann. Prod: Warner Bros. Dist: United Artists.
    Cast: Billy Mauch, Frank Craven, Spring Byington.
    Penrod gets into wild escapades with G-Men and bank robbers. *Note: Penrod was a character who appeared in several novels and stories. Original screen stories based on this character were also written. Other "Penrod" films are Penrod and His Twin Brother, Penrod's Double Trouble.

TATE, SYLVIA

Man on the Run in *American Magazine* (April 1948)
    Woman on the Run
    77 min.   b&w   1950
    Dir: Norman Foster. Sp: Alan Campbell, Norman Foster. Prod: Universal.
    Cast: Ann Sheridan, Dennis O'Keefe.
    Drama. A beautiful woman tries to find her husband, who witnessed a gangland killing, before the mobsters do.

TAYLOR, ERIC

Unidentified story
  Romance on the Run
  54 min.   b&w   1938
  Dir: Gus Meins. Prod: Republic. Dist: Ivy.
  Cast: Donald Woods, Edward Brophy.
  Jewel thieves appear in a now-you-got-it, now-you-don't plot.

TAYLOR, GRANT

Riders of the Terror Trail
  The Terror Trail
  58 min.   b&w   1933
  Dir: Armand Schaefer. Prod: Universal.
  Cast: Tom Mix, Naomi Judge.
  Western. A crooked sheriff aids horse thieves.

TAYLOR, KRESSMAN

Address Unknown in *Address Unknown* (N.Y., Simon and Schuster, 1939)
  Address Unknown
  72 min.   b&w   1944
  Dir: William Menzies. Prod: Columbia.
  Cast: Paul Lukas, Carl Esmond.
  Drama. A Businessman in Germany embraces the Nazi Party; his partner in
America takes his revenge.

TAYLOR, MATT

Safari in Manhattan
  More Than a Secretary
  77 min.   b&w   1936
  Dir: Alfred E. Green. Prod: Columbia
  Cast: Jean Arthur, George Brent.
  Comedy. The secretary to the publisher of a health magazine falls for him.

TAYLOR, SAMUEL W.

Fever
  Bait
  79 min.   b&w   1954
  Dir: Hugo Haas. Sp: Taylor. Prod: Columbia.
  Cast: Hugo Haas, Cleo Moore, John Agar.
  An old prospector married to a sexy blonde tries to kill his partner.

TAYLOR, SAMUEL W. (cont'd)

The Man Who Came to Life
  The Man Who Came to Life
  6 reels   b&w   1941
  Dir: Lew Landers. Sp: Gordon Rigby. Prod: Columbia.
  Cast: John Howard.
  A B-picture. A man leaves town to get a fresh start but later learns that someone
is on trial for supposedly murdering him.

A Situation of Gravity in *Liberty Magazine*
  The Absent Minded Professor
  97 min.   b&w   1961
  Dir: Robert Stevenson. Prod: Walt Disney Prod. Dist: Macmillan, Twyman, Roa's,
      Swank.
  Cast: Fred MacMurray, Nancy Olsen.
  A loveable but bumbling science teacher accidently invents an incredible anti-
gravity substance which he calls "flubber." He puts it to work as the energy source
of his Model T and finds it can now fly. Son of Flubber was a movie sequel produced in 1962 by Disney.

TELLEZ, HERNANDO

Just Lather, That's All
  Just Lather, That's All
  21 min.   color   1976
  Dir: John Sebert. Sp: Joan Overaker. Dist: Learning Corp.
  A Latin American army captain strolls into a barber shop for a shave. He is the
only customer. With an attitude of calmness he begins discussing killing revolutionaries. As the barber prepares his shaving tools, it becomes increasingly clear that
the barber is a revolutionary.

TERHUNE, ALBERT PAYSON

Driftwood in *Redbook* (September 1918)
  Daring Love
  6 reels   sil.   b&w   1924
  Dir: Roland G. Edwards. Adap: Roland West, Willard Mack. Prod: Hoffman Prod.
  Cast: Elaine Hammerstein, Huntly Gordon.
  Society melodrama. John Stedman, a heavy drinker, divorces his wife and then
reforms and marries again.

Grand Larceny in *Cosmopolitan* (December 1920)
  Grand Larceny
  6 reels   sil.   b&w   1922
  Dir: Wallace Worsley. Prod: Goldwyn Pictures.

TERHUNE, ALBERT PAYSON (cont'd)

Grand Larceny (cont'd)
Cast: Claire Windsor, Elliott Dexter.
Society melodrama. Finding her in the arms of another man, John divorces his wife without waiting for an explanation.

The Hero in *New Narratives*, ed. by B. C. Williams (N.Y., Appleton-Century-Crofts, 1944)
Whom the Gods Destroy
7 reels   b&w   1934
Dir: Walter Lang. Adap: Fred Niblo, Jr. Prod: Columbia.
Cast: Robert Young, Walter Connolly, Doris Kenyon.
A theatrical producer, believed dead, secretly helps his son become a producer.

The Hunch in *Redbook Magazine* (September 1920)
Knockout Reilly
7 reels   sil.   b&w   1927
Dir: Malcolm St. Clair. Sp: Pierre Collings, Kenneth Raisbeck. Prod: Famous
    Players—Lasky.
Cast: Richard Dix, Mary Brian, Jack Renault.
Melodrama. A New Jersey steel worker named Dundee falls in love with Mary Malone, sister of a defeated boxer, who then trains Dundee to box. Dundee, however, is framed for a shooting.

TERRETT, COURTENAY

Public Relations
Made on Broadway
7 reels   b&w   1933
Dir: Harry Beaumont. Sp: Gene Markey. Prod: M-G-M.
Cast: Robert Montgomery, Madge Evans.
A story about the manufacture of a star through effective publicity.

TERRILL, LUCY STONE

Clothes in *Saturday Evening Post*
Clothes
b&w   1929
Prod: Pathe Exchange Inc.

Face in *Saturday Evening Post* (January 26, 1924)
Unguarded Women
6 reels   sil.   b&w   1924
Dir: Alan Crosland. Prod: Famous Players—Lasky.

TERRILL, LUCY STONE (cont'd)

Unguarded Women (cont'd)
Cast: Bebe Daniells, Richard Dix.
Melodrama. Douglas, guilt-ridden for allowing his buddy to die during the war, offers to marry the dead man's widow.

THERY, JACQUES

Yolanda and the Thief (jt. author Ludwig Bemelmans)
Yolanda and the Thief
110 min.   color   1945
Dir: Vincente Minnelli. Prod: M-G-M. Dist: Films Inc.
Cast: Fred Astaire, Lucille Bremer.
Musical. The story of a con man and a little girl.

THOM, ROBERT

The Day It All Happened, Baby in *Esquire* (December 1966)
Wild in the Streets
95 min.   color   1968
Dir: Barry Shear. Dist: Budget, Macmillan, Modern.
Cast: Christopher Jones, Shelley Winters, Ed Begley.
A liberal congressman seeks youngsters' support; when he wins, he offers to get the voting age lowered to 14. Later the kids pour LSD into the Washington, D.C., water supply.

THOMPKINS, JULIET WILBUR

Fanny Foley Herself
Fanny Foley Herself
1931
Prod: RKO.

THOMPSON, HAMILTON

The Ark Angel in *Saturday Evening Post*
The Rowdy
5 reels   sil.   b&w   1921
Dir: David Kirkland. Prod: Universal.
Cast: Rex Roselli, Anna Hernandez.
Melodrama. A retired skipper raises a child found in a storm.

THOMPSON, MARY AGNES

A Call from Mitch Miller.
Loving You
101 min.   1957

THOMPSON, MARY AGNES (cont'd)

Loving You (cont'd)
Dir: Hal Kanton. Prod: Paramount.
Cast: Elvis Presley, Lizabeth Scott, Wendell Corey.
A small-town boy becomes an overnight sensation when he is signed to sing
with a band.

THOMPSON, MORTON

Lewie, My Brother Who Talked to Horses in *Joe, the Wounded Tennis Player*
My Brother Talks to Horses
93 min.   b&w   1946
Dir: Fred Zinnemann. Sp: Thompson. Prod: M-G-M. Dist: Films Inc.
Cast: Butch Jenkins, Peter Lawford.
A child's gift for talking to animals proves lucrative when he talks to race horses.

THURBER, JAMES

The Catbird Seat in *Best American Stories of 1943*, ed. by Martha Foley.
The Battle of the Sexes
83 min.   b&w   1960
Dir: Charles Crichton. Rel: Continental Dist. Corp. Dist: Budget, Twyman.
Cast: Peter Sellers, Constance Cummings, Robert Morley.
The Old World head of the accounting department of a Scottish firm is dis-
comfited by a female efficiency expert.

The Night the Ghost Got In
James Thurber's The Night the Ghost Got In
15½ min.   color   1977
Dir: Robert Stitzel. Dist: BFA.
While taking a bath, young James hears a noise, which his brother believes is a
ghost.

The Secret Life of Walter Mitty
The Secret Life of Walter Mitty
110 min.   color   1947
Dir: Norman Z. McLeod. Prod: Samuel Goldwyn Prod. Dist: Macmillan.
Cast: Danny Kaye, Virginia Mayo.
Henpecked by his mother and a finicky fiancée, Mitty dreams of sailing the Seven
Seas, dogfighting the Red Baron, facing down gunmen, and other heroic feats.

THURBER, JAMES (cont'd)

Suggested by the writings of Thurber and his cartoons
    The War Between Men and Women
    110 min.   color   1972
    Dir: Melville Shavelson. Dist: Film Center.
    Cast: Jack Lemmon, Barbara Harris, Jason Robards.
    Lemmon is a gruff, grumpy cartoonist who dislikes women, children, and dogs.
Harris is an attractive divorcee with three kids and a pregnant dog whose ex-husband
periodically re-appears and on one occasion gets drunk with Lemmon.

A Unicorn in the Garden
    A Unicorn in the Garden
    8 min.   color   1953
    Prod: UPA. Dist: Learning.
    The whimsical tale of a domineering wife who tries to get her meek husband
carted off to the booby-hatch because he saw a unicorn in the garden.

TILDESLEY, ALICE L.

What Can You Expect? in *Saturday Evening Post*
    Short Skirts
    5 reels   sil.   b&w   1921
    Dir: Harry B. Harris. Prod: Universal.
    Cast: Gladys Welton, Ena Gregory.
    Society melodrama. A young girl of 17 tries to ruin the election of her mother's
fiancé.

TINSLEY, THEODORE A.

Five Spot
    Panic on the Air
    6 reels   b&w   1936
    Dir: D. Ross Lederman. Sp: Harold Shumate. Prod: Columbia.
    Cast: Lew Ayres, Florence Rice.
    A far-fetched comedy about a sports announcer with a flair for uncovering
mysteries.

Manhattan Whirligig
    Manhattan Shakedown
    6 reels   b&w   1937
    Dir: Leon Barsha. Sp: Edgar Edwards. Prod: Warwick Pictures.
    Cast: John Galloudet, Rosalind Keith.
    A columnist wants to run a blackmailing doctor out of town.

TITUS, HAROLD

Stuff of Heroes
The Great Mr. Nobody
71 min.   b&w   1941
Dir: Ben Stoloff. Prod: Warner Bros. Dist: United Artists.
Cast: Eddie Albert, Joan Leslie.
Comedy about a salesman who is perpetually in hot water. Prior movie title was
Bashful Hero.

How Baxter Butted In
7 reels   sil.   b&w   1925
Dir: William Beaudine. Adap: Julien Josephson. Prod: Warner Bros.
Cast: Dorothy Devore, Matt Moore.
Comedy. A shy clerk in the circulation department of a large newspaper dreams
of performing heroic deeds. He falls in love with a pretty stenographer.

TOLSTOY, LEO

Father Sergius
Father Sergius (U.S.S.R.)
81 min.   sil.   b&w   1917
Dir: Yakov Protazanov. Sp: Alexander Volkov. Dist: Macmillan.
Cast: Ivan Mozhukhin, Vera Dzheneyeva.
On the eve of his wedding to a beautiful woman, a handsome officer at the court
of Czar Nikolai I breaks his engagement, gives up his estate, and becomes a monk.

Martin the Cobbler
Martin the Cobbler
28 min.   color   1977
Prod: Frank Moynihan. Dist: Mass Media.
A cobbler who has lost his family, loses all interest in life and hopes to die. In a
dream he hears a voice, which he assumes is the Lord's, promising to come and visit
him the next day. The next day, not the Lord, but people in need arrive and he helps
them. By caring for others he finds new hope in life. Done in 3-dimensional clay
animation.

TOMPKINS, JULIET

Once There Was a Princess
Misbehaving Ladies
75 min.   b&w   1931
Dir: William Beaudine. Prod: First National Pictures. Dist: United Artists.
Cast: Louise Fazenda, Lila Lee, Ben Lyon.
A girl returns home incognito.

TOOHEY, JOHN PETER

On the Back Seat in *Collier's* (September 12, 1925)
Outcast Souls
6 reels   sil.   b&w   1928
Dir: Louis Chaudet. Prod: Sterling Pictures.
Cast: Pricilla Bonner, Charles Delaney.
A husband's father and his wife's mother meet and fall in love after trying
unsuccessfully to live with their children.

TORS, IVAN

Jumpin' Joe
Below the Deadline
7 reels   b&w   1946
Dir: William Beaudine. Sp: Harvey H. Gates, Forrest Judd. Prod: Monogram.
Cast: Warren Douglas, Ramsay Ames.
A returning G.I. gets involved in the rackets.

TRAVEN, BRUNO

The Third Guest
Macario (Mex.)
90 min.   1960
Dir: Roberto Gavaldon. Prod: Azteca Films.
Cast: Ignacio Lopez Tarso, Pina Pellicer.
A hungry peasant refuses to share food with God and the Devil, but shares it
with Death, who cures the dying when willing. Then the peasant is arraigned by
the Inquisition as a wizard. Nominated for an Academy Award in the Foreign
Language Film Category in 1960.

TREYNOR, ALBERT

Highway Robber
It's a Small World
7 reels   b&w   1935
Dir: Irving Cummings. Sp: Gladys Lehman, Sam Hellman. Prod: Fox.
Cast: Spencer Tracy, Wendy Barrie.
Two St. Louis big-timers who smash their cars near a small Louisiana town are
stranded there until the cars car be repaired.

TRUMBELL, WALTER see Bits of Life under WILEY, HUGH

TUPPER, TRISTRAM

Four Brothers in *Saturday Evening Post* (April 7, 1928)
  First Kiss
  6 reels   sil.   b&w   1928
  Dir: Rowland V. Lee. Prod: Paramount Famous Players—Lasky.
  Cast; Fay Wray, Gary Cooper, Land Chandler.
  The Talbot family is going downhill. To finance an education for his brothers, the
second son decides to rob ships in the Chesapeke Bay.

Three Episodes in the Life of Timothy Osborn in *Saturday Evening Post* (April 9,
  1927)
  Lucky Star
  10 reels   sil. or sd.   1929
  Dir: Frank Borzage. Prod: Fox.
  Cast: Charles Farrell, Janet Gaynor.
  After World War I, a farm girl chooses a disabled veteran over a war hero against
the wishes of her widowed mother.

TURGENEV, IVAN

Bezhin Meadow
  Bezhin Meadow
  30 min.   b&w   1935
  Dir: Sergei Eisenstein. Dist: Audio Brandon.
  Cast: E. Vitka, Boris Zakhava, Yelena Teleshova.
  A story about the gallant work of Russian youths on a collective farm. Young
Stepok, guarding the harvest at night, is shot down by his father, a mad saboteur.

First Love (novella)
  First Love
  90 min.   color   1970
  Dir: Maximilian Schell. Prod: Schell, Barry Levinson. Dist: Audio Brandon.
  Cast: Maximilian Schell, Dominique Sanda, John Moulder Brown.
  During an era of social decay and impending revolution, a 16-year-old boy
becomes infatuated with an impoverished princess.

Mumu
  Mumu
  71 min.   b&w   1960
  Dir: Anatoli Bobrovsky, Yevgeni Teterin. Dist: Audio Brandon.
  Cast: Afanasi Kochetkov, Nina Grebeshkova, Leonid Kmit.
  Gerasim, the huge powerful deaf-mute, is a village serf. He loves the land, his work,
and the people around him. When his mistress decides to take him to Moscow, he
is lonely and derided, and seeks out the company of Vanya, a laundress. But Vanya
is sent away. When his puppy Mumu is taken from him he rebels.

TURNER, GEORGE KIBBE

Companionate*
  Half Marriage
  7 reels   sil. or sd.   b&w   1929
  Dir: William J. Cowen. Prod: RKO.
  Cast: Olive Borden, Morgan Farley.
  Romantic drama. Following a party, Judy Page elopes with Dick Carroll, who
is employed by her father. Dick hides when her mother arrives at her apartment and
insists that Judy go home with her. *Note: According to the AFI, publication of
this story was not determined.

A Passage to Hong Kong
  Roar of the Dragon
  s.m. a story by Merian C. Cooper, Jane Bigelow.
  8 reels   b&w   1932
  Dir: Wesley Ruggles. Sp: Howard Estabrook. Prod: RKO.
  The American captain of an Oriental steamship defends the foreign population
from a murderous bandit.

The Street of Forgotten Men in *Liberty Magazine* (February 14, 1925)
  The Street of Forgotten Man
  7 reels   sil.   b&w   1925
  Dir: Herbert Brenon. Prod: Famous Players–Lasky. Dist: Thunderbird.
  Cast: Grace Fleming.
  Melodrama. Charlie disguises himself as a cripple.

TUTTLE, W. C.

Baa, Baa Black Sheep in *Short Stories*
  Black Sheep
  5 reels   sil.   b&w   1921
  Dir: Paul Hurst. Prod: Chaudet-Hurst Prod.
  Cast: Neal Hart, Ted Brooks.
  Western melodrama. A complicated story about cattlemen versus sheepmen.

The Devil's Dooryard in *Adventure Magazine* (May 3, 1921)
  The Devil's Dooryard
  5 reels   sil.   b&w   1923
  Dir: Lewis King. Prod: Ben Wilson Prod.
  Cast: William Fairbanks, Ena Gregory.
  Western melodrama. Paul Stevens recovers stolen money.

TUTTLE, W. C. (cont'd)

Fate of the Wolf in *Short Stories* (June 25, 1925)
Driftin' Sands
5 reels   sil.   b&w   1928
Dir: Wallace W. Fox. Adap: Oliver Drake. Prod: FBO Pictures.
Cast: Bob Steele, Gladys Quartaro.
Western melodrama. A wealthy Mexican hires Driftin' Sands to guard his daughter.

Henry Goes to Arizona
Henry Goes to Arizona
7 reels   b&w   1939
Dir: Edwin Marin. Sp: Florence Ryerson, Milton Merlin. Prod: Loew's.
Cast: Frank Morgan.
Comedy western. Henry is a rent-beating vaudevillian who heads West. Prior movie title was Spats to Spurs.

The Law Rustlers in *Adventure Magazine* (September 1, 1921)
The Law Rustlers
5 reels   sil.   b&w   1923
Dir: Lewis King. Prod: Ben Wilson Prod.
Cast: William Fairbanks, Edmund Cobb.
On their way to Alaska a pair of drifters help a young woman stand up to a corrupt town council.

Peaceful in *Short Stories Magazine*
Peaceful Peters
5 reels   sil.   b&w   1922
Dir: Lewis King. Prod: Ben Wilson Prod.
Cast: William Fairbanks, Harry La Mont.
The last words of a dying prospector bring danger, excitement, romance, and fortune to Peaceful Peters.

The Red Head from Sun Dog
The Red Rider (series)
2 reels each   b&w   1934
Dir: Lew Landers. Prod: Universal.
Cast: William Fairbanks.
Fifteen films. A sheriff sacrifices his job when he lets his friend, a convicted murderer, out of jail. He sets off to find the real killer.

The Sheriff of Sun-Dog in *Adventure Magazine* (November 30, 1921)
The Sheriff of Sun-Dog
4,949'   sil.   b&w   1922
Dir: Lewis King. Prod: Berwilla Film Corp.

TUTTLE, W. C. (cont'd)

The Sheriff of Sun-Dog (cont'd)
Cast: William Fairbanks, Robert McKenzie.
Western melodrama. Sheriff "Silvent" Davidson is framed.

Sir Piegan Passes
Cheyenne Kid
6 reels   b&w   1933
Dir: Robert Hill. Sp: Jack Curtis.
Cast: Tom Keene.
A danger-loving cowboy is mistaken for a killer.

The Fargo Kid
64 min.   b&w   1940
Prod: RKO.
Cast: Tim Holt.
The Fargo Kid outwits a professional gunman.

Spawn of the Desert in *Short Stories* (May 10, 1922)
Spawn of the Desert
5 reels   sil.   b&w   1923
Dir: Lewis King. Prod: Berwilla Film Corp.
Cast: William Fairbanks, Florence Gilbert.
Western melodrama. Le Saint is in search of the man who destroyed his home.

Straight Shooting in *Short Stories Magazine*
The Border Sheriff
56 min.   b&w   sil.   1926
Dir: Robert North Bradbury. Prod: Universal. Dist: Em Gee.
Cast: Jack Hoxie.
Leaving a conference on drug smuggling in Washington, Cultus Collins, the
sheriff of Cayuse County, goes to San Francisco to rescue a millionaire rancher from
a Chinatown dive.

The Yellow Seal in *Liberty Magazine* (January 10, 1925)
The Prairie Pirate
5 reels   sil.   b&w   1925
Dir: Edmund Mortimer. Adap: Anthony Dillon. Dist: Film Classic Exchange.
Cast: Harry Carey, Jean Dumas.
Western tale of murder, revenge, and romance: a bandit and a gambler battle over
a woman.

TWAIN, MARK

The Celebrated Jumping Frog of Calaveras County
    The Best Man Wins
    75 min.   b&w   1948
    Prod: Columbia.
    Cast: Edgar Buchanan, Anna Lee.
    A man who returns home after many years raises money by jumping his frog.

    The Legend of Mark Twain
    32 min.   color   1969
    Prod: ABC News. Dist: Benchmark
    The story recounts the life of Mark Twain, dramatizing this story and segments
of *The Adventures of Hucklebery Finn.*

The Million Pound Bank Note
    Man with a Million (Br.)
    90 min.   color   1953
    Dir: Ronald Neame. Sp: Jill Craigie. Prod: Group Film Prod. Dist: Macmillan,
        United Artists.
    Cast: Gregory Peck, A. E. Matthews.
    An impoverished American stranded in London comes into possession of a
million-pound bank note. No one can make change for it, but it brings the man
luxury.

Unidentified story
    Double-Barrelled Detective Story
    90 min.   b&w   1965
    Dir and Sp: Adolfas Mekas. Prod: Saloon Prod.
    Cast: Jeff Siggra, Greta Thyssen, Hurd Hatfield.
    Mystery comedy drama. A preposterous story of a wronged women who trains
her son to track down his father for revenge.

ULMAN, WILLIAM A., JR.

A Gun in His Hand*
  Sergeant Madden
  8 reels   b&w   1939
  Dir: Josepf von Sternberg. Sp: Wells Root. Prod: M-G-M. Dist: Films Inc.
  Cast: Wallace Beery, Laraine Day.
  A bad copy story. *Note: One source questioned whether or not this story was
published.

UPDIKE, JOHN

The Music School
  The Music School
  30 min.   color   1977
  Dir and Sp: John Korty. Dist: Perspective.
  A contemporary writer struggles during a 24-hour period to find meaning in his
life. The implication of religion, technology, contemporary violence, and social
change all emerge in vivid images, and then he takes his daughter to music school.

UPSON, WILLIAM HAZLETT

A series of unidentified stories in *Saturday Evening Post*
  Earthworm Tractors
  69 min.   b&w   1936
  Dir: Ray Enright. Prod: First National Pictures and Vitaphone. Dist: WNET/13.
  Cast: Joe E. Brown, June Travis.
  Salesman Alexander Botts blunders into trouble.

VADNAI (AKA VADNAY), LADISLAUS

Josette
  Josette
  s.m. Jo and Josette, a play by Paul Frank and George Fraser in turn based on
    the story
  6,241'   b&w   1938
  Dir: Allan Dwan. Sp: James Edward Grant. Prod: 20th Century Fox.
  Cast: Simone Simon, Robert Young, Don Ameche.
  Farce. Two brothers pressure the wrong girl.

VANCE, HENRY C.

Pin Money in *Snappy Stories* (December 2, 1921)
  Diamond Handcuffs
  6,070'   sil.   b&w   1928
  Dir: John P. McCarthy. Adap: Willis Goldbeck. Prod: Cosmopolitan Prod.
  Cast: Lena Malena, Charles Stevens, Conrad Nagel.
  Three episodes about a cursed diamond.

VANCE, LOUIS JOSEPH

Lone Wolf in Paris*
  Lone Wolf in Paris
  7 reels   b&w   1938
  Dir: Albert S. Rogell. Sp: Arthur T. Horman. Prod: Columbia.
  Cast: Francis Lederer, Francis Drake.
  Rival thieves. *Note: The Lone Wolf, a jewel thief, was a character who appeared
in a number of novels and stories, as well as in original screen stories. Among the Lone
Wolf films are the following: Last of the Lone Wolf, The Lone Wolf and His Lady,
Lone Wolf in London, Lone Wolf in Mexico, The Lone Wolf Meets a Lady, The
Lone Wolf Returns, Lone Wolf Spy Hunt, The Lone Wolf Strikes, The Lone Wolf
Takes a Chance, The Lone Wolf's Laughter.

VAN LOAN, CHARLES E.

Scrap Iron in *Saturday Evening Post*
  Scrap Iron
  7 reels   b&w   sil.   1921
  Dir: Charles Ray. Adap: Finis Fox. Prod: Charles Ray.

VAN LOAN, CHARLES E. (cont'd)

Scrap Iron (cont'd)
Cast: Charles Ray, Lydia Knott.
A mill worker gives up amateur boxing at the request of his invalid mother and is ostracized by co-workers and his girlfriend. He later redeems himself.

VAN RIPPER, DONALD

Dying Lips
Sealed Lips
s.m. radio show Street and Smith's Detective Story Magazine Hour
17 min.   b&w
Dir: Kurt Neuman. Sp: Samuel Freedman. Prod: Universal.

VESZI, MARGIT

Unidentified story
All in a Night's Work
s.m. a play by Owen Elford
94 min.   color   1961
Dir: Joseph Anthony. Prod: Paramount. Dist: Association, Macmillan.
Cast: Dean Martin, Shirley MacLaine.
Romantic comedy. A playboy matches wits with a zany and lovely employee of his publishing company, whom he suspects of having had an affair with the company's previous owner.

VONNEGUT, KURT, JR.

Next Door in *Welcome to the Monkey House*
Next Door
24 min.   color   1975
Dir: Andrew Silver. Dist: Phoenix Films.
The parents of an 8-year-old boy forgot to call the sitter, and go to the movies anyway.

VROMAN, MARY ELIZABETH

See How They Run
Bright Road
69 min.   b&w   1953
Dir: Gerald Mayer. Prod: M-G-M. Dist: Films Inc.
Cast: Dorothy Dandridge, Harry Belafonte.
A story about a problem pupil.

WALLACE, EDGAR

Criminal at Large
  Criminal at Large (Br. title The Frightened Lady)
  s.m. play by Wallace
  70 min.   b&w   1932
  Dir: T. Hayes Hunter. Prod: Gainsborough and Helber.
  Cast: Emlyn Williams, Cathleen Nesbit, Norman McKinnel.
  A man commits murder during spells of insanity.

Death Watch
  Before Dawn
  60 min.   b&w   1933
  Dir: Irving Pichel. Sp: Garret Fort, Marian Dix, Ralph Block.
  Cast: Stuart Erwin, Dorothy Wilson, Warner Oland.
  Fantasy. A clairvoyant girl is mixed up in murders.

The Feathered Serpent
  The Menace
  7 reels   color   1932
  Dir: Roy William Neill. Adap: Charles Logue. Prod: Columbia.

The Greek Poropulos in *Mystery Companion*, ed. by Abraham Louis (N.Y.,
  Lantern Press, 1946)
  Born to Gamble
  8 reels   b&w   1935
  Dir: Phil Rosen. Prod: Liberty Pictures.

Unidentified stories
  Death Trap (Br.)
  56 min.   b&w   1966
  Dir: John Moxey. Sp: John Roddick. Prod: Anglo Guild Prod.
  Cast: Albert Lieven, Barbara Shelley.
  Mystery. The money of a deceased girl disappears.

WALLACE, EDGAR (cont'd)

Incident at Midnight (Br.)
58 min.   b&w   1966
Dir: Norman Harrison. Prod: Merton Park Studios.
Cast: Anton Diffring, William Sylvester.
A former Nazi is spotted in a drug store by an undercover agent of the narcotics squad.

The £20,000 Kiss (Br.)
57 min.   b&w   1962
Dir: John Moxey. Prod: Merton Park Studios.
Cast: Dawn Addams, Michael Goodliffe.
An extortion ring tries to blackmail a member of Parliament, which leads to murder.

WALPOLE, HUGH

The Silver Mask
  Kind Lady
  s.m. film based on the play Kind Lady by Edward Chodorov in turn based on
    this story
  78 min.   b&w   1951
Dir: John Sturges. Prod: M-G-M. Dist: Films Inc.
Cast: Ethel Barrymore, Maurice Evans, Angela Lansbury, Keenan Wynn.
A wealthy old lady befriends a charming artist, who, by a clever ruse, gets into her home and with several of his criminal friends keeps her prisoner while they sell off her possessions.

WALSH, MAURICE

Green Rushes
  The Quiet Man
  129 min.   color   1952
Dir: John Ford. Prod: Republic. Dist: Ivy.
Cast: John Wayne, Maureen O'Hara, Barry Fitzgerald, Ward Bond.
Comedy. A boxer returns to Ireland and falls for a fiery colleen. Nominated for an Academy Award as the Best Written American Comedy.

WALSH, THOMAS

Home Coming (suggestion for)
  Don't Turn 'em Loose
  65 min.   b&w   1936
Dir: Ben Stoloff. Sp: Harry Segall, Ferdinand Reyher. Prod: RKO.
Cast: Lewis Stone, Bruce Cabot, Betty Grable.
Crime melodrama. Parole board member watches his own son become a criminal.

WALSH, THOMAS (cont'd)

Husk
    We're Only Human
    7 reels   b&w   1936
    Dir: James Flood. Sp: Rian James. Prod: RKO.
    Cast: Preston Flood, Jane Wyatt.
    A detective loses his job when he lets a bandit escape, but eventually clears
himself.

WARE, DARRELL

A series of unidentified stories
    Life Begins at College
    110 min.   b&w   1937
    Dir: William A. Seiter. Prod: Fox.
    Cast: Ritz Brothers, Joan Davis.
    Slapstick football comedy.

WARE, LEON

The Search
    In Self Defense
    1947
    Prod: Monogram.

Unidentified story
    Peggy
    77 min.   color   1950
    Dir: Frederick de Cordova. Sp: George F. Slavin, George W. George. Prod and
        Dist: Universal.
    Cast: Diana Lynn, Charles Coburn.
    Comedy. Two beautiful sisters compete for the title of Queen of the Tournament
of Roses, but one of them is secretly married.

WATKINS, MARY T.

Stolen Thunder in *Saturday Evening Post* (June 7, 1930)
    Oh, for a Man!
    9 reels   b&w   1930
    Dir: Hamilton MacFadden. Prod: Fox.
    Cast: Jeanette MacDonald, Reginald Denny.
    An opera singer falls for and marries a former burglar, with the intention of
making a singer out of him.

WAUGH, ALEX

Small Back Room in St. Marylebone in *Esquire* (March 1953)
    Circle of Deception (Br.)
    100 min.   b&w   1961
    Dir: Jack Lee. Prod: 20th Century Fox. Dist: Select.
    Cast: Bradford Dillman, Suzy Parker.
    War melodrama. An intelligence agent on a dangerous mission in Germany gets
caught.

WEBB, JAMES R.

A Baby for Midge
    Close to My Heart
    90 min.   b&w   1951
    Dir: William Keighley. Prod: Warner Bros.
    Cast: Gene Tierney, Ray Milland, Fay Bainter.
    A soap opera about a couple who adopt the child of a convicted murderer.

Fugitive from Terror (magazine serial)
    Woman in Hiding
    92 min.   b&w   1950
    Dir: Michael Gordon. Sp: Oscar Saul. Prod: Universal.
    Cast: Ida Lupino, Howard Duff.
    Drama. A woman pretends she was killed in a car crash in order to prove that her
husband killed her father.

WEIDMAN, JEROME

R.S.V.P.
    Invitation
    84 min.   b&w   1952
    Dir: Gottfried Reinhardt. Sp: Paul Osborn. Prod: M-G-M. Dist: Films Inc.
    Cast: Van Johnson, Dorothy McGuire.
    Soap opera. A rich father bribes a young man to marry his daughter who has
only one year to live.

WEIMAN, RITA

Curtain in *Saturday Evening Post*
    Curtain
    5 reels   b&w   sil.   1927
    Dir and Adap: James Young. Prod: Katharine MacDonald Picture Corp.

WEIMAN, RITA (cont'd)

Footlights in *Saturday Evening Post* (May 17, 1919)
    The Spotlight
    5 reels   sil.   b&w   1927
    Dir: Frank Tuttle. Prod: Paramount Famous Players—Lasky
    Cast: Esther Ralston, Neil Hamilton.
    Romantic drama of an obscure actress who rises to stardom by pretending to
be an exotic Russian.

On Your Back in *Liberty Magazine* (February 22, 1930)
    On Your Back
    8 reels   b&w   1930
    Dir: Guthrie McClintic. Prod: Fox.
    Cast: Irene Rich, Raymond Hackett.
    A college student becomes engaged to a showgirl, who is having an affair with a
powerful broker in business with the student's mother, the owner of a fashionable
Fifth Avenue salon.

One Man's Secret (novelette)
    Possessed
    108 min.   b&w   1949
    Dir: Curtis Bernhardt. Prod: Warner Bros. Dist: United Artists.
    Cast: Joan Crawford, Van Heflin.
    The dramatic story of a pretty schizophrenic who is entangled in a love triangle
and becomes involved in a murder case.

The Stage Door in *More Aces* (New York, 1925)
    After the Show
    6 reels   sil.   b&w   1921
    Dir: William De Mille. Prod: Famous Players—Lasky.
    Cast: Jack Holt, Lila Lee, Charles Ogle, Eve Southern.
    Melodrama. Pop O'Malley, a stage door keeper, takes a paternal interest in
Eileen, a chorus girl. A millionaire backer of the show takes an interest in Eileen
also, and Pop objects.

To Whom It May Concern in *Cosmopolitan* (February 1922)
    The Social Code
    5 reels   sil.   b&w   1923
    Dir: Oscar Apfel. Prod: Metro.
    Cast: Viola Dana, Malcolm McGregor.
    Mystery drama. A girl saves her lover from the electric chair.

WELCH, DOUGLASS

We Go Fast in *Mr. Digby*
  We Go Fast
  5,790'   b&w   1941
  Dir: William McGann. Prod: 20th Century Fox.
  Cast: Marjorie Weaver, John Hubbard.
  Ten people sign a pact whereby $200,000 goes to the last survivor.

WELLS, H(ERBERT) G(EORGE)

The Man Who Could Work Miracles
  The Man Who Could Work Miracles (Br.)
  82 min.   b&w   1937
  Dir: Alexander Korda. Prod: London Film Prod. Dist: Budget, Mogull's,
    Institutional Cinema.
  Cast: Roland Young, Joan Gardner.
  An obscure little clerk in a small English country town discovers he has the
power to work miracles. When this power is abused, the world is on the brink of
disaster.

WEST, REBECCA

Abiding Vision
  A Life of Her Own
  108 min.   b&w   1950
  Dir: George Cukor. Sp: Isobel Lennart. Prod: M-G-M. Dist: Films Inc.
  Cast: Lana Turner, Ray Milland, Ann Dvorak.
  A story about two photographic models—one on her way up, the other on her
way down.

WEST, WALTON

Big Bend Bucharoo
  Riding Avenger
  50 min.   b&w   1936
  Dir: Harry Fraser. Prod: Walter Futter. Dist: United Films.
  Cast: Hoot Gibson.

WESTMAN, LOLITA ANN

Lawless Honeymoon
  The Perfect Clue
  7 reels   b&w   1935
  Dir: Robert G. Vignola. Adap: Albert De Mond. Prod: Majestic Producers Corp.
  Cast: David Manners, Skeets Gallagher.
  A too-perfect clue almost thwarts the detectives.

WESTON, GARNETT

Mounted Patrol, a serial in *Saturday Evening Post*
  Pony Soldier
  82 min.   b&w   1952
  Dir: Joseph M. Newman. Prod: 20th Century Fox. Dist: Films Inc.
  Cast: Tyrone Power, Cameron Mitchell, Robert Horton.
  A Mountie tries to stop a tribe of rebellious Indians from waging war.

WESTON, GEORGE

The Open Door in *Saturday Evening Post* (January 8, 1921)
  Is Life Worth Living?
  5 reels   sil.   b&w   1921
  Dir: Alan Crosland. Prod: Selznick Pictures.
  Cast: Eugene O'Brian, Winifred Westover.
  Melodrama. On parole, a man wrongly accused of a crime becomes a salesman,
but he can't succeed. He buys a revolver and goes to Central Park to kill himself.
There he sees a young girl who faints from hunger, and he resolves to take care of
her.

Taxi! Taxi! in *Saturday Evening Post* (July 25-August 8, 1925)
  Taxi! Taxi!
  7 reels   sil.   b&w   1927
  Dir: Melville W. Brown. Prod: Universal.
  Cast: Edward Everett Horton, Marian Nixon.
  Romantic farce. A murder is committed in a taxi.

WETJEN, RICHARD ALBERT

Wallaby Jim of the Islands
  Wallaby Jim of the Islands
  7 reels   b&w   1937
  Dir: Charles Lamont. Sp: Bennett Cohen, Houston Branch. Prod: Edward L.
    Alperson. Dist: Mogull's.
  Cast: Ian Keith, George Houston.
  Pearl pirates roam the waters of the South Seas.

WHEELIS, ALLEN

The Illusionless Man and the Visionary Maid in *Commentary* (May 1964)
  The Crazy Quilt
  80 min.   b&w   1967
  Dir: John Korty. Prod: Continental. Dist: Walter Reade 16.
  Cast: Tom Rosqui, Ina Mela.
  Drama. A story about the 50-year marriage of a pragmatic man and a romantic
dreamer.

WHITE, E. B.

A Preposterous Parable in *New Yorker*
  The Family That Dwelt Apart
  8 min.   color   1973
  Prod: National Film Board of Canada. Dist: Learning Corp.

A tall and salty Yankee story about a family done in by do-gooders. The Pruitt family, seven members strong, live in euphoric independence on an island off the New Hampshire coast until they are marooned by a winter freeze and the mainlanders mount a massive campaign to save them. It is the beginning of the end for them.

WHITE, LESLIE T.

Five Thousand Trojan Horses
  Northern Pursuit
  94 min.   b&w   1942
  Dir: Raoul Walsh. Prod: First National Pictures. Dist: United Artists.
  Cast: Errol Flynn, Julie Bishop.
  A Canadian Mountie pursues a Nazi.

Six Weeks South of Texas (AKA Trouble in Paradise, a magazine serial)
  The Americano
  85 min.   color   1954
  Dir: William Castle. Sp: Guy Trosper. Prud: Robert Stillman Prod. Dist: Ivy.
  Cast: Glenn Ford, Frank Lovejoy, Cesar Romero.

An adventure melodrama. A Texan delivering three bulls to cattlemen in Brazil becomes involved in a feud.

WHITE, NELIA GARDNER

The Little Horse
  The Gift of Love
  105 min.   color   1958
  Dir: Jean Negulesco. Prod: 20th Century Fox. Dist: Films Inc.
  Cast: Lauren Becall, Robert Stack.

After the death of his wife, a man adopts a precocious child who desperately tries to fill the void in his life.

Sentimental Journey
  55 min.   b&w   1946
  Dir: Walter Land. Prod: 20th Century Fox. Dist: Films Inc.
  Cast: Maureen O'Hara.

WHITE, STEWART EDWARD

Leopard Woman
    Leopard Woman
    77 min.   sil.   b&w   1920
    Dist: Em Gee, Blackhawk.
    Cast: Louise Glaum.
    An epic of passion, intrigue, and espionage in the Equatorial jungle.

The Shepper-Newfounder in *Saturday Evening Post* (March 29, 1930)
    Part Time Wife
    6,500'   b&w   1930
    Dir: Leo McCarey. Prod: Fox.
    Cast: Edmund Lowe, Leila Hyams.
    A husband, who is married to his business activities, is re-united with his estranged wife on the golf course.

The Two Gun Man in *Famous Story Magazine* (October 1925)
    Under a Texas Moon
    8 reels   tinted   1930
    Dir: Michael Curtiz. Sp: Gordon Rigby. Prod: Warner Bros.
    Cast: Frank Fay, Raquel Torres.
    Romantic western drama. A dashing Mexican adventurer captures rustlers and wins the heart of his girl.

WHITE, WILLIAM C.

Unidentified story
    Beg, Borrow or Steal
    8 reels   b&w   1937
    Dir: William Thiele. Sp: Leonard Lee, Harry Ruskin, Marion Parsonnet. Prod: M-G-M.
    A B-movie about con men on the Riviera.

WHITFIELD, RAOUL

Inside Job
    High Tide
    70 min.   b&w   1947
    Dir: John Reinhardt. Prod: Monogram.
    Cast: Don Castle, Lee Tracy, Anabel Shaw.
    A newspaperman combats corruption.

WHITTAKER, WAYNE

Chicago Lulu
  The Bamboo Blonde
  67 min.   b&w   1946
  Dir: Anthony Mann. Prod: RKO. Dist: Films Inc.
  Cast: Frances Langford.
  A South Pacific pilot names his bomber after a night club singer, thereby
bringing her fame.

WHITTIER, JOHN GREENLEAF

The Barefoot Boy
  The Barefoot Boy
  6 reels   sil.   b&w   1923
  Dir: David Kirkland. Prod: Mission Film Corp.
  Cast: John Bowers, Marjorie Daw, Sylvia Breamer.
  Rural drama. Mistreated by his stepfather and wrongly accused of setting fire to
the school, Dick Alden runs away but returns home years later.

WHITTINGTON, HARRY

Wyoming Wildcatters
  Black Gold
  98 min.   1961
  Dir: Leslie Martinson. Prod: Warner Bros.
  Cast: Philip Carey, Diane McBain, James Best.
  Melodrama. An adventurer stakes everything on the chance of striking oil.

WILBUR, RICHARD

A Game of Catch
  A Game of Catch
  7 min.   color   1974
  Dir: Steven K. Witty. Dist: Audio Brandon.
  Two young boys exclude another boy from their game.

WILDE, OSCAR

The Canterville Ghost
  The Canterville Ghost
  95 min.   b&w   1944
  Dir: Jules Dassin. Prod: M-G-M. Dist: Films Inc.
  Cast: Robert Young, Charles Laughton.
  Condemned for his cowardice, a ghost must haunt the ancestral castle until some-
one in the family line performs a heroic act.

WILDE, OSCAR (cont'd)

The Canterville Ghost (cont'd)
   The Canterville Ghost
   15 min.   b&w   1955
   Prod: Dynamic Films. Dist: Audio Brandon.
   Cast: Monty Woolley.
   A modern version of the story about a weary ghost and children.

The Happy Prince
   The Happy Prince
   25 min.   color   1974
   Prod: Reader's Digest. Dist: Pyramid.
   A swallow strips the gold off a statue of a prince to help the poor.

Lord Arthur Saville's Crime
   Flesh and Fantasy
   s.m. two unidentified stories, one by Laslo Vadnai, and the other by Ellis
      St. Joseph.
   94 min.   b&w   1943
   Dir: Julien Duvivier. Prod: Universal. Dist: Twyman, Universal.
   Cast: Edward G. Robinson, Charles Boyer, Barbara Stanwyck, Robert Bench-
      ley, Robert Cummings, Betty Field, Thomas Mitchell.
   The theme of superstition links three stories: one depicts the ugly duckling
fable; in another, a man is obsessed by murder; and the last concerns the inner
struggle of a superstitious circus performer.

The Nightingale and the Rose
   The Nightingale and the Rose
   14 min.   color   1967
   Dir: Joseph Karbert. Dist: Audio Brandon.
   A two-dimensional animated rendering of this story.

The Remarkable Rocket
   The Remarkable Rocket
   25 min.   color   1975
   Prod: Reader's Digest. Dist: Pyramid.
   David Niven narrates this witty story about the fireworks ready to be set off
during a royal wedding ceremony.

The Selfish Giant
   The Selfish Giant
   27 min.   color   1972
   Prod: Reader's Digest. Dist: Pyramid.
   A giant won't let the children play in his garden and therefore Spring is kept away.

WILDE, PERCIVAL

The Extreme Airiness of Duton Lang
   The Rise of Duton Lang
   7 min.   color   1955
   Dir: Osmond Evans. Prod: Bosustow.

WILEY, HUGH

Hop in *Jade and Other Stories* (New York, 1921)
   Bits of Life
   s.m. "The Man Who Heard Everything," by Walter Trumbell in *Smart Set*
      (April 1921)
   6 reels   sil.   b&w   1921
   Dir: A. Marshall Neilan. Prod: First National Pictures.
   Cast: Wesley Barry, Rockliffe Fellowes.
   Melodrama. Four episodes about good versus evil.

James Lee Wong stories and the character
   Doomed to Die
   67 min.   b&w   1940
   Dir: William Nigh. Prod: Monogram. Dist: Budget, United Artists.
   Cast: Boris Karloff, Marjorie Reynolds, Grant Withers.
   James Lee Wong joins the police in solving a murder in order to prevent a tong
war while tracking down stolen bonds.

   The Fatal Hour
   68 min.   b&w   1940
   Dir: William Nigh. Prod: Monogram.
   Cast: Boris Karloff.

   Mr. Wong, Detective
   69 min.   b&w   1938
   Dir: William Nigh. Prod: Monogram. Dist: Budget, Mogull's.
   Cast: Boris Karloff, Grant Withers.
   Wong traps a killer who acts guilty to avoid suspicion.

   Mr. Wong in Chinatown
   70 min.   b&w   1939
   Dir: William Nigh. Prod: Monogram.
   Cast: Boris Karloff, Grant Withers.

WILEY, HUGH (cont'd)

The Spoils of War in *Saturday Evening Post* (May 9, 1925)
    Behind the Front
    5,555'   sil.   b&w   1926
    Dir: Edward Sutherland. Prod: Paramount. Dist: Em Gee.
    Cast: Mary Brian.
    A story of misadventures at the front where a couple of wise guys try to make the
war go the way they want it to go.

WILKINSON, RODERICK see Three Cases of Murder under MAUGHAM,
    W. SOMERSET

WILLIAMS, BEN AMES

More Stately Mansions in *Good Housekeeping* (October-November 1920)
    Extravagance
    6 reels   sil.   b&w   1921
    Dir: Philip E. Rosen. Prod: Metro Pictures.
    Cast: May Allison, Robert Edeson.
    Society melodrama. A young lawyer finds that his wife's extravagant tastes are
beyond his financial means and forges a check to obtain money.

Prodigal's Daughter
    Johnny Trouble
    80 min.   b&w   1957
    Dir: John H. Auer. Prod: Clarion Enterprises; rel. Warner Bros.
    Cast: Stuart Whitman, Ethel Barrymore.
    Drama. A guy on the road turns over a new leaf when he meets a woman who has
never given up hope that her long-lost son will return. A re-make of Someone to
Remember.

    Someone to Remember
    8 reels   b&w   1943
    Dir: Robert Siodmak. Sp: Frances Hyland. Prod: Republic.

A Son of Anak in *Saturday Evening Post* (November 10-December 13, 1928)
    Masked Emotions
    7 reels   mus. and sd. effects   b&w   1929
    Dir: David Butler, Kenneth Hawks. Prod: Fox.
    Cast: George O'Brien, Nora Lane.
    On a sailing vessel used to smuggle Chinese laborers, two brothers encounter
action and romance.

WILLIAMS, BEN AMES (cont'd)

Three in a Thousand in *All-Story Weekly* (October 20, 1917)
    The Fighting Lover
    5 reels   sil.   b&w   1921
    Dir: Fred Leroy Granville. Prod: Universal.
    Cast: Frank Mayo, Elinor Hancock.
    Comedy mystery. Andrew bets his friend $10,000 that he will fall in love with
one of three girls.

A Very Practical Joke in *Saturday Evening Post* (December 5, 1925)
    Man Trouble
    8 reels   b&w   1930
    Dir: Berthold Viertel. Adap: George M. Watters, Marion Orth. Prod: Fox.
    Cast: Milton Sills, Dorothy Mackaill.
    Against the wishes of her bootlegger boyfriend, a cabaret singer falls in love
with a newspaper columnist.

    Inside Story
    87 min.   b&w   1938
    Dir: Allan Dwan. Prod: Fox.
    Cast: William Lundigan, Marsha Hunt.
    Comedy drama. On a bank holiday during the Depression a $1,000 bill is
suddenly put into circulation.

WILLIAMS, GENE

Sticky My Fingers, Fleet My Feet in *New Yorker*
    Sticky My Fingers, Fleet My Feet
    23 min.   color   1973
    Prod: American Film Institute. Dist: Time-Life.
    Norman, a fortyish executive addicted to Sunday touch football, is drawn to
New York's Central Park to engage in ritual combat with his contemporaries. But
their dreams of glory turn to dust when a 15-year-old boy is allowed to join the
game. Academy Award nomination.

WILLIAMS, JESSE L.

Not Wanted in *Best American Stories of 1919-24*, ed. by B. C. Williams.
    Too Many Parents
    s.m. "Too Many Parents," an unpublished story by George Templeton
    75 min.   b&w   1936
    Prod: Paramount.
    Cast: Frances Farner, Billy Lee.
    Story about a group of boys at a military academy.

WILLIAMS, MONA

May the Best Man Win
  Woman's World
  94 min.   color   1954
  Dir: Jean Negulesco. Prod: 20th Century Fox. Dist: Films Inc.
  Cast: Lauren Becall, Clifton Webb, June Allyson.
  A story about the world of fashion.

WILLIAMS, TENNESSEE

Man, Bring This Up Road
  Boom (It.)
  s.m. based on the play The Milk Train Doesn't Stop Here Anymore in turn based
    on this story
  110 min.   color   1968
  Dir: Joseph Losey. Prod: Universal. Dist: Twyman, Universal.
  Cast: Elizabeth Taylor, Richard Burton, Noel Coward.
  In her private kingdom on an unnamed Mediterranean Island, Flora Goforth, who
has driven six husbands to the grave, builds a fortress against death. In comes Chris
Flander, nicknamed "Angel of Death."

WILLIAMSON, ALICE MURIEL

Honeymoon Hate in *Saturday Evening Post* (July 9-16, 1927)
  Honeymoon Hate
  6 reels   sil.   b&w   1927
  Dir: Luther Reed. Prod: Paramount Famous Players—Lasky
  Cast: Florence Vidor, Tullio Carminati, William Austin.
  Romantic comedy. The impetuous daughter, Gail, of a wealthy steel magnate
demands the Imperial Suite in a hotel in Venice. Looking for royal furnishings, the
hotel manager agrees to buy the contents of Prince Dantarini's villa. The Prince
escorts Gail around the city.

WILLSON, DIXIE

God Gave Me Twenty Cents in *Cosmopolitan*
  God Gave Me Twenty Cents
  7 reels   sil.   b&w   1926
  Dir: Herbert Brenon. Adap: John Russell. Prod: Famous Players—Lasky.
  Cast: Lois Moran, Jack Mulhall.
  Melodrama. The story of the whirlwind courtship and marriage of a sailor.

WILLSON, DIXIE (cont'd)

Help Yourself to Hay in *Hearst's International Cosmopolitan*
    Three-Ring Marriage
    6 reels   sil.   b&w   1928
    Dir: Marshall Neilan. Prod: First National.
    Melodrama. Wealthy Anna joins the circus.

Here Y' Are Brother in *Best Love Stories of 1924-25*, ed. by Muriel Miller
    Humphrey (Boston, 1925)
    7 reels   sil.   b&w   1927
    Dir: Millard Webb. Prod: First National.
    Cast: Lewis Stone, Billie Dove, Lloyd Hughes.
    Romantic drama. An inventor returns to his wife with the help of his friend.

WILSON, JOHN FLEMING

The Man Who Married His Own Wife in *Hearst's International Cosmopolitan*
    The Man Who Married His Own Wife (jt. author Mary Ashe Miller)
    5 reels   sil.   b&w   1922
    Dir: Stuart Paton. Prod: Universal.
    Cast: Frank Mayo, Sylvia Breamer.
    A disfigured sea captain married to the heiress he once rescued, undergoes plastic
surgery and learns social graces, only to find that his wife loved him as he was.

The Salving of John Somers in *Everybody's*
    The Bonded Woman
    6 reels   sil.   b&w   1922
    Dir: Philip E. Rosen. Prod: Famous Players.
    Cast: Betty Compson, John Bowers.
    Romantic drama. Angela rehabilitates a drunken first mate and gives him
money to buy a ship.

WINTER, LOUISE

The Mad Dancer in *Young's Magazine* (December 1924)
    The Mad Dancer
    7 reels   sil.   b&w   1925
    Dir: Burton King. Prod: Jans Prod.
    Cast: Ann Pennington, Johnny Walker.
    A woman's romance with the son of a U.S. senator is threatened when a sculp-
tor unveils a nude statue of her.

WITNER, H. C.

Cain and Mabel
  Cain and Mabel
  90 min.   b&w   1936
  Dir: Lloyd Bacon. Prod: Warner Bros. Dist: United Artists.
  Cast: Clark Gable, Marion Davies, Allen Jenkins.
  Comedy. A musical comedy star tangles with a boxing champion over a publicity
stunt.

  The Great White Way
  10 reels   tinted   sil.   1924
  Dir: E. Mason Hopper. Prod: Cosmopolitan.
  Cast: Anita Stewart, Tom Lewis.
  Comedy drama. A press agent romantically links the names of his two most popu-
lar clients, a fighter and a Follies dancer, and then they really fall in love.

Unidentified stories in *Cosmopolitan*
  The Beauty Parlor
  2 reels   sil.   b&w   1926
  Dir: Arvid E. Gillstrom, Reggie Morris. Adap: Tom McNamara. Prod: R-C Pictures.

WODEHOUSE, P. G.

The Small Bachelor in *Liberty Magazine* (September 18-December 25, 1926)
  The Small Bachelor
  7 reels   sil.   b&w   1927
  Dir: William A. Seiter. Prod: Universal.
  Cast: Barbara Kent, André Beranger.
  Comedy. Molly's mother plots to break up the marriage plans of Molly and Finch,
a bashful artist.

The Watchdog (suggestion for)
  Dizzy Dames
  9 reels   b&w   1935
  Dir: William Nigh. Sp: George Waggner. Prod: Liberty Pictures.

WOHL, LUDWIG VON

Jimmy the Crook
  Century Daredevil
  b&w   1929
  Prod: American General.

WONDERLY, WILLIAM CAREY

The Viennese Charmer (novelette)
    Four Jacks and a Jill
    68 min.   1941
    Dir: Jack Hively. Prod: RKO.
    Cast: Ray Bolger, Desi Arnaz.
    The trials and tribulations of a band and a girl.

    Street Girl
    9 reels   b&w   1929
    Dir: Wesley Ruggles. Prod: RKO.
    Cast: Betty Compson, John Harron.
    Romantic drama. A Hungarian violinist, rescued by a band, later teams up with
them and they become well-known.

    That Girl from Paris
    105 min.   b&w   1937
    Dir: Leigh Jason. Prod: RKO.
    Cast: Lily Pons, Gene Raymond.
    An opera star flees from her wedding and follows a band.

WOODBURY, HERBERT A.

A Fool and His Gold
    Riders in the Sky
    70 min.   b&w   1949
    Dir: John English. Prod: Gene Autry.
    Cast: Gene Autry.
    Western. A singing country investigator tracks down evidence that convicts a
murderer.

WOOLRICH, CORNELL

The Boy Cried Murder (novelette) in *Mystery Book Magazine* (March 1947)
    The Boy Cried Murder
    88 min.   color   1966
    Dir: George Breakston. Sp: Robin Estridge. Prod: Universal. Dist: Cine-Craft.
    Cast: Veronica Hurst, Frasher (Fizz) MacIntosh, Phil Brown.
    Thriller. A young boy witnesses a murder but no one believes him except the
killer.

    The Window
    73 min.   b&w   1948
    Dir: Ted Tetzlaff. Prod: RKO. Dist: Films Inc.
    Cast: Bobby Driscoll, Barbara Hale.

WOOLRICH, CORNELL (cont'd)

The Window (cont'd)
Ten-year-old Tommy, living in a New York tenement house, has a neighborhood reputation for telling tall tales. When he witnesses a murder, no one believes him except the killers.

Children of the Ritz in *College Humor*
Children of the Ritz
7 reels   sd. effects and mus.   b&w   1929
Dir: John Francis Dillon. Prod: First National.
Cast: Dorothy Mackaill, Jack Mulhall.
Comedy drama. A rich girl amuses herself by trying to seduce the chauffeur.

Cocaine
Fall Guy
63 min.   b&w   1947
Dir: Reginald Le Borg. Prod: Monogram. Dist: Ivy.
Cast: Robert Armstrong, Clifford Penn.
A man is the fall guy for a murder he didn't commit.

Face Work
Convicted
6 reels   b&w   1938
Dir: Leon Barsha. Sp: Edgar Edwards. Prod: Columbia.
Cast: Rita Hayworth, Marc Lawrence.
A detective convicts a boy of murder and is later convinced that the boy is innocent.

Nightmare
Fear in the Night
72 min.   b&w   1947
Dir and Sp: Maxwell Shane. Prod: Paramount.
Cast: Paul Kelly, De Forrest Kelly, Ann Doran.
A man, hypnotized and forced to murder, recalls the murder in a nightmare.

Rear Window in *After Dinner Stories*, by William Irish (Lippincott, 1944)
Rear Window
122 min.   b&w   1954
Dir: Alfred Hitchcock. Prod: Patron.
Cast: James Stewart, Grace Kelly, Raymond Burr.
A photographer laid up in his apartment watches his neighbors through binoculars and witnesses a murder. Nominated for an Academy Award for Best Written American Drama.

WOOLRICH, CORNELL (cont'd)

Two Men in a Furnished Room
    The Guilty
    70 min.   b&w   1947
    Dir: John Reinhardt. Prod: Monogram.
    Cast: Don Castle, Bonita Granville.
    Mystery. Two friends are in love with the same girl, who has a twin. One of the twins is murdered.

WORMSER, ANNE

The Baby's Had a Hard Day
    West Point Widow
    64 min.   b&w   1941
    Dir: Robert Siodmak. Prod: Paramount.
    Cast: Anne Shirley, Richard Carlson.
    Romance. A nurse secretly marries an Army football star, but her pregnancy jeopardizes the secret.

WORMSER, RICHARD

It's All in the Racket
    Sworn Enemy
    8 reels   b&w   1936
    Dir: Edwin Marin. Sp: Wells Root. Prod: M-G-M.
    Cast: Joseph Calleia, Robert Young, Florence Rice.
    Crime drama.

Right Guy
    The Frame-Up
    6 reels   b&w   1937
    Dir: D. Ross Lederman. Sp: Harold Shumate. Prod: Columbia.
    Cast: Paul Kelly, Jacqueline Wells.
    A strong-arm romance between a track sleuth and a secretary.

The Road to Carmichaels
    The Big Steal
    70 min.   b&w   1949
    Dir: Don Siegel. Prod: RKO. Dist: Films Inc.
    Cast: Robert Mitchum, Jane Greer.
    A robbery caper set in the Southwest and Mexico with Mitchum after the heisters and Greer.

WORMSER, RICHARD (cont'd)

Sleep All Winter in *Esquire* (jt. author Dan Gordon)
Showdown
86 min.   b&w   1950
Dir: Darrell McGowan. Prod: Republic. Dist: Ivy.
Cast: Walter Brennan, Leif Ericson.
Western. A former state trooper looks for his brother's killer and finds the
suspects in a gambling house.

WORTS, GEORGE FRANK

Out Where the Worst Begins in *Argosy All-Story Weekly* (January 5-February 2,
1924)
Where the Worst Begins
6 reels   sil.   b&w   1925
Dir: John McDermott. Prod: Co-Artists Prod.
Cast: Ruth Roland, Alec B. Francis.
Western comedy. A young lady kidnaps Donald and he falls in love with her.

Red Darkness in *Argosy All-Story Weekly* (November 18-December 9, 1922)
Madness of Youth
5 reels   sil.   b&w   1923
Dir: Jerome Storm. Prod: Fox.
Cast: John Gilbert, Billie Dove.
A youthful crook, who, when pulling jobs, poses as an evangelist, falls in love
with the daughter of a potential victim.

WRIGHT, RICHARD

Almos' a Man
Almos' a Man
39 min.   color   1977
Dir: Stan Lathan. Sp: Leslie Lee. Dist: Perspective.
Cast: LeVar Burton.
Set in the Deep South during the late 1930, David's parents protectively deprive
him of independence, yet he persuades his mother to give him part of his earnings
for a used handgun. While practicing, he accidentally kills a mule and is bonded by
the landowner to work 25 months without pay.

WYLIE, IDA ALEXA ROSS

The Gay Banditti in *Saturday Evening Post* (February 26, 1938)
The Young in Heart
s.m. *The Young in Heart*, a novel
86 min.   b&w   1938
Dir: Richard Wallace. Prod: Selznick International Pictures. Dist: Mogull's.

WYLIE, IDA ALEXA ROSS (cont'd)

The Young in Heart (cont'd)
Cast: Douglas Fairbanks, Jr., Janet Gaynor.
Comedy. A dizzy family of cardsharps and fortune hunters is reformed by the kindness of a sweet old lady.

Grandma Bernie Learns Her Letters in *Saturday Evening Post* (September 11, 1926)
Four Sons
100 min.   mus. and sd. effects.   b&w   1928
Dir: John Ford. Prod: Fox.
Cast: Margaret Mann, James Hall.
A Bavarian widow with four sons loses them one by one until only Joseph is left. He migrates to America, fights with the Allies, and after the war asks his mother to join him and his family.

Four Sons
89 min.   1940
Dir: Archie Mayo. Prod: Fox.
Cast: Don Ameche.
Drama. A Czech family is torn apart by the Nazi invasion. Far removed from the original story.

Jungle Law in *Good Housekeeping*
A Man Must Live
7 reels   sil.   b&w   1925
Dir: Paul Sloane. Prod: Famous Players—Lasky.
Cast: Richard Dix, Jacqueline Logan.
A scandal sheet reporter finds a story when an old war buddy gets arrested on narcotics charges. When he falls in love with his buddy's sister, he tries to kill the story.

Pilgrimage
Pilgrimage
90 min.   b&w   1933
Dir: John Ford. Prod: Fox. Dist: Films Inc.
Cast: Henrietta Crossman, Heather Angel.
An old woman who breaks up her son's romance by sending him off to war, lives to regret it.

Vivacious Lady (published later as a 3-act comedy)
Vivacious Lady
90 min.   b&w   1938
Dir: George Stevens. Prod: RKO. Dist: Films Inc.
Cast: James Stewart, Ginger Rogers.

WYLIE, IDA ALEXA ROSS (cont'd)

Vivacious Lady (cont'd)

Comedy. A college professor marries a nightclub singer and then has trouble getting his family to accept her.

Why Should I Cry
Torch Song
90 min.   color   1953
Dir: Charles Walters. Sp: John Michael Hayes, Jan Lustig. Prod: M-G-M. Dist: Films Inc.
Cast: Joan Crawford, Michael Wilding.
Singer/dancer Crawford loves a blind pianist.

Young Nowheres in *Saturday Evening Post* (April 16, 1927)
That Man's Here Again
58 min.   b&w   1937
Dir: Louis King. Prod: Warner Bros. Dist: United Artists.
Cast: Hugh Herbert, Tom Brown.
An apartment dweller furthers a romance.

Young Nowheres
7 reels   sil. or sd.   b&w   1929
Dir: Frank Lloyd. Prod: First National.
Cast: Richard Barthelmess, Marion Nixon.
Romantic drama. A poor boy takes his sick girlfriend to the luxurious apartment of his employer, which makes the employer angry.

WYLIE, PHILIP

Death Flies East
Death Flies East
7 reels   b&w   1935
Dir: Phil Rosen. Prod: Columbia.

Death in Paradise Canyon
Fair Warning
68 min.   b&w   1937
Dir: Norman Foster. Prod: Fox.
Cast: Jay Edward Bromberg, Betty Furness, John Payne.
Fashionable winter resort turns into bedlam when a mysterious death puts the guests under suspicion.

WYLIE, PHILIP (cont'd)

Murderess Welcome
  Under Suspicion
  63 min.   b&w   1937
  Dir: Lewis D. Collins. Prod: Columbia.
  Cast: Jack Holt, Katherine De Mille, Craig Reynolds.
  Auto magnate plans to retire and is almost killed.

Unidentified story
  Cinderella Jones
  88 min.   b&w   1946
  Dir: Busby Berkeley. Prod: Warner Bros. Dist: United Artists.
  Cast: Joan Leslie, Robert Alda.
  To collect her inheritance, a girl must marry a brainy man.

Worship the Sun (suggestion for)
  Springtime in the Rockies
  91 min.   color   1942
  Prod: 20th Century Fox.
  Cast: Betty Grable, John Payne.
  Musical about show people and a broken romance.

WYNDHAM, JOHN

Random Quest
  Quest for Love (Br.)
  91 min.   color   1971
  Dir: Ralph Thomas. Sp: Bert Batt. Prod: Peter Rogers Prod.
  Cast: Joan Collins, Tom Bell, Denholm Elliott.
  A man finds himself in a world where disasters don't occur.

U

YERKOW, CHARLES

Island Freighter
  Sea Tiger
  75 min.   b&w   1952
  Dir: Frank McDonald. Prod: Monogram. Dist: Ivy.

YERKOW, CHARLES (cont'd)

Sea Tiger (cont'd)
Cast: Marguerite Chapman, John Archer.
A man, cleared of collusion with the Japanese, becomes a murder suspect.

YOUNG, GORDON RAY

Hurricane Williams stories
Hurricane Smith
90 min.   b&w   1952
Dir: Jerry Hopper. Prod: Paramount.
Cast: John Ireland, Yvonne de Carlo.
A fugitive on a South Seas island captures a ship.

ZANGWILL, ISRAEL

Merely Mary Ann
Merely Mary Ann
b&w   1931
Prod: Fox.

ZILAHY, LAJAS

The General
The Virtuous Sin
81 min.   b&w   1930
Dir: George Cukor, Louis Gasnier. Prod: Paramount Publix. Dist: Universal.
Cast: Walter Huston, Kay Francis.
Melodrama. The wife of a Russian medical student bribes her way into a brothel
in order to persuade a general to exempt her husband from military service. When
the husband finds out, he plans to kill the general.

ZOLOTOW, MAURICE

Little Boy Blue
Let's Dance
112 min.   color   1950

ZOLOTOW, MAURICE (cont'd)

Let's Dance (cont'd)
Dir: Norman Z. McLeod. Prod: Paramount.
Cast: Fred Astaire, Betty Hutton.

An ex-actress and her former partner fight her wealthy mother-in-law when she tries to take her son away.

DIRECTORY OF DISTRIBUTORS

Alba House
7050 Pinehurst
P.O. Box 35
Dearborn, MI 48126

Arcus Films
1225 Broadway
New York, NY 10001

Audio Brandon
34 MacQuesten P'way S.
Mt. Vernon, NY 10550

BFA Educational Media
2211 Michigan Ave.
Santa Monica, CA 90404

Benchmark Films
145 Scarborough Rd.
Briarcliff Manor, NY 10510

Blackhawk
Eastin-Phelan Corp.
Davenport, IA 52808

Stephen Bosustow Productions
1649 Eleventh St.
Santa Monica, CA 90904

Buchan Pictures
122 W. Chippewa St.
Buffalo, NY 14202

Budget Films
4590 Santa Monica Blvd.
Los Angeles, CA 90029

Carousel Films
1501 Broadway
New York, NY 10036

Charard Motion Pictures
2110 E. 24th St.
Brooklyn, NY 11229

Cine Craft
1720 N.W. Marshal
P.O. Box 4126
Portland, OR 97209

Cine Service Vantage Films
85 Exeter St.
Bridgeport, CT 06606

Cinema Eight
91 Main St.
Chester, CT 06412

Classic Film Museum
4 Union Sq.
Dover-Foxcroft, ME 04426

Clem Williams Films
2240 Noblestown Rd.
Pittsburgh, PA 15205

Contemporary/McGraw-Hill
1221 Avenue of the Americas
New York, NY 10020

ESO-S Pictures
47th and Holly
Kansas City, MO 64112

Educational Communications
2814 Virginia
Houston, TX 77098

Em Gee Film Library
4931 Gloria Ave.
Encino, CA 91316

Encyclopaedia Britannica Educational
   Corp.
425 N. Michigan Ave.
Chicago, IL 60611

Film Classic Exchange
1914 S. Vermont Ave.
Los Angeles, CA 90007

Film Images
17 W. 61st St.
New York, NY 10023

Films Inc.
1144 Wilmette Ave.
Wilmette, IL 60091

Griggs-Moviedrome
263 Harrison St.
Nutley, NJ 07110

Hurlock Cine World
13 Arcadia Rd.
Old Greenwhich, CT 06870

Images
2 Purdy Ave.
Rye, NY 10580

Indiana University
A-V Center
Bloomington, IN 47401

Institutional Cinema Service
915 Broadway
New York, NY 10010

Ivy Film
165 W. 46th St.
New York, NY 10036

Janus Films
745 Fifth Ave.
New York, NY 10022

Kerr Film Exchange
3034 Canon St.
San Diego, CA 92106

Killiam Shows
6 E. 39th St.
New York, NY 10016

Kit Parker Films
P.O. Box 227
Carmel Valley, CA 93924

LSB Productions
1310 Monaco Dr.
Pacific Palisades, CA 90272

Learning Corp. of America
1350 Avenue of the Americas
New York, NY 10019

Lewis Film Service
1425 E. Central
Wichita, KS 67214

Macmillan Films
34 MacQuesten P'way S.
Mt. Vernon, NY 10550

Mass Media Ministries
2116 N. Charles St.
Baltimore, MD 21218

McGraw-Hill Films
1221 Avenue of the Americas
New York, NY 10020

Modern Sound Pictures
111402 Howard St.
Omaha, NE 68102

Mogull's
235 E. 46th St.
New York, NY 10036

Museum of Modern Art
11 W. 53rd St.
New York, NY 10019

National Film Board of Canada
1251 Avenue of the Americas
New York, NY 10020

New Line Cinema
853 Broadway, 16th Floor
New York, NY 10003

New Yorker Films
43 W. 61st St.
New York, NY 10023

Newman Film Library
400 32nd St. SE
Grand Rapids, MI 49508

Perspective Films
369 W. Erie St.
Chicago, IL 60610

Phoenix Films
470 Park Ave. S.
New York, NY 10016

Pyramid Films
P.O. Box 1048
Santa Monica, CA 90406

Roa's Films
1696 N. Astor St.
Milwaukee, WI 53202

Select Film Library
115 W. 31st St.
New York, NY 10001

Swank Motion Pictures
201 S. Jefferson Ave.
St. Louis, MO 63166

Sylvan Films
P.O. Box 622
Brevard, NC 28712

Syracuse University
1455 E. Colvin St.
Syracuse, NY 13210

"The" Film Center
908 12th St. NW
Washington, DC 20005

Thunderbird Films
3501 Eagle Rock Blvd.
Los Angeles, CA 90054

Time-Life
Time-Life Bldg.
1271 Avenue of the Americas
New York, NY 10020

Trans-National Films
48 W. 69th St.
New York, NY 10023

Twyman Films
329 Salem Ave.
Dayton, OH 45401

United Artists 16
720 Seventh Ave.
New York, NY 10019

United Films
1425 S. Main St.
Tulsa, OK 74119

Universal 16
445 Park Ave.
New York, NY 10022

Viewfinders, Inc.
2550 Green Bay Rd.
Box 1665
Evanston, IL 60204

Walter Reade 16
241 E. 34th St.
New York, NY 10016

Warner Brothers
Non-Theatrical Div.
4000 Warner Blvd.
Burbank, CA 91522

Welling Motion Pictures
454 Meacham Ave.
Elmont, NY 11003

Westcoast Films
25 Lusk St.
San Francisco, CA 94107

Wholesome Film Center
20 Melrose St.
Boston, MA 02116

Willoughby-Peerless
110 W. 32nd St.
New York, NY 10001

Xerox Films
245 Long Hill Rd.
Middletown, CT 06457

FILM TITLE INDEX

SHORT STORY TITLE INDEX